D0321806

WITHDRAWN

THE
PAUL HAMLYN
LIBRARY

DONATED BY
THE PAUL HAMLYN
FOUNDATION
TO THE
BRITISH MUSEUM

opened December 2000

ANIMALS AND HUMAN SOCIETY

To the memory of
Professor David Wood-Gush, FRSE
1922–1992

ANIMALS AND HUMAN SOCIETY

Changing perspectives

Edited by

*Aubrey Manning and
James Serpell*

THE
BRITISH
MUSEUM

London and New York

THE BRITISH MUSEUM
THE PAUL HAMLYN LIBRARY

WITHDRAWN

304.2 MAN

First published 1994
by Routledge
11 New Fetter Lane, London EC4P 4EE

Simultaneously published in the USA and Canada
by Routledge
29 West 35th Street, New York, NY 10001

Reprinted 2000, 2001

Routleage is an imprint of the Taylor & Francis Group

© Selection and editorial matter 1994
Aubrey Manning and James Serpell;
individual chapters © 1994 respective author

Typeset in Garamond by
Ponting–Green Publishing Services, Chesham, Bucks
Printed and bound in Great Britain by
T.J.I. Digital, Padstow, Cornwall

All rights reserved. No part of this book may be
reprinted or reproduced or utilized in any form or by
any electronic, mechanical, or other means, now
known or hereafter invented, including photocopying
and recording, or in any storage or information
retrieval system, without permission in writing
from the publishers.

British Library Cataloguing in Publication Data
A catalogue record for this book is available from
the British Library

Library of Congress Cataloging in Publication Data
Animals and human society: changing perspectives /
[edited by] Aubrey Manning and James Serpell.
p.   cm.
Includes bibliographical references and index.
1. Human–animal relationships–Congresses
2. Animals–Social aspects–Congresses.
I. Manning, Aubrey.   II. Serpell, James.
QL85.A53   1993
304.2–dc20   93–10557

ISBN 0–415–09155–1

CONTENTS

v

CONTENTS

LIST OF PLATES

LIST OF PLATES

Between pages 126–7

Every attempt has been made to obtain permission to reproduce copyright material. If there are omissions, please contact Routledge's London office.

NOTES ON CONTRIBUTORS

Arnold Arluke is Professor of Sociology and Anthropology at Northeastern University in Boston. His publications focus on how modern cultures manage their contradictory treatment of animals.

Juliet Clutton-Brock retired recently as Archaeozoologist at the Natural History Museum in London. Her publications include *A Natural History of Domesticated Mammals* and *Horse Power*.

Esther Cohen is Senior Lecturer in Medieval History at Ben Gurion University of the Negev, Israel. She is the author of *The Crossroads of Justice*.

Tim Ingold is Professor of Social Anthropology at the University of Manchester. His books include *Hunters, Pastoralists and Ranchers* and *The Appropriation of Nature*.

Stephen Kellert is a Professor at the Yale University School of Forestry and Environmental Studies. He has published extensively on the subject of human values and perceptions regarding animals and nature.

Andreas-Holger Maehle is Lecturer in the History of Medicine at the University of Göttingen, and Wellcome Research Fellow at the Wellcome Institute for the History of Medicine in London. His published works include *Johan Jakob Wepfer (1620–1695) als Toxikologe* and *Kritik und Verteidigung des Tierversuchs*.

Aubrey Manning is Professor of Natural History at the University of Edinburgh, Chairman of the Scottish Wildlife Trust, and a Fellow of the Royal Society of Edinburgh. He is the author of *An Introduction to Animal Behaviour*.

Mary Midgley was formerly Senior Lecturer in Philosophy at the University of Newcastle-upon-Tyne. She is the author of *Beast and Man*, *Animals and Why They Matter*, and *Wickedness, Science and Salvation*.

Elizabeth Paul is RSPCA Research Fellow in the Department of Psychology, University of Edinburgh. Her studies are concerned with the development of attitudes to animals.

Harriet Ritvo is Professor of History at Massachusetts Institute of Technology, and the author of *The Animal Estate: the English and other Creatures in the Victorian Age*.

James Serpell was recently appointed Associate Professor of Humane Ethics and Animal Welfare in the School of Veterinary Medicine, University of Pennsylvania. He is editor of *Companion Animals in Society* and author of *In the Company of Animals*.

Calvin Schwabe is Professor Emeritus of Epidemiology in the School of Veterinary Medicine (Davis) and the School of Medicine (San Francisco), and Adjunct Professor in the Agricultural History Center (Davis) of the University of California. His books include *Veterinary Medicine and Human Health* and *Cattle, Priests and Progress in Medicine*.

INTRODUCTION

Animals have always formed and will always form a central feature of the human world. We may remain in total ignorance of, or choose to ignore, the vast majority of them (and after all over two-thirds of living species are insects) but those with which we do interact have a profound significance. The sharing of life itself – the 'vital spark' – is crucial, and however mysterious the nature of animals may be, they are, as Robert Burns recognized when addressing a mouse, fellow mortals.

The nature of our relationships with them and the way in which they have been regarded has depended on how we human beings see ourselves and our place in the pattern of existence. The modern environmental or 'green' stance, which sees a vital link between animals and ourselves and tries to re-establish a balance, has something in common with the views of the earliest human societies, the hunter-gatherers. Both would see a continuity between them and us, both regard animals as essential for our own existence, though setting this conclusion in completely different contexts.

The wheel may have come full circle in some senses but along the way over some ten millennia and in diverse cultures the animal/human relationship has taken some extraordinary forms. Animals have been worshipped as gods, reviled as evil spirits, endowed with souls, or regarded as mindless machines. They have been killed for food with careful respect but also slaughtered for sport. Whilst some species have been objects of terror or loathing, others have been taken into our homes and treated as if human themselves. We can record periods when extreme cruelty was commonplace, others when concern for animal welfare has been a high priority and regarded as a model for human relationships.

This volume, and the conference from which it derives, arose from a conviction that this diversity of attitudes and the paradoxes which it presents are not only of great intrinsic interest, its investigation is a necessary base from which to develop a sensible, yet sensitive approach to animals in the modern world.

The chapters that follow consider animals and society both across time and across cultures. They provide some fascinating accounts of the incomparably strange and the utterly familiar. The concluding chapters deal with ourselves in our time. No matter how much technology appears to cut us off and buffer our societies from the so-called natural world, it remains pervasive and indeed we are presented with some issues concerning animals as pressing as at any time in history. Ruth Harrison's book on factory farming was called *Animal Machines*, a title which harks back ironically to Descartes. Modern agriculture, the pet industry, transgenic animals and the conservation movement offer some striking contrasts for us to contemplate. These phenomena coexist, and proponents of each may be able to learn from the others. Mary Midgley calls her summing up 'Bridge-building at last'. We hope this volume will play a part.

The conference on which this volume is based was held under the auspices of the Royal Society of Edinburgh. The Editors are grateful to the Society for its support and also to the International Fund for Animal Welfare, the Royal Society for the Prevention of Cruelty to Animals, the St Andrew's Animal Fund, the Scottish Society for the Prevention of Cruelty to Animals, Waltham Centre for Pet Nutrition and Wood Green Animal Shelters who generously sponsored us.

We also wish to thank Professor Forbes Robertson, Professor Frank Willet and the late Professor David Wood-Gush who helped us greatly with the organization. Miss Sandra McDougall and Mrs Paula Couts of the Royal Society ran the logistics of the meeting with great skill. Finally we wish to express our gratitude to Andrew Wheatcroft and Moira Taylor of Routledge for their consistent encouragement and patience on the way to publication.

Aubrey Manning
James Serpell

1

FROM TRUST TO DOMINATION
An alternative history of human–animal relations

Tim Ingold

Just as humans have a history of their relations with animals, so also animals have a history of their relations with humans. Only humans, however, construct *narratives* of this history. Such narratives range from what we might regard as myths of totemic origin to supposedly 'scientific' accounts of the origins of domestication. And however we might choose to distinguish between myth and science, they have in common that they tell us as much about how the narrators view their own humanity as they do about their attitudes and relations to non-human animals. I aim to show that the story we tell in the West about the human exploitation and eventual domestication of animals is part of a more encompassing story about how humans have risen above, and have sought to bring under control, a world of nature that includes their *own* animality.

In this story, a special role is created for that category of human beings who have yet to achieve such emancipation from the natural world: known in the past as wild men or savages, they are now more politely designated as hunters and gatherers. I shall be looking at how hunter-gatherers have come to be stereotypically portrayed, in western anthropological accounts, as surviving exemplars of the 'natural' condition of mankind, and more particularly at how this is reflected in the depiction of hunters' relations toward their animal prey. I shall then go on to contrast this depiction with the understandings that people who actually live by hunting and gathering have of their relations with the environmental resources on which they depend: again, since our concern is specifically with relations towards animals, I shall concentrate on hunting rather than gathering whilst recognizing, of course, that it is not a simple matter to determine where the former ends and the latter begins (Ingold 1986a: Ch. 4).

Taking the hunter-gatherer understandings as a baseline, I shall attempt to construct an alternative account of the transformation in human–animal relations that in western discourse comes under the rubric of 'domestication',

1

otherwise known as 'the origins of food production'. My concern, in particular, will be to contrast human–animal relations under a regime of hunting with those under a regime of pastoralism. And a leading premiss of my account will be that the domain in which human persons are involved as social beings with one another cannot be rigidly set apart from the domain of their involvement with non-human components of the environment. Hence, any qualitative transformation in environmental relations is likely to be manifested similarly both in the relationships that humans extend towards animals and in those that obtain among themselves in society.

HUMANITY, NATURE AND HUNTER-GATHERERS

Let me begin, then, with the portrayal of the savage hunter-gatherer in western literature.[1] There are countless instances, especially in the writings of nineteenth-century anthropologists, of pronouncements to the effect that hunter-gatherers 'live like animals' or 'live little better than animals'. Remarks of this kind carry force only in the context of a belief that the proper destiny of human beings is to *overcome* the condition of animality to which the life of all other creatures is confined. Darwin, for example, found nothing shocking, and much to marvel at, in the lives of non-human animals, yet his reaction on encountering the native human inhabitants of Tierra del Fuego, during his round-the-world voyage in the *Beagle*, was one of utter disgust. 'Viewing such men,' he confided to his journal, 'one can hardly make oneself believe that they are fellow-creatures and inhabitants of the same world' (Darwin 1860: 216). It was not just that their technical inferiority left them completely at the mercy of their miserable environment; they also had no control over their own impulses and desires, being by nature fickle, excitable and violent. 'I could not have believed,' Darwin wrote, 'how wide was the difference between savage and civilised man; it is greater than between a wild and domesticated animal, inasmuch as in man there is a greater power of improvement' (1860: 208, see Plate 1.1).

Now Darwin, like many of his contemporaries and followers, was in no doubt that these human hunter-gatherers were innately inferior to modern Europeans. This is a view that no longer commands acceptance today. If you wanted to compare, say, the innate capacities of humans and chimpanzees, it would make no difference whatever whether your human subjects were – say – Australian Aboriginal hunter-gatherers or British university professors. Nevertheless, the belief persists in many quarters that even though, *biologically*, hunter-gatherers are fully human, their way of life makes them comparable to other animals in a way that people in pastoral, agricultural or urban societies are not. As recently as 1957, the American archaeologist Robert Braidwood wrote that 'a man who spends his whole life following animals just to kill them to eat, or moving from one berry patch to another, is really living just like an animal himself (1957: 122). Indeed, this idea of hunters

2

and gatherers, as living in a pristine world of nature rather than an artificial, man-made environment, is virtually given by definition. To see why this should be so, we need to return to that very dichotomy which Darwin used as the measure of the distance from savagery to civilization, namely that between the wild and the domestic.

Hunting and gathering, of course, are terms that denote particular kinds of activity. How, then, are these activities to be defined? The conventional answer is that hunters and gatherers exploit 'wild' or *non-domesticated* resources, whereas farmers and herdsmen, by contrast, exploit *domesticated* ones (e.g. Ellen 1982: 128). The precise meaning of domestication has remained a topic of scholarly debate for well over a century, and I shall return in a moment to examine some of the suppositions that underlie this debate. Suffice it to say at this point that every one of the competing definitions introduces some notion of human *control* over the growth and reproduction of animals and plants. Wild animals, therefore, are *animals out of control*. Hunter-gatherers, it seems, are no more able to achieve mastery over their environmental resources than they are to master their own internal dispositions. Like other animal predators, hunters are engaged in the continual pursuit of fugitive prey, locked in a struggle for existence which – on account of the poverty of their technology – is not yet won. Indeed the ubiquity, in western archaeo-zoological literature, of the metaphors of pursuit and capture is extremely striking: hunters forever pursue, but it is capture that represents the decisive moment in the onset of domestication (cf. Ducos 1989: 28). Feral animals, in turn, are likened to convicts on the loose. Notice how the relation between predator and prey is presented as an essentially *antagonistic* one, pitting the endurance and cunning of the hunter against the capacities for escape and evasion of his quarry, each continually augmented by the other through the ratchet mechanism of natural selection. The encounter, when it comes, is forcible and violent.

Then again, hunters and gatherers are conventionally defined as *collectors* rather than *producers* of their food. The history of this dichotomy is an intriguing one. Long ago, Marx and Engels argued that production was the essential criterion that set mankind apart from other animals. Men, they said, 'begin to distinguish themselves from animals as soon as they begin to *produce* their means of subsistence' (Marx and Engels 1977: 42). Animals, by contrast, were supposed to collect whatever nature has to offer. But later on, the archaeologist V. Gordon Childe (1942) was to adopt exactly the same dichotomy, between food production and food collection, not to distinguish humans from animals, but to distinguish human agriculturalists and pastoralists from hunter-gatherers (or 'foragers') whether human or non-human. These terms have since become part of the stock-in-trade of prehistorians, who still speak of hunter-gatherers as food collectors, and of the domestication of plants and animals as marking the inception of food production. Indeed, this is just one of many examples of the way in which criteria originally introduced to specify the distinction between animals and humans have tended to slide on to the quite different distinction between domesticators and non-domesticators, so placing non-domesticating humans on the side of the animals (for other examples, see Ingold 1986a: 11, 236).

Behind these oppositions between the wild and the domestic, and between collection and production, there lies a much more fundamental metaphysical dualism – one that seems peculiar to the discourse which, as a convenient shorthand, we can call 'western', to the extent of being its defining feature. This is the separation of two mutually exclusive domains of being to which we attach the labels 'humanity' and 'nature'. All animals, according to the principle of this separation, belong wholly in the world of nature, such that the differences between species are differences within nature. Humans, however, are the sole exception: they are different because the essence of their humanity *transcends* nature; and by the same token, that part of them that remains *within* nature presents itself as an undifferentiated amalgam of animal characteristics (Ingold 1990a: 210). Thus human beings, uniquely among animals, live a split-level existence, half in nature and half out: they are conceived as biological *and* cultural beings, organisms with bodies and persons with minds. Now as Raymond Williams has pointed out,

> to speak of man 'intervening' in natural processes is to suppose that he might find it possible not to do so, or decide not to do so. Nature has to be thought of ... as separate from man, before any question of intervention or command, and the method and ethics of either, can arise.
>
> (1972: 154)

It follows that when we speak of production and domestication as interventions in nature, as we are inclined to do, humanity's transcendence of the natural world is already presupposed.

Consider, for example, the meaning of production, classically defined by Engels as 'the transforming reaction of man on nature' (1934: 34). In order to produce, humans have to achieve such command or mastery over nature as to be able to impress their own premeditated designs upon the face of the earth: 'The further removed men are from animals ... the more their effect on nature assumes the character of premeditated, planned action directed towards definite preconceived ends' (Engels 1934: 178).

In other words, to the extent that the human condition transcends nature, so nature herself comes to stand as raw material to human projects of construction. In their realization, these projects establish a division, *within* the material world, between the natural and the artificial, the pristine and the man-made, nature in the raw and nature transformed. Hunters and gatherers, as the human inhabitants of a still pristine environment, cannot produce, for in the very act of production the world is irreversibly altered from its natural state. The virgin forest, for example, becomes a neatly ordered patchwork of cultivated fields, naturally occurring raw materials are turned into tools and artefacts, and plants and animals are bred to forms that better serve human purposes. The field, the plough and the ox, though they all belong to the physical world, have been engineered to designs that in every case had their origins in the minds of men, in human acts of envisioning.

Since our present concern is with the history of human–animal relations, or rather with a particular narration of that history, I want to stress the way 'domestication' figures in this account as a feat of engineering, as though the ox were man-made, an artificial construction put together like the plough. (The possibility of actually engineering animals is, of course, one that has opened up only very recently.) Darwin, to his credit, was at pains to stress that the power of humans to intervene in natural processes is in reality rather limited: above all, humans cannot *create* novel variants, but can only select retroactively from those that arise spontaneously. 'It is an error,' Darwin wrote, 'to speak of man "tampering with nature" and causing variability' (1875: 2). Nevertheless, and despite Darwin's careful distinction between intentional and unintentional selection, the belief has persisted that the husbandry of animals and the cultivation of crops, to qualify at all as forms of productive activity, must necessarily entail the deliberate, planned modification of the species involved. Thus it was assumed that to husband animals or plants was, in essence, to breed them, so that both husbandry and breeding came to be lumped indiscriminately under the concept of domestication. Instances where one appeared without the other, such as the 'domesticated wild barley' cultivated by early Neolithic villagers in Southwest Asia (Jarman 1972), and the reindeer of northern Eurasian pastoralists which fall within the range of variation of the 'wild' form (Ingold 1980: Ch. 2), were dismissed as anomalies or as unstable, transitional states of 'semi-domestication'.

Such anomalies arise since making things, not growing things, had been taken as the paradigm for production. According to this paradigm, production is conceived as a 'shaping up', through the operations of construction or reconfiguration, of raw materials already brought forth in nature. In other words, nature provides the substance, human reason the form; production lies in the inscription of form upon substance.[2] It is this paradigm, as we have seen, that specifies the artefact as an object of nature transformed through the imposition of external, conceptual design. For pastoralists and farmers, who cannot exactly construct their animals and plants, the closest thing to making is breeding. And so it is in those modifications to the morphology and behaviour of animals brought about by 'controlled breeding' (Bökönyi 1969: 219; 1989: 22) – or more technically by 'artificial selection' – that the essence of their domestication has been supposed to lie. And just as the distinction between the artefact and the naturally given object (such as a living organism) depends on the notion that the 'building plan' by which the artefact is constructed is extrinsic rather than intrinsic to the material (see Monod 1972: 21), so likewise artificial selection can only be distinguished from natural selection on the premiss that the former is guided by a 'preconceived end', an

5

ideal preserved in the collective representations of a human community, suspended above the inter- and intra-generational variability of the material world. As Durkheim wrote of concepts in general, the blueprint for selection stands 'as it were, outside of time and change' (1976: 433), situated on the ethereal platform from which the human mind launches its selective interventions into the natural world.

The separation of humanity and nature which is implicit in the definition of domestication as a process of artificial selection reappears in a competing definition which emphasizes its social (or cultural) rather than its biological aspect.[3] 'Domestication,' Ducos writes, 'can be said to exist when living animals are integrated as objects into the socio-economic organisation of the human group' (1978: 54; 1989; see also Ingold 1986a: 113, 168, 233). They become a form of property which can be owned, inherited and exchanged. Property, however, is conceived here as a relation between persons (subjects) in respect of things (objects), or more generally, as a social appropriation of nature. Human beings, as social persons, can own; animals, as natural objects, are only ownable. Thus the concept of appropriation, just as the concept of intervention, sets humanity, the world of persons, on a pedestal above the natural world of things. As I have remarked elsewhere, in connection with the concept of land tenure, 'one cannot appropriate that within which one's being is wholly contained' (Ingold, 1986a: 135). It follows that hunters and gatherers, characterized in western discourse as exemplars of man in the state of nature, 'at or near the absolute zero of cultural development' (ibid.), can no more own their resources than they can intervene in their reproductive processes. The advent of domestication, in both senses, had to await the breakthrough that liberated humanity from the shackles of nature, a breakthrough that was marked equally by the emergence of institutions of law and government, serving to shackle *human* nature to a social order.

Implied here is the evolutionary premiss that the level of being that sets mankind above the animal kingdom has to be *achieved*, in the course of an ascent from savagery to civilization, just as it has to be achieved in the development of every individual from childhood to maturity. That man's rise to civilization was conceived to have had its counterpart in the domestication of nature is evident from the interchangeable use of the concept of culture to denote both processes. Edward Tylor's *Primitive Culture* of 1871, the first comprehensive study of human cultural variation, began with the words 'Culture or Civilisation', by which he meant the cultivation of intellectual potentialities common to humanity (1871, I: 1, see Ingold 1986b: 44). Darwin, for his part, introduced his equally compendious study, *The Variation of Animals and Plants Under Domestication*, with the remark that 'from a remote period, in all parts of the world, man has subjected many animals and plants to domestication or culture' (1875: 2). The cultivation of nature was thus presented as the logical corollary of man's cultivation of himself, of his own powers of reason and morality. As the former gave rise to modern domesticated breeds, so did the latter culminate in the emergence of that most perfect expression of the human condition, namely civil society.

Let me conclude this section by returning to Darwin's observation of the native inhabitants of Tierra del Fuego. When it came to his own kind, Darwin remained forever convinced of the necessity and inevitability of progress towards civilization, yet he was unequivocal in his estimation that the Fuegians had not made it. In the spheres of religion, law, language and technology they fell far short of a truly human level of existence. Thus

> we have no reason to believe that they perform any sort of religious worship ... then different tribes have no government or chief ... the language of these people, according to our notions, scarcely deserves to be called articulate ... their [technical] skill in some respects may be compared to the instinct of animals, for it is not improved by experience.
> (1860: 208, 217–18)

Biologically, Darwin seems to be saying, these people are certainly human beings, they are of the same species as ourselves, yet in terms of their level of civilization they are so far from *being human* that their existence may justifiably be set on the same plane as that of the animals. That being so, any influence that they may have had on the non-human animals in their environment, and on which they depend, cannot differ in kind from the influence that such animals have had on one another.

HOW HUNTERS AND GATHERERS PERCEIVE THEIR ENVIRONMENTS

So much for the construction of hunter-gatherers, as *somewhat ambiguously* human, within the framework of concepts bequeathed by western thought. Let me turn now to the hunter-gatherers themselves. How do these peoples who derive a livelihood, at least in part, from hunting and gathering, actually perceive their relations with their environments?

Much of our information about the traditional ways of life of hunters and gatherers – prior to their transformation or destruction in the wake of European invasion of their lands – comes from the writings of early anthropologists, missionaries, traders and explorers. They tended to depict hunter-gatherer life as a constant struggle for existence. Equipped with the most rudimentary technology in a harsh environment, hunters and gatherers were thought to have to devote every moment of their lives to the quest for food. In this respect, Darwin's description of the natives of Tierra del Fuego, apparently beset by hunger and famine and without the wit to improve their miserable condition, was entirely typical. More recent ethnographic studies, however, have shown this picture to be grossly exaggerated, if not entirely false. The new view of hunter-gatherer economy that emerged from these studies was put forward in its most outspoken form in a now celebrated article

7

by Marshall Sahlins, originally presented to the 1966 Symposium on 'Man the Hunter', and provocatively entitled 'The original affluent society' (subsequently revised and published in Sahlins 1972: Ch. 1).

Unlike the individual in modern western society who always wants more than he can get, however well-off he may be, the wants of the hunter-gatherer, Sahlins argued, are very limited. What one has, one shares, and there is no point in accumulating material property that would only be an impediment, given the demands of nomadic life. Moreover, for hunter-gatherers who know how to get it, food is always abundant. There is no concept of scarcity. Hunter-gatherers fulfil their limited needs easily and without having to expend very much effort. Two points go along with this. The first is an apparent lack of foresight, or of concern for the future. Hunter-gatherers, in Sahlins's depiction, take what they can get opportunistically, as and when they want it. And what they have they consume. The important thing, for them, is that food should 'go round' rather than that it should 'last out'. And so whatever food is available is distributed so that everyone has a share, even though this means that there may be none left on the morrow. No attempt is made to ration food out from one day to the next, as explorers do when they go on expeditions. After all, for hunter-gatherers the 'expedition' is not time out from ordinary life but is rather life itself, and this life rests on the assumption that more food will eventually be found (Ingold 1986a: 211–12). The second point, which follows directly from this, is that hunter-gatherers are unconcerned about the storage of food. Stored surpluses impede mobility, and given that food is all around in the environment, hunter-gatherers treat the environment itself as their storehouse, rather than setting aside supplies of harvested food for the future.

One of the studies on which Sahlins drew for evidence in presenting this picture of hunter-gatherer affluence was that undertaken by the anthropologist James Woodburn, of the Hadza people of Tanzania. But Woodburn himself, in a series of recent articles, has sought to qualify this view by distinguishing between different *kinds* of hunter-gatherer economy (Woodburn 1980, 1982, 1988). The major distinction is between what he calls *immediate-return* and *delayed-return* economies. In an immediate-return system, people go out on most days to obtain food, which they consume on the day they obtain it or very soon after. The equipment they use is simple and quickly made without involving much time or effort, nor do they invest any effort in looking after the resources they exploit. Moreover, there is little or no storage of harvested food. This picture, according to Woodburn, is consistent with the Hadza data, and also with Sahlins's general picture of hunter-gatherer affluence. In a delayed-return system, by contrast, there may be a substantial advance investment of labour in the construction of hunting or trapping facilities or (for fishermen) boats and nets. People might devote considerable effort to husbanding their resources, and there may also be extensive storage.

The significance of this distinction lies in what it suggests about people's commitments both to the natural environment and to one another. Such commitments, Woodburn thinks, are likely to be far greater in a delayed-return system than in an immediate-return one. Obviously, people depend in an immediate-return system, just as much as they do in a delayed-return one, both on the resources of their natural environment and on the support of other people in the social environment. But what is striking about the immediate-return system is the *lack* of investment in, or commitment towards, *particular* resources or persons. An individual, say in Hadza society, relies on other people *in general*, and on the resources of the environment *in general*, rather than building up relationships with particular people and particular resources. As Woodburn puts it, 'people are not dependent on *specific* other people, for access to basic requirements' (1982: 434).

The more, however, that we learn about hunter-gatherer perceptions of the environment, and of their relations with it, the more unlikely this picture of the immediate-return system seems. If what Woodburn says about the Hadza is correct, then they appear more as the exception than the rule. Over and over again we encounter the idea that the environment, far from being seen as a passive container for resources which are there in abundance for the taking, is saturated with personal powers of one kind or another. It is *alive*.[4] And hunter-gatherers, if they are to survive and prosper, have to maintain relationships with these powers, just as they must maintain relationships with other human persons. In many societies, this is expressed by the idea that people have to *look after* or *care for* the country in which they live, by ensuring that proper relationships are maintained. This means treating the country, and the animals and plants that dwell in it, with due consideration and respect, doing all one can to minimize damage and disturbance.

Let me present one example, which will serve to direct our attention from the general context of hunter–gatherers' relations with the environment towards the more specific context of the hunters' relations with their animal prey. Among the Cree Indians of northern Canada, it is believed that animals intentionally present themselves to the hunter to be killed. The hunter consumes the meat, but the soul of the animal is released to be reclothed with flesh. Hunting there, as among many northern peoples, is conceived as a rite of regeneration: consumption follows killing as birth follows intercourse, and both acts are integral to the reproductive cycles, respectively, of animals and humans. However, animals will not return to hunters who have treated them badly in the past. One treats an animal badly by failing to observe the proper, respectful procedures in the processes of butchering, consumption and disposal of the bones, or by causing undue pain and suffering to the animal in killing it. Above all, animals are offended by *unnecessary* killing: that is, by killing as an end in itself rather than to satisfy genuine consumption needs. They are offended, too, if the meat is not properly shared around all those in the community who need it. Thus, meat and other usable products should on no account be wasted (see Feit 1973; Tanner 1979; cf. Ingold 1986a: Ch. 10).

This emphasis on the careful and prudent use of resources, and on the avoidance of waste, seems a far cry from the image, presented by Sahlins, of original affluence, of people opportunistically collecting whatever is on offer. Moreover, the idea that success in present hunting depends on personal relationships built up and maintained with animal powers through a history of previous hunts, quite contradicts Woodburn's notion of immediate returns. For in the Cree conception, the meat that the hunter obtains now is a return on the investment of attention he put in on a previous occasion, when hunting the same animal or its conspecifics, by observing the proper procedures. Indeed it could be argued that in their concern to look after their environments, and to use them carefully, hunter-gatherers practise a conscious policy of conservation. They could, in other words, be said to manage their resources, as has been suggested by one recent collection of anthropological studies of North American and Australian hunter-gatherers, which was pointedly entitled *Resource Managers* (Williams and Hunn 1982).

Yet the environmental conservation practised by hunter-gatherers, if such it is, is fundamentally different from the so-called 'scientific' conservation advocated by western wildlife protection agencies. Scientific conservation is firmly rooted in the doctrine, which I have already spelled out, that the world of nature is separate from, and subordinate to, the world of humanity. One corollary of this doctrine is the idea that merely by virtue of inhabiting an environment, humans – or at least civilized humans – are bound to transform it, to alter it from its 'natural' state. As a result, we tend to think that the only environments that still exist in a genuinely natural condition are those that remain beyond the bounds of human civilization, as in the dictionary definition of a *wilderness*: 'A tract of land or a region . . . uncultivated or uninhabited by human beings'. Likewise the wild animal is one that lives an authentically natural life, untainted by human contact. It will, of course, have contacts with animals of many other, non-human species, but whereas these latter contacts are supposed to reveal its true nature, any contact with human beings is supposed to render the animal 'unnatural', and therefore unfit as an object of properly scientific inquiry. Clutton-Brock, in the next chapter, draws our attention to the way in which, by according to domestic animals a second-class status in this regard, the investigation of their behaviour has been impeded. Domestic animals, it seems, are to be exploited but not studied; wild animals to be studied but not exploited.

Scientific conservation operates, then, by sealing off portions of wilderness and their animal inhabitants, and by restricting or banning human intervention. This is like putting a 'do not touch' notice in front of a museum exhibit: we can observe, but only from a distance, one that excludes direct participation or active 'hands-on' involvement. It is consequently no accident that regions designated as wilderness, and that have been brought under externally imposed regulations of conservation, are very often regions inhabited by hunters and gatherers. Allegedly lacking the capability to control and transform nature, they alone are supposed to occupy a still unmodified, 'pristine' environment. The presence of indigenous hunter-gatherers in regions designated for conservation has often proved acutely embarrassing for the conservationists. For there is no way in which native people can be accommodated within schemes of scientific conservation except as *parts of the wildlife*, that is as constituents of the nature that is to be conserved. They cannot themselves be conservers, because the principles and practice of scientific conservation enjoin a degree of detachment which is incompatible with the kind of involvement with the environment that is essential to hunting and gathering as a way of life.

The sense in which hunters and gatherers see themselves as conservers or custodians of their environments should not, then, be confused with the western scientific idea of conservation. This latter, as I have shown, is rooted in the assumption that humans – as controllers of the natural world – bear full responsibility for the survival or extinction of wildlife species. For hunter-gatherers this responsibility is inverted. In the last resort, it is those powers that animate the environment that are responsible for the survival or extinction of humans. Summarizing the view of the Koyukon, an indigenous hunting people of Alaska, the anthropologist Richard Nelson writes:

> The proper role of humankind is to serve a dominant nature. The natural universe is nearly omnipotent, and only through acts of respect and propitiation is the well-being of humans ensured. . . . In the Koyukon world, human existence depends on a morally based relationship with the overarching powers of nature. Humanity acts at the behest of the environment. The Koyukon must move *with* the forces of their surroundings, not attempting to control, master or fundamentally alter them. They do not confront nature, they yield to it.
>
> (Nelson 1983: 240)

For the Koyukon, as for other hunting and gathering peoples, there are not two separate worlds, of humanity and nature. There is one world, and human beings form a rather small and insignificant part of it.

Given this view of the world, everything depends on maintaining a proper balance in one's relationships with its manifold powers. Thus, rather than saying that hunter-gatherers *exploit* their environment, it might be better to say that they aim to *keep up a dialogue* with it. I shall turn in the next section to what this means in terms of hunters' relations with animals. At this juncture, the point I wish to stress is that for hunters and gatherers, *there is no incompatibility between conservation and participation*. It is through a direct engagement with the constituents of the environment, not through a detached, hands-off approach, that hunters and gatherers look after it. Indeed, caring for an environment is like caring for people: it requires a deep, personal and affectionate involvement, an involvement not just of mind or body but of one's entire, undivided being. We do not feel forced in the social world – for

11

example in the field of our relations with kin – to choose between either exploiting others for personal profit or avoiding all direct contact. Yet in the context of relations with animals, this is precisely the choice that is forced on us by the conventional dichotomy between wildness and domestication. It is time now to suggest some alternative terms.

FROM TRUST TO DOMINATION

It should by now be clear that the characterization of hunting as the human pursuit of animals that are 'wild', though it speaks volumes about our western view of hunters, is quite inappropriate when it comes to the hunters' view of animals. For they are not regarded as strange alien beings from another world, but as participants in the same world to which the people also belong. They are not, moreover, conceived to be bent on escape, brought down only by the hunter's superior cunning, speed or force. To the contrary, a hunt that is successfully consummated with a kill is taken as proof of amicable relations between the hunter and the animal that has willingly allowed itself to be taken. Hunters are well known for their abhorrence of violence in the context of human relations,[5] and the same goes for their relations with animals: the encounter, at the moment of the kill, is – to them – essentially *non*-violent. And so, too, hunting is not a failed enterprise, as it is so often depicted in the West: a failure marked by the technical inability to assert or maintain control; pursuit that is not ultimately crowned by capture. It is rather a highly successful attempt to draw the animals in the hunters' environment into the familiar ambit of social being, and to establish a working basis for mutuality and coexistence.

For hunters and gatherers, animals and plants in the environment play a nurturing role, as do human care-givers. In a recent article concentrating on peoples of the tropical forest for whom gathering is rather more important than hunting, Nurit Bird-David has adopted the phrase 'the giving environment' to capture this understanding (Bird-David 1990). She has gone on to suggest that hunters and gatherers model their relationships with life-giving agencies in their environments on the institution of sharing, which is the foundation for interpersonal relations within the human community. Thus in their nurturing capacity, these non-human agencies 'share' with you, just as you share what you receive from the environment with other people. Both movements, from non-human to human beings, and among the latter themselves, are seen to constitute a single system which Bird-David (1992) calls the 'cosmic economy of sharing'. However, whilst people may indeed draw an analogy between the relations with animals and plants activated in hunting and gathering, and the relations among humans activated in sharing, it seems to me that these two sets of relations are, at a more fundamental level of principle, not just analogous but identical. This principle which, I maintain, inheres equally in the activities of sharing and in those of hunting and gathering, is that of *trust*.

12

The essence of trust is a peculiar combination of *autonomy* and *dependency*. To trust someone is to act with that person in mind, in the hope and expectation that she will do likewise – responding in ways favourable to you – so long as you do nothing to curb her autonomy to act otherwise. Although you depend on a favourable response, that response comes entirely on the initiative and volition of the other party. Any attempt to *impose* a response, to lay down conditions or obligations that the other is bound to follow, would represent a betrayal of trust and a negation of the relationship. For example, if I force my friend to assist me in my enterprise, this is tantamount to a declaration that I do not trust him to assist me of his own accord, and therefore that I no longer count him as a friend at all. Offended by my infidelity, his likely response will be to withdraw his favour towards me. Trust, therefore, always involves an element of risk – the risk that the other on whose actions I depend, but which I cannot in any way control, may act contrary to my expectations (see Gambetta, 1988, for some excellent discussions of this point).

Now this combination of autonomy and dependency is, I believe, the essence of what is commonly reported in ethnographic studies of hunting and gathering societies under the rubric of 'sharing'. People in hunter-gatherer communities *do* depend on one another for food and for a variety of everyday services, though these exchanges may be the surface expression of a deeper concern with *companionship*, characterized by Tom Gibson as 'shared activity in itself' (Gibson 1985: 393). Noteworthy in Gibson's account is the connection he draws between companionship and autonomy: 'a relationship based on companionship is voluntary, freely terminable and involves the preservation of the personal autonomy of both parties' (1985: 392). He contrasts this kind of relationship with the kind that is involuntary, non-terminable and places the parties under obligation (see Ingold 1986a: 116–17). Bird-David (1990) draws essentially the same contrast under the terms 'giving' and 'reciprocating', referring respectively to the relationships that hunter-gatherers and cultivators see themselves as having with the environment of the tropical forest. Clearly, both hunter-gatherers and cultivators depend on their environments. But whereas for cultivators this dependency is framed within a structure of reciprocal obligation, for hunter-gatherers it rests on the recognition of personal autonomy. In my terms, the contrast is between relationships based on *trust* and those based on *domination*. I shall turn to the latter in a moment, but first I should like to specify more precisely the meaning of trust in the context of relations between hunters and their animal prey.

I shall do so by drawing a further, analytic distinction between *trust* and *confidence* (following Luhmann 1988). Both terms are commonly and casually used in characterizations of hunter-gatherer attitudes towards the environment. Sahlins, for example, uses the terms freely and interchangeably in his account of the 'pristine affluence' of hunter-gatherer economic arrangements, marked, he claims, by a *trust* in the abundance of nature's resources rather than despair at the inadequacy of human means. My point is that otherwise curious heathen devices became understandable by the people's *confidence*, a confidence which is the reasonable human attribute of a generally successful economy.

(1972: 29, my emphases)

Now Sahlins writes as though, for hunters and gatherers, the environment existed as a world of nature 'out there', quite separate from the world of human society and its interests. In this he uncritically projects on to the hunter-gatherer way of thinking a nature/society dichotomy which, as we have seen, is of western provenance. According to this view, nature – which the people make no attempt to control or modify – is seen to go its own way, subject to ups and downs regardless of human actions or dispositions towards it. If it yields, or fails to yield, this is not because it has the hunter-gatherer in mind. And the hunter-gatherer has to assume that it *will* yield, since life itself is predicated on this expectation. The alternative, in Luhmann's words, 'is to withdraw expectations without having anything with which to replace them' (1988: 97).

Now all of us have to make these kinds of assumption all the time: they are what enable us to get by in a world full of unforeseen and unconsidered dangers. The world may stop revolving or be knocked off course by a meteoric collision, but we have to assume that it will not, and for the most part the possibility never enters our heads. Likewise, according to Sahlins, hunter-gatherers assume the providence of nature and do not consider the possibility of starvation. It is this attitude that I denote by the concept of confidence. And the crucial aspect of confidence to which I wish to draw attention is that it presupposes no engagement, no active involvement on our part, with the potential sources of danger in the world, so that when trouble does strike it is attributed to forces *external* to the field of our own relationships, forces which just happen to set the 'outside world', under its own momentum, on a collision course with our expectations. But with the attitude that I denote by the concept of trust, it is quite otherwise. Trust presupposes an active, prior engagement with the agencies and entities of the environment on which we depend; it is an inherent quality of our relationships towards them. And my contention is that in this strict sense, trust rather than confidence characterizes the attitude of hunters and gatherers towards their non-human environment, just as it characterizes their attitude towards one another.

The animals in the environment of the hunter do not simply go their own way, but are supposed to act with the hunter in mind. They are not just 'there' for the hunter to find and take as he will, rather they *present themselves* to him (see Plate 1.2). The encounter, then, is a moment in the unfolding of a continuing – even lifelong – relationship between the hunter and the animal kind (of which every particular individual encountered is a specific instance).

The hunter hopes that by being good to animals, they in turn will be good to him (see, for example, Fienup-Riordan 1990: Ch. 8 on the Yup'ik Eskimos). But by the same token, the animals have the power to withhold if any attempt is made to coerce what they are not, of their own volition, prepared to provide. For coercion, the attempt to extract by force, represents a betrayal of the trust that underwrites the willingness to give. Animals thus maltreated will desert the hunter, or even cause him ill fortune. This is the reason why, as I mentioned above, the encounter between hunter and prey is conceived as basically non-violent. It is also the reason why hunters aim to take only what is revealed to them and do not press for more. To describe this orientation as 'opportunism' is misleading, for it is not a matter of taking what you can get but of accepting what is given. The same applies in the context of intra-community sharing: one may indeed ask for things that others have, but not for more. 'Practically, would-be-recipients request what they *see* in the possession of others and do not request them to produce what they do not appear to have' (Bird-David 1992: 30).

By regarding the relation between hunters and their prey as one of trust, we can also resolve the problem inherent in Woodburn's distinction between immediate-return and delayed-return systems. Woodburn was concerned to discover the basis for the pronounced emphasis on personal autonomy in many hunter-gatherer societies, and he put it down to the lack of specific commitments and enduring relationships in an immediate-return economy. Yet we find that at least among hunters, people are enmeshed in highly particularistic and intimate ties with both human and non-human others. Contrary to expectations, however, their sense of autonomy is not compromised. Woodburn's error, as we can now see, was to assume that dependency on specific other people entails loss of autonomy. This is not necessarily so, for it is precisely in relations of trust that autonomy is retained *despite* dependency. But trust, as I have noted, inevitably entails risk, and this is as much the case in hunters' relations with animals as it is within the human community. Thus, of the 'other-than-human' persons which inhabit the world of the Ojibwa, Hallowell observes – taking up the perspective of an Ojibwa subject – that

> I cannot always predict exactly how they will act, although most of the time their behaviour meets my expectations . . . . They may be friendly and help me when I need them but, at the same time, I have to be prepared for hostile acts, too. I must be cautious in my relations with other 'persons' because appearances may be deceptive.
>
> (1960: 43)

That is why hunters attach such enormous importance to *knowledge* and its acquisition. This is not knowledge in the natural scientific sense, of things and how they work. It is rather as we would speak of it in relation to persons: to 'know' someone is to be in a position to approach him directly with a fair expectation of the likely response, to be familiar with that person's past history and sensible to his tastes, moods and idiosyncrasies. You get to know other human persons by sharing with them, that is by experiencing their companionship. And if you are a hunter, you get to know animals by hunting. I have argued elsewhere (Ingold 1990b: 12–13) that the weapons of the hunter, far from being instruments of control or manipulation, serve this purpose of acquiring knowledge. Through them, the hunter does not transform the world, rather the world opens itself up to him. Like words, the hunter's tools are caught up in chains of personal (not mechanical) causation, serving to reveal the otherwise hidden intentions of non-human agents in a world where, as Harvey Feit remarks of the Cree, it is 'always appropriate to ask "who did it?" and "why?" rather than "how does that work?"' (1973: 116). In short, the hunter does not seek, and fail to achieve, control over animals; he seeks revelation. Robin Ridington has put the point concisely in his observation that hunter-gatherers, 'instead of attempting to control nature . . . concentrate on controlling their relationship with it' (1982: 471).

It is quite otherwise with pastoralists. Like hunters, they depend on animals, and their relationship with these animals may similarly be characterized by a quality of attentive, and at times even benevolent, regard. Herdsmen do indeed care for their animals, but it is a care of a quite different kind from that extended by hunters. For one thing, the animals are presumed to lack the capacity to reciprocate. In the world of the hunter, animals, too, are supposed to care, to the extent of laying down their lives for humans by allowing themselves to be taken. They retain, however, full control over their own destiny. Under pastoralism, that control has been relinquished to humans. It is the herdsman who takes life-or-death decisions concerning what are now 'his' animals, and who controls every other aspect of their welfare, acting as he does as protector, guardian and executioner. He sacrifices them; they do not sacrifice themselves to him (Ingold 1986a: 272–3). They are cared for, but they are not themselves empowered to care. Like dependants in the household of a patriarch, their status is that of jural minors, subject to the authority of their human master (Ingold 1980: 96). In short, the relationship of pastoral care, quite unlike that of the hunter towards animals, is founded on a principle not of trust but of domination (see Plate 1.3).

These principles of relationship are mutually exclusive: to secure the compliance of the other by imposing one's will, whether by force or by more subtle forms of manipulation, is an abrogation of trust, entailing as it does the denial rather than the recognition of the autonomy of the other on whom one depends. The very means by which the herdsman aims to secure access to animals would, for the hunter, involve a betrayal which would have the opposite effect of causing them to desert. The instruments of herding, quite unlike those of hunting, are of control rather than revelation: they include the whip, spur, harness and hobble, all of them designed either to restrict or to induce movement through the infliction of physical force, and sometimes acute pain. Should we conclude, then, that whilst the concept of wildness is clearly inapplicable as a description of the hunter's perception of animals with whom he enjoys a relation of trust and familiarity, the opposite concept of domestication – with its connotations of mastery and control – is perfectly apt to describe the pastoralist's relation with the animals in his herd?

The answer depends on precisely how we understand the nature of this mastery and control, and this, in turn, hinges on the significance we attach to the notion of physical force. Consider the slave-driver, whip in hand, compelling his slaves to toil through the brute infliction of severe pain. Clearly the autonomy of the slave in this situation to act according to his own volition is very seriously curtailed. Does this mean that the slave responds in a purely mechanical way to the stroke of the whip? Far from it. For when we speak of the application of force in this kind of situation, we impute to the recipient powers of resistance – powers which the infliction of pain is specifically intended to break down. That is to say, the use of force is predicated on the assumption that the slave is a being with the capacity to act and suffer, and in that sense a person. And when we say that the master *causes* the slave to work, the causation is personal, not mechanical: it lies in the *social* relation between master and slave, which is clearly one of domination. In fact, the original connotation of 'force' was precisely that of action intentionally directed against the resistance of another sentient being, and the metaphorical extension from the domain of interpersonal relations to that of the movements of inanimate and insentient things, like planets or billiard balls, is both relatively recent and highly specialized (see Walter 1969: 40 for a discussion of this point).

Now if by the notion of domestication is implied a kind of mastery and control similar to that entailed in slavery, then this notion might indeed be applicable to the pastoralist's relation with the animals in his herd (see Tapper, 1988: 52–3; Tani 1986: 40–1). Western thought, however, recoils from the idea of such similarity, on the grounds that whereas the master–slave relationship, occurring between human beings, exists on the level of society, domestication represents the social appropriation of – or intervention in – the separate domain of nature, within which animal existence is fully contained. In a revealing comment, Marx argued that relations of domination, such as obtain between master and slave, cannot obtain between humans and domestic animals, because the latter lack the power of intentional agency: 'Beings without will, such as animals, may indeed render services, but their owner is not thereby lord and master' (1964: 102; see Ingold 1980: 88). Domination and domestication are here distinguished, on the premise that the one is a form of social control exercised over subject-persons, and the other a form of mechanical control exercised over object-things. But this is not, to my knowledge, a distinction that any pastoralist people make themselves. They may rank animals hierarchically below freemen, but they are not assigned to a separate domain of being. And although the relations they establish with animals are quite different from those established by hunters, they rest, at a more fundamental level, on the same premiss, namely that animals are, like human beings, endowed with powers of sentience and autonomous action which have either to be respected, as in hunting, or overcome through superior force, as in pastoralism.

To sum up: adopting an indigenous perspective, my contention is that the transition in human–animal relations that in western literature is described as the domestication of creatures that were once wild, should rather be described as a transition from trust to domination. The former is not to be understood in a purely negative sense, as the absence of control, nor is the latter contingent on humans' achieving a state of being that somehow transcends the world in which all other creatures live. In both cases, humans and animals are understood as fellow inhabitants of the *same* world, engaging with one another not in mind or body alone but as undivided centres of intention and action, as whole beings. Trust and domination, in the account I have presented, describe alternative modes of such engagement, neither of which is in any sense more advanced than the other. Moreover, the relations thus constituted exist not only between humans and non-human animals, but also, and equally, among human beings themselves. It is to the implications of this point that I now turn.

CONCLUSION

Writing of Koyukon hunters of Alaska, Nelson remarks that, for them, 'the conceptual distance between humanity and nature is narrow' (1983: 240). On the evidence of his own account, and many others, it would be nearer the truth to say that there is no conceptual distance at all, or rather that what *we* distinguish as humanity and nature merge, for them, into a single field of relationships. And indeed, we find nothing corresponding to the western concept of nature in hunter-gatherer representations, for they see no essential difference between the ways one relates to humans and to non-human constituents of the environment. We have seen how both sharing (among humans) and hunting (of animals by humans) rest on the same principle of trust, and how the sense in which hunters claim to know and care for animals is identical to the sense in which they know and care for other human beings. One could make the same argument for pastoralism: I have shown elsewhere, in the case of northern Eurasian reindeer herdsmen, how the transition from hunting to pastoralism led to the emergence, in place of egalitarian relations of sharing, of relations of dominance and subordination between herding leaders and their assistants (Ingold 1980: 165–9). Evidently, a transition in the quality of relationship, from trust to domination, affects relations with humans and non-humans alike. Hallowell's observation that in the world of the Ojibwa, 'vital social relations transcend those which are maintained with human beings' (1960: 43) could apply equally to other hunting peoples, and indeed to pastoralists as well.

This observation, however, plays complete havoc with the established western dichotomies between animals and society, or nature and humanity. The distinction between the human and the non-human no longer marks the limits of the social world, as against that of nature, but rather maps a domain within it whose boundary is both permeable and easily crossed. It comes as no surprise, then, that anthropology, as an intellectual product of the western tradition, has sought to contain the damage by relativizing the indigenous view and thereby neutralizing the challenge it presents to our own suppositions. Thus we are told that the hunter-gatherer view is just another cultural construction of reality. When hunters use terms drawn from the domain of human interaction to describe their relations with animals, they are said to be indulging in *metaphor* (Bird-David 1992). But to claim that what is literally true of relations among humans (for example, that they share), is only figuratively true of relations with animals, is to *reproduce* the very dichotomy between animals and society that the indigenous view purports to reject. We tell ourselves reassuringly that this view the hunters have, of sharing with animals as they would with people, however appealing it might be, does not correspond with what actually happens. For nature, we say, does not *really* share with man. When hunters assert the contrary it is because the image of sharing is so deeply ingrained in their thought that they can no longer tell the metaphor from the reality. But *we* can, and we insist – on these grounds – that the hunters have got it wrong.

This strikes me as profoundly arrogant. It is to accord priority to the western metaphysics of the alienation of humanity from nature, and to use *our* disengagement as the standard against which to judge *their* engagement. Faced with an ecological crisis whose roots lie in this disengagement, in the separation of human agency and social responsibility from the sphere of our direct involvement with the non-human environment, it surely behoves us to reverse this order of priority. I began with the point that whilst both humans and animals have histories of their mutual relations, only humans narrate such histories. But no one can construct a narrative who does not already dwell in the world, and in the dwelling we must inevitably enter into relationships with its constituents, both human and non-human. I am suggesting that we rewrite the history of human–animal relations, taking this condition of active engagement, of being-in-the-world, as our starting point. We might speak of it as a history of human *concern* with animals, in so far as this notion conveys a caring, attentive regard, a 'being with'. And I am suggesting that those who are 'with' animals in their day-to-day lives, most notably hunters and herdsmen, can offer us some of the best possible indications of how we might proceed.

NOTES

1 For more detailed reviews and analysis of the 'savage' in literature, see Street (1975), Berkhofer (1979) and Barnard (1989).
2 Gudeman (1986): Ch. 4) has traced the logical structure of this argument to eighteenth-century Physiocracy, and to the philosophy of John Locke. For the Physiocrats, however, productive agency was assigned to nature in bringing forth the material, rather than to human labour in transforming it. It was left to Marx to turn this view on its head, making the labourer, and not nature, the real producer of value.
3 In the context of this opposition, the term 'social' refers to that domain within which human beings are constituted as persons. This is not to be confused with the interactive sense of sociality commonly encountered in the literature on animal behaviour. See Ingold (1989) for a discussion of these alternative senses.
4 For a particularly fine account, albeit from a society which Woodburn would regard as having a delayed-return system, see Hallowell (1960) on the Ojibwa.
5 For examples, see Marshall (1961) on Kalahari Bushmen, Turnbull (1978) on the Mbuti Pygmies, Dentan (1968) and Robarchek (1989) on the Semai, Briggs (1970) on the Inuit and Howell (1989) on the Chewong.

REFERENCES

Barnard, A. (1989) 'The lost world of Laurens van der Post?', *Current Anthropology* 30: 104–14.
Berkhofer, R. F. Jr. (1979) *The White Man's Indian: Images of the American Indian from Columbus to the Present*, New York: Vintage.
Bird-David, N. (1990) 'The giving environment: another perspective on the economic system of gatherer-hunters', *Current Anthropology* 31: 183–96.
—— (1992) '"The Original Affluent Society": beyond Sahlins' seminal essay on hunter-gatherers' economies', *Current Anthropology* 33: 25–47.
Bökönyi, S. (1969) 'Archaeological problems and methods of recognising animal domestication', in P. J. Ucko and G. W. Dimbleby (eds) *The Domestication and Exploitation of Plants and Animals*, London: Duckworth.
—— (1989) 'Definitions of animal domestication', in J. Clutton-Brock (ed.) *The Walking Larder: Patterns of Domestication, Pastoralism and Predation*, London: Unwin Hyman.
Braidwood, R. J. (1957) *Prehistoric Men*, 3rd edn, Chicago Natural History Museum Popular Series, Anthropology, 37.
Briggs, J. (1970) *Never in Anger: Portrait of an Eskimo Family*, Cambridge, Mass.: Harvard University Press.
Darwin, C. (1860) *Journal of Researches During the Voyage of HMS 'Beagle'*, 2nd edn, London: Collins.
—— (1875) *The Variation of Animals and Plants under Domestication*, 2nd edn, London: John Murray.
Dentan, R. K. (1968) *The Semai: A Nonviolent People of Malaya*, New York: Holt, Rinehart & Winston.
Ducos, P. (1978) '"Domestication" defined and methodological approaches to its recognition in faunal assemblages', in R. H. Meadows and M. A. Zeder (eds) *Approaches to Faunal Analysis in the Middle East*, Cambridge, Mass.: Harvard University, Peabody Museum Bulletin 2.
—— (1989) 'Defining domestication: a clarification', in J. Clutton-Brock (ed.) *The Walking Larder: Patterns of Domestication, Pastoralism and Predation*, London: Unwin Hyman.

Durkheim, E. (1976) *The Elementary Forms of the Religious Life*, trans. J. W. Swain, 2nd edn, London: Allen & Unwin. First published 1915.

Ellen, R. F. (1982) *Environment, Subsistence and System: The Ecology of Small-Scale Social Formations*, Cambridge: Cambridge University Press.

Engels, F. (1934) *Dialectics of Nature*, trans. C. Dutton, Moscow: Progress.

Feit, H. (1973) 'The ethnoecology of the Waswanipi Cree: or how hunters can manage their resources', in B. Cox (ed.) *Cultural Ecology: Readings on the Canadian Indians and Eskimos*, Toronto: McClelland & Stewart.

Fienup-Riordan, A. (1990) *Eskimo Essays: Yup'ik Lives and How We See Them*, New Brunswick, NJ: Rutgers University Press.

Gambetta, D. (ed.) (1988) *Trust: Making and Breaking Co-operative Relations*, Oxford: Blackwell.

Gibson, T. (1985), 'The sharing of substance versus the sharing of activity among the Buid', *Man* (NS) 20: 391–411.

Gudeman, S. (1986) *Economics as Culture: Models and Metaphors of Livelihood*, London: Routledge & Kegan Paul.

Hallowell, A. I. (1960) 'Ojibwa ontology, behaviour and world view', in S. Diamond (ed.) *Culture in History: Essays in Honor of Paul Radin*, New York: Columbia University Press.

Howell, S. (1989) '"To be angry is not to be human, but to be fearful is": Chewong concepts of human nature', in S. Howell and R. Willis (eds) *Societies at Peace: Anthropological Perspectives*, London: Routledge.

Ingold, T. (1980) *Hunters, Pastoralists and Ranchers: Reindeer Economies and their Transformations*, Cambridge: Cambridge University Press.

—— (1986a) *The Appropriation of Nature: Essays on Human Ecology and Social Relations*, Manchester: Manchester University Press.

—— (1986b) *Evolution and Social Life*, Cambridge: Cambridge University Press.

—— (1989) 'The social and environmental relations of human beings and other animals', in V. Standen and R. A. Foley (eds) *Comparative Socioecology*, Oxford: Blackwell Scientific.

—— (1990a) 'An anthropologists looks at biology', *Man* (NS) 25: 208–29.

—— (1990b) 'Society, nature and the concept of technology', *Archaeological Review from Cambridge* 9 (1): 5–17.

Jarman, H. N. (1972) 'The origins of wheat and barley cultivation', in E. S. Higgs (ed.) *Papers in Economic Prehistory*, Cambridge: Cambridge University Press.

King, P. P., FitzRoy, R. and Darwin, C. (1839) *Narrative of the Surveying Voyages of HMS 'Adventure' and 'Beagle' between the Years 1826 and 1836*, London: H. Colburn.

Luhmann, N. (1988) 'Familiarity, confidence, trust: problems and alternatives', in D. Gambetta (ed.) *Trust: Making and Breaking Co-operative Relations*, Oxford: Blackwell.

Marshall, L. (1961) 'Sharing, talking and giving: relief of social tensions among !Kung Bushmen', *Africa* 31: 231–49.

Marx, K. (1964) *Pre-Capitalist Economic Formations*, trans. J. Cohen, ed. E. J. Hobsbawm, London: Lawrence & Wishart.

Marx, K. and Engels, F. (1977) *The German Ideology*, ed. C.J. Arthur, London: Lawrence & Wishart.

Monod, J. (1972) *Chance and Necessity*, trans. A Wainhouse, London: Collins.

Nelson, R. K. (1983) *Make Prayers to the Raven: A Koyukon View of the Northern Forest*, Chicago: University of Chicago Press.

Newberry, P. E. (1893) *Beni Hasan*, part I, in F. L. Griffith (ed.) *Archaeological Survey of Egypt*, Egypt Exploration Fund, London: Kegan Paul, Trench, Trübner.

Ridington, R. (1982) 'Technology, world view and adaptive strategy in a northern hunting society', *Canadian Review of Sociology and Anthropology* 19: 469–81.

Robarchek, C. A. (1989) 'Hobbesian and Rousseauan images of man: autonomy and individualism in a peaceful society', in S. Howell and R. Willis (eds) *Societies at Peace: Anthropological Perspectives*, London: Routledge.

Sahlins, M. D. (1972) *Stone Age Economics*, London: Tavistock.

Saladin d'Anglure, B. (1979) *Inuit and Caribou* (Inuit texts and illustrations concerning caribou, collected by Saladin d'Anglure), Inuksiutiit Allaniagait 2, Association Inuksiutiit Katimajiit, Département d'Anthropologie, Université Laval, Quebec.

Street, B. V. (1975) *The Savage in the Literature: Representations of 'Primitive' Society in English Fiction, 1858–1920*, London: Routledge & Kegan Paul.

Tani, Y. (1986) 'Two types of human interventions into the sheep flock: intervention into the mother–offspring relationship, and raising the flock leader', in Y. Tani (ed.) *Domesticated Plants and Animals of the Southwest Eurasian Agro-pastoral Complex (2): Pastoralism*, Kyoto: Kyoto University Research Institute for Humanistic Studies.

Tanner, A. (1979) *Bringing Home Animals: Religious Ideology and Mode of Production of the Mistassini Cree Hunters*, London: Hurst.

Tapper, R. (1988) 'Animality, humanity, morality, society', in T. Ingold (ed.) *What is an Animal?*, London: Unwin Hyman.

Turnbull, C. (1978) 'The politics of non-aggression (Zaire)', in A. Montagu (ed.) *Learning Non-aggression: The Experience of Non-literate Societies*, Oxford: Oxford University Press.

Tylor, E. B. (1871) *Primitive Culture*, 2 vols, London: John Murray.

Walter, E. V. (1969) *Terror and Resistance*, New York: Oxford University Press.

Williams, N. M. and Hunn, E. S. (eds) (1982) *Resource Managers: North American and Australian Hunter-Gatherers*, Boulder, Colo.: Westview Press.

Woodburn, J. (1980) 'Hunters and gatherers today and reconstruction of the past', in E. Gellner (ed.) *Soviet and Western Anthropology*, London: Duckworth.

—— (1982) 'Egalitarian Societies', *Man* (NS) 17: 431–51.

—— (1988) 'African hunter-gatherer social organisation: is it best understood as a product of encapsulation?', in T. Ingold, D. Riches and J. Woodburn (eds) *Hunters and Gatherers, I: History, Evolution and Social Change*, Oxford: Berg.

2

THE UNNATURAL WORLD
Behavioural aspects of humans and animals in the process of domestication

Juliet Clutton-Brock

INTRODUCTION

In western thought, the natural world is perceived as those parts of the land and its inhabitants that are untouched by human activity and culture. Everything that is controlled by humanity is considered to be unnatural and the more *civilized* people become the more they yearn to be, as Dryden wrote in *The Conquest of Granada* in the seventeenth century:

> as free as Nature first made man,
> Ere the base laws of servitude began,
> When wild in woods the noble savage ran.

In the preceding chapter Tim Ingold has written of present-day attitudes to the noble savage and of the domination of nature that accompanied the transformation of hunter-gatherers into agriculturalists and pastoralists. I wish to take up the discourse from there and to write about the behavioural and cultural changes brought about in mammals by the process of domestication. Apart from some notable exceptions, such as Konrad Lorenz, *Man Meets Dog*, 1954, this has been a neglected area of study among biologists. Until recently, many have considered the tame animal to be unnatural and, as fieldworkers, have gained higher status by watching wild animals in a supposedly natural state. As discussed by Ingold (see Ch. 1) any contact with human beings (except those likewise regarded as wild or savage) is considered to render an animal outside nature and therefore unworthy of study because its behaviour must be abnormal.

I believe that there is no dichotomy between the natural world and the human environment, and it is time to realize that the interactions of humans and animals are as much a part of evolution and as worthy of study as the extinction of the dinosaurs or the behaviour of chimpanzees. The change from gathering wild plants and hunting animals to cultivation and domestication was a survival strategy for, by keeping animals alive and near at hand, hunters

23

were able to escape from the controls set on a predator species by the availability of the prey. The beginnings of livestock husbandry 9,000 years ago enabled human populations not only to survive but also to increase in regions, such as western Asia, where the supplies of wild food were becoming depleted as a result of a combination of climatic change and over-exploitation.

WOLVES AND HUMANS AS CO-OPERATIVE HUNTERS

The predatory mammal may be either a solitary hunter like the cats or the fox, partly social like the jackal, or highly social like the African hunting dog, wolf, or human being. During the Pleistocene period the hunting of large ungulates was probably one of the formative activities that led to the integration and co-ordination of all other behavioural patterns in the social evolution of humans. It was this communal way of life that enabled Palaeolithic peoples to achieve worldwide distribution by the exploitation of other animals in their environment, whether these were fish, reptiles, birds or mammals (Nitechi and Nitechi 1986).

Humans were not the only beings to have been so successful as broad-spectrum social hunters; half a million years ago the wolf was equally successful but it was pushed into second place by the ever-improving technology of human hunters – at first the long-distance projectile and the poisoned arrow, and later the gun.

The oldest and most important of all interactions of humans and animals is that of predator and prey, and the hunting traditions of western Europe remain with us today in language. A wild animal is one that runs away on sight, a fierce animal is one that fights back, and a tame animal is one that allows itself to be handled and has no concept of itself as potential prey. We expect all wild animals to flee on sight and if they do not, like the dodo, they are described as stupid, (the name 'dodo' comes from the Portugese *doudo* meaning a simpleton or fool). A tame animal on the other hand is dependent on humans and will stay close to them of its own free will. All mammals can be tamed if they are taken from their mothers and reared in association with a human protector from a very young age. Whether they will remain tame as adults depends to a great extent on the degree of development of their innate social behavioural patterns, that is whether they are solitary or social in their way of life.

Human hunters were the most social of all mammals and I believe that the enfolding of other species of animal within early communities was a natural outcome of extending the practices of sharing, nurturing and protecting the weaker members of the human group. It was the development of these social patterns that made the way of life of early hunter-gatherers so successful, and a decisive part of this pattern was the fact that human young were carried about by their mothers. They were not left in a den as are the young of most carnivores and it was as easy to carry or even suckle a puppy or other young mammal as it was a human baby.

I believe that the young of many species of mammal would have been tamed in a haphazard sort of way by Palaeolithic peoples, and kept in captivity for short periods. This is how I see the first associations with the wolf, which may have happened from time to time in many parts of the world from half a million years ago onwards. The young of other carnivores, such as foxes and jackals, would have been kept as young animals but being less social in their behavioural patterns, the association would not have extended into the animals' adult lives because they would not have remained habituated to the human group as they matured.

During the late Pleistocene, wolves and humans would have been close competitors preying on the vast herds of ungulates living on the grass plains of Eurasia. Because both were co-operative hunters, living in tightly structured social groups, it is not surprising that they should have been capable of forming an alliance (Hall and Sharp 1978). It would not have taken long for humans to realize that wolves, reared from pups as part of the community, could increase the hunters' success by joining in the detection and tracking of prey.

FORAGERS AND FARMERS

A persistent problem that archaeologists and anthropologists still argue about is why the seemingly successful and relatively easy life of the hunter-gatherers of 10,000 years ago was replaced by the drudgery of farming. People will not ordinarily change their way of life unless there is great pressure to do so. Since the 1960s, and the now famous first conference on 'Man the Hunter' (Lee and Devore 1968), it has been widely accepted that there must have been considerable environmental stress to force nomadic hunters into the sowing of seeds and the rearing of livestock. Growing crops have to be watered, weeded, manured and protected from marauding ungulates, while animals have to be controlled, fed, and protected from predators. The idea put forward by Cohen (1977) that it was the increasing pressure of expanding human populations that provided the impetus for change has been criticized on the grounds that there is no evidence for malnutrition in the human remains of the Epi-palaeolithic, the period just preceding the beginnings of agriculture (Rindos 1989). But whatever the causes, and presumably they were many and complex, the earliest widespread evidence for the change-over from hunting to agri-culture is found on archaeological sites in western Asia (Uerpmann 1987). In the early Holocene, this region, although it includes the so-called Fertile Crescent, was not sufficiently abundant in natural resources to support expanding human populations. It was and is a zone of great environmental and climatic extremes, bordered by inhospitable areas which could have been colonized only with the aid of new techniques. In the cold north, meat and fish could be stored through times of scarcity by smoking, drying, and even freezing, but in the extreme heat of western Asia meat soon rotted even when dried and it became essential to have a store of food for periods of scarcity.

Evidence for the storage of plant foods in specially dug pits appears first in the Natufian, the name for the Mesolithic period in western Asia, dating to around 11,000 years ago. Once grain could be kept from one season of germination to the next, it could be transported and planted in new areas. This grain, together with meat stored in the form of live animals, would have greatly extended the range for human settlement, even when the climate became increasingly arid, as it appears to have done following the last ice age.

The necessity to drive marauding animals away from growing crops could well have provided an added inducement to keep a few tethered goats and sheep as a live store of meat. These small groups of early domestic animals may have been reproductively isolated and become inbred. Their body size evidently decreased with poor nutrition and selection for small animals that were easy to handle (Tchernov and Horwitz 1991). Other bodily features were also altered and the animals soon began to look markedly different from their wild progenitors. The shape of the horn in goats, for example, changed from the long scimitar of the wild species to a short twist, and the fleece of sheep became white. Animals that looked as different as possible from the wild species would have been preferred, because they could be easily distinguished from wild crop-robbers that had to be driven away from the settlement (Clutton-Brock 1992). In northern Europe, today, a few black sheep in a flock are encouraged because they help shepherds to see their sheep in the snow (A. Manning, personal communication). Sheep-dogs were certainly selected to be white, as described by the Roman writer Columella:

> The shepherd prefers a white dog because it is unlike a wild beast, and sometimes a plain means of distinction is required when one is driving off wolves in the obscurity of early morning or even at dusk, lest one strike a dog instead of a wild beast.
>
> (XII, 3. Forster and Heffner 1968)

DEFINITIONS OF DOMESTICATION

At what point can the tamed animal be called 'domestic'? Domestication, though it has to be a progression from taming, is in my view quite distinct. Domestication has had many definitions (Bökönyi 1989). I have defined a domesticated animal as one that has been bred in captivity, for purposes of subsistence or profit, in a human community that maintains complete mastery over its breeding, organization of territory, and food supply (Clutton-Brock 1989). The exception, of course, is the cat which walks by itself (Clutton-Brock 1993).

During the 1960s Eric Higgs and his school of palaeoeconomists at Cambridge argued that the red deer in Europe and the gazelle in Asia were herded and selectively slaughtered. They postulated that there was little difference between this form of exploitation and domestication (see Higgs

1972). Others, including myself (Clutton-Brock 1979, 1987), disagree and wish to restrict the term 'domestication' to animals that are kept under conditions of controlled breeding (there is, in any case, no substantive archaeological evidence for any human control or domination of the deer or gazelle). That is not to deny, however, that people may have followed the wild herds and purposefully ranged over the same area as the animal populations. In Chapter 1 Ingold discusses the differing perceptions of animals by hunters and pastoralists. His two concepts of trust and domination are divided by a thin line, which is crossed only when the concept of personal ownership of animals becomes integral to human society (for further discussion of herding and pastoralism see Ingold 1980 and Khazanov 1984).

The end product of domestication is the breed, which may be defined as a group of animals that has been bred by humans to possess uniform characteristics which are heritable and distinguish it from other animals within the same species.

Harris (1989) and Zeuner (1963) regard domestication as a form of symbiosis from which both humans and animals derive benefit. I do not agree because, like Darwin, I believe only humans benefit from the association. According to Darwin (1868: 4):

> It can, also, be clearly shown that man, without any intention or thought of improving the breed, by preserving in each successive generation the individuals which he prizes most, and by destroying the worthless individuals, slowly, though surely, induces great changes. As the will of man thus comes into play we can understand how it is that domestic races of animals and cultivated races of plants often exhibit an abnormal character, as compared with natural species; for they have been modified not for their own benefit, but for that of man.

It is true that the numbers and worldwide distribution of the common domestic animals, such as cattle and horses, have greatly increased over those ever attained by their wild ancestors, but this has been achieved by an irretrievable loss of genetic diversity and evolutionary autonomy.

NATURAL BEHAVIOUR OF DOMESTIC ANIMALS

Clues to the history of the domestication of animals can be found in the natural behavioural patterns of their wild progenitors. Ten thousand years ago the large herbivores that provided meat for the hunter-gatherers and their domestic dogs were, in Europe, red deer and reindeer, wild cattle, wild boar, and dwindling numbers of wild horse. In western Asia the principal sources of meat were gazelle, followed by wild goat and sheep, deer, wild cattle, wild boar and onager. Of these animals, hunting of red deer and gazelles continued but they were not domesticated in the prehistoric period. The goat and sheep were domesticated first, around 9,000 years ago, followed by cattle and pigs.

Domestication of the horse came later, with its main centre being in the Ukraine, around 5,000 years ago (Clutton-Brock 1987, 1992).

The ideal progenitor of a domestic herbivore comes from a species that is not territorial, lives in large, wide-ranging herds of mixed sexes, organized in hierarchies, has a wide tolerance of different food plants, a short flight distance, and a relatively slow response to danger (Hale 1962: 28; Garrard 1984; Clutton-Brock 1987). Sheep (*Ovis orientalis*), goats (*Capra aegagrus*), cattle (*Bos primigenius*), and pigs (*Sus scrofa*) all share these characteristics, while horses (*Equus ferus*), camels (*Camelus dromedarius*), and reindeer (*Rangifer tarandus*) have some of them.

Being mountain animals, wild goats and sheep are particularly well adapted for domestication. They are gregarious, live in mixed herds, and are not territorial (Garrard 1984). Their survival depends more on finding enough to eat than on the ability to escape fast from predators. Therefore they are not such swift runners as, say, the plains-living gazelles whose slender legs would soon be broken in a high-speed chase across craggy mountains.

The social behaviour of gazelles (belonging to the genus *Gazella*) differs from that of goats and sheep. The sexes are split into separate herds, except during the mating season, the males are strongly territorial, and they are very nervous, that is they take fright easily (have a long flight distance) and have very fast reactions to danger.

So it is easy, on the premises of social behaviour, to speculate on why goats and not gazelles were domesticated in the early Holocene but it is not easy to see why the native Americans did not domesticate the Bighorn sheep (*Ovis canadensis*), or the ancient Egyptians the Barbary sheep (*Ammotragus lervia*), or perhaps the Australian Aborigines various species of kangaroo. The reasons why these species and others such as the eland (*Tragelaphus oryx*), which had a close association with the !Kung San of southern Africa, were not domesticated have to be sought in human ecology and culture, rather than in the biology of the animals.

DOMESTICATION AS A CULTURAL PROCESS

It can be argued that breeds of domesticated animals undergo cultural evolution as much as do human societies. The adaptations of the natural behavioural patterns of domesticated species to the human cultures in which the animals are reared is an important aspect of sociobiology, but it has been very little studied. Until the 1960s the idea that animals could exhibit cultures was considered to be anthropomorphic; only humans and their hominid ancestors could have a culture and all other animals were assumed to be precultural (Steward 1968). Today we are prepared to be more flexible and it is generally agreed that there are cultural aspects to animal behaviour. The problems mostly arise from the changing definitions of what constitutes culture. To Dr Johnson culture was synonymous with cultivation, and

Darwin (1868, I: 2) was using the word in this sense when he wrote that:

> From a remote period, in all parts of the world, man has subjected many
> plants and animals to domestication or culture. . . . He unintentionally
> exposes his animals and plants to various conditions of life, and
> variability supervenes, which he cannot even prevent or check.

Today, many archaeologists still describe culture in terms of artefacts; for
example 'stone age culture'. Others describe it in behavioural terms and use
the word to mean learned behaviour that is passed down through imitation
and/or education. I agree that the concept of culture should be applied in this
latter sense and suggest the following definition: a culture is a way of life
imposed over successive generations on a society of humans or animals by its
elders. Where the society includes both humans and animals then the humans
act as elders.

I should like to look at the example of the dodo in this context. The cultural
attitudes of European sailors would inform them that when they landed on an
island the indigenous wild animals were there to be hunted and that as prey
they would flee as fast as possible on the sight of man. But, as everyone knows,
the dodos on Mauritius did not flee – they just sat and looked at the sailors,
who therefore believed the birds to be extraordinarily stupid.

The dodos were not stupid, but because these birds had evolved in the
complete absence of predators they had no mechanisms for escape. They were
flightless and had no need to acquire escape behaviour either instinctively, i.e.
in the absence of learning or practice, or culturally, by copying their elders.
Thus dodos were naturally tame. No doubt, over the sixty years or so that
they survived on Mauritius, after the arrival of humans at the beginning of the
seventeenth century, the dodos did learn that humans and the introduced pigs,
which ate their eggs, were enemies, but they had no physical means of escape.
If greater numbers of dodos had been brought alive to Europe and had been
bred in captivity they would probably now be more widespread as domestic
fowls than the turkey.

A domestic animal is a cultural artefact of human society but, in addition,
the process of taming an animal such as a wild goat can be seen as changing the
cultural transmission of its behaviour. The animal is removed from the
environment in which it learns from birth to flee on sight from any potential
predator, and brought into a protected place where there are no life-
threatening events either to itself or to its progeny, except of course when it is
finally slaughtered by the hand that fed it. In this context it is not hard to
envisage the terror of livestock animals that are held, sometimes for many
hours, in a slaughterhouse surrounded by the smell of blood, after a gruelling
journey packed into a jolting truck. This is one of the many practices of
modern husbandry that, as we all know, need drastic revision.

I should like to argue that domestic animals live in as many different cultural
situations as humans and that their learned behaviour is responsive to all these

differences. If a human baby and a puppy from the !Kung San hunter-gatherers were brought together to a European city, they would both grow up to be indistinguishable in culture from any other European person or dog. Neither would learn the skills of the hunter and forager. The person would sit at a desk all day; the dog would learn to walk the streets on a lead, and its puppies would learn to sleep on beds and not to defecate in the house.

That animal societies can acquire and transmit behaviour that is specific to them but also relates to human culture has been demonstrated by Thomas (1990) in her remarkable account of the lions of the Kalahari Desert and their interaction with the Bushmen (!Kung San). During the 1950s these people were still living as hunter-gatherers in the western Kalahari and they shared their territory with several packs of lions. There was effectively a truce between the two groups of hunters who were equally matched. They often robbed each other's kills, but otherwise left each other alone. In a study of the causes of death among 3,000 San going back a hundred years, out of 1,500 remembered deaths, only one was caused by a lion. Twenty years later the equilibrium of the Kalahari had been destroyed; the people had given up hunting, the truce with the lions was broken and their culture changed, not once, but several times as the wild animals came and went and were replaced by cattle. These cattle had acquired their own adaptive behaviour and took precautions against the lions. When going out to graze, which they did unattended, they always walked in single file, varied their direction, and returned well before sunset. However, when a foreign bull was introduced to the herd all this adaptation was disrupted, and the result was a massacre of the cattle by thirty lions.

In the absence of predators, domestic animals adapt to the culture of their human owners and so closely do they fit within it that they seem to have lost all links with their wild progenitors. Just as a human can live as a hunter-gatherer or in a prison cell, so a cow can live as a free-ranging grazer or in a factory farm. But neither the human nor the cow actually changes their inherent behavioural impulses or their innate powers of perception, although these may be suppressed by lack of opportunity. This can be seen for example in the experiments on nesting behaviour in pigs which have been kept in intensive conditions. When given bedding material the pigs will use it in the same way to make nests as do free-ranging pigs (Wood-Gush 1985; Kerr et al. 1988).

THE PERCEPTUAL WORLD OF DOMESTIC ANIMALS

Hemmer (1990) has proposed a useful way of looking at the process of domestication as a change in the perceptual world of the animals (the *Merkwelt*). The essence of his theory is that selection under domestication resulted in markedly reduced responsiveness to stress. This is also associated with a reduction in the cranial capacity of the domesticates together with the appearance of many other physical features, including change of coat colour, length of coat, and carriage of the ears and tail. This hypothesis appears to reflect the facts – the perceptual world of a Pekinese dog must be very different from that of a wolf – but then so is the environment in which it lives (Plate 2.1). Perception can also be enhanced in one direction and lowered in another. For example, as a result of selective breeding, a greyhound may see better than a wolf (as well as run faster) but its hearing may be much less acute.

DOMESTIC ANIMALS AS SLAVES AND MEDIATORS

Relationships between humans and animals have probably changed relatively little over the last 10,000 years. I should like to give thought here to some of these relationships, the first of which is the resemblance between the husbanding of livestock and the keeping of slaves. Human families, like wolf families, are hierarchical and are based on the control of subordinate individuals by dominant leaders. Domestic animals have always been at the bottom of this pyramid of dominance, and often they are treated as property rather than as sentient beings with their own interests. It is only within the last 200 years that the same attitude to human slaves has been outlawed in most societies. The following quotations from the Roman writers Varro and Cato, writing on agriculture, neatly summarize the attitudes of owners to their slaves which lasted for 4,000 years and which still prevail today towards animals: Varro on the three aids to men without which they cannot cultivate the land (Hooper and Ash 1967: 225):

> The class of instruments which is articulate, the inarticulate, and the mute; the articulate comprising the slaves, the inarticulate comprising the cattle, and the mute comprising the vehicles .... Slaves should be neither cowed nor high-spirited. Avoid having too many slaves of the same nation, for this is a fertile source of domestic quarrels ... and they should have mates from among their fellow-slaves to bear them children; for by this means they are made more steady and more attached to the place.

Cato, on taking over a new farm (Hooper and Ash 1967: 9):

> Look over the livestock and hold a sale. ... Sell worn-out oxen, blemished cattle, blemished sheep, wool, hides, an old wagon, old tools, an old slave, a sickly slave, and whatever else is superfluous. The master should have the selling habit not the buying habit.

The second aspect of human–animal relationships that I wish to discuss concerns castration. In the ancient world it was probably rare to castrate a dog or cat but there is evidence for the castration of male farm animals from early in the Neolithic period. By 2000 BC it was a well established practice throughout Eurasia. Castration is a physiological aid to taming. It enables all male animals to be more easily handled; the behaviour of the bull, ram, boar and

31

stallion is transformed by the removal of their testes. Castration also produces other benefits to the owners of livestock: if it is carried out before growth has ceased, the animals grow larger and become fat, which in oxen and sheep was of very great value in producing tallow before fossil fuels became widespread. When the famous Shorthorn Durham ox died, aged 11 years, in 1807, the weight of the tallow (fat) alone from the carcass was 11 st 12 lb (75.3 kg), and this was after the ox had been ailing with a dislocated hip for eight weeks (Plate 2.2). Moreover, castrated cattle and horses not only become fat and placid they are also powerful animals that can be used for haulage and ploughing.

Removing the animal's interest in sexual activity with its own kind enables interspecific associations to be strengthened. Usually these close associations are between a domestic animal and a human but they can equally well be between two species of animals. An interesting example of this was described by Darwin (1845: 142) for the sheep-dogs of Argentina. These dogs are trained to carry out many of the functions of a shepherd without a human being present. Darwin recounted how he saw, when out riding, flocks of sheep several miles from any human and guarded only by one or two dogs. He also described the training of these dogs. A puppy was taken from its mother and was reared entirely with the sheep. It was put to suck from a ewe and had a bed of wool in the sheep pen. From this time on the dog had no other contact with humans except that he came to the house once a day for meat. The dog was castrated and both he and the flock of sheep behaved as though he was the senior ram. The sheep followed the dog wherever he directed and went with him to the house at an appointed time each evening. What is more, the other dogs belonging to the house recognized that this dog was different. When he came to the house for meat they would attack and pursue him but when the dog reached his flock of sheep and turned, barking, on his pursuers they would flee, and neither they nor any other dogs would attack the sheep while the guardian dog was with them. Darwin thought it strange that a single dog could protect a flock of sheep on its own but he concluded that:

> The shepherd-dog ranks the sheep as its fellow-brethren, and thus gains confidence; and the wild dogs, though knowing that the individual sheep are not dogs, but are good to eat, yet partly consent to this view when seeing them in a flock with a shepherd-dog at their head.

In some other parts of the world, notably in Turkey, and in experiments in the USA at the present day (Coppinger and Coppinger 1982) dogs are trained to guard sheep on their own, but mostly their role is to supplement that of the human shepherd. However, dogs are not the only animals to perform such tasks, for since ancient times, in many countries of southern Europe and western Asia the bell-wether or flock-leader has fulfilled this role. As described by Tani (1989), this leader is a specially trained sheep or goat that may be of either sex, but is most often a castrated male, which has been hand-reared by the shepherd and will follow his verbal instructions (Plate 2.3). The flock-leader holds a unique position in terms of the relationship between the human (dominant) and the domestic animal (dominated). In so far as the shepherd views the castrated male leader as a member of the flock, he belongs to the category of the dominated group. However, being castrated, he is no longer an essential element of the flock's reproductive process. From the point of view of the culture or learned behaviour of the sheep the flock-leader is an agent of the dominator. Tani's thesis is that the guide-wether is a mediator between the dominating shepherd and the dominated flock, and if most of the flock consists of ewes, the wether takes the role of the guardian of the female group.

Tani (1989) further proposes that the position of the eunuch in ancient human societies corresponded to that of the castrated male flock-leader. The eunuch was a mediator between the king (dominator) and his harem (dominated). When I first read this suggested analogy it seemed very far-fetched, but since then I have come to believe that there was probably very little difference in the attitudes and treatment of animals and human slaves by the dominant members of human societies. This view is supported by the deductions of Maekawa (1980) who has shown that the Sumerian term amar-KUD, which is common in texts of the Ur III period (2100 BC), was used not only for young castrated equids and oxen but also for young human castrates (eunuchs). These young men were the sons of slave women who worked in a specialized weaving industry (Plate 2.4). Their daughters were recruited into this work but their sons were castrated and had a low position in society, working as stable boys and labourers. In this, Maekawa sees an analogy with the management of cattle herds where the females are kept in the breeding herd but the males are castrated and used as beasts of burden.

THE ANIMAL AS AN INDIVIDUAL

Finally, I should like to mention the attitude of humans to animals as individuals. It is a characteristic of every human society that its individual members are enormously variable in intelligence, powers of leadership, levels of energy and so on. Until relatively recently ethologists have concentrated on the behaviour of a species without taking into account the 'personalities' of the individual animals. This is now recognized as being quite inadequate, at least for advanced vertebrates. Anyone who has raised a newborn lamb on a bottle, or hand-milked a cow, knows that there are subtle differences of character in each animal. One cow will be restless and difficult to milk while another will be quite placid, and every animal shows a different response to the attentions of its human owner. In the ancient world, people lived very close to their livestock, often even sharing the same house with them, and however cruel they may have been at times, they treated their animals as individuals who could suffer like themselves. In the first century AD, for example, Columella advised that:

The delivery of a pregnant ewe should be watched over with as much care as midwives exercise; for this animal produces its offspring just in the same way as a woman, and its labour is painful even more often since it is devoid of all reasoning.

(VII, iii, 16. Forster and Heffner 1968)

But it is inevitable that once the number of animals owned becomes large, say in the thousands, their individual identities are lost. This has been the inevitable result of industrial farming in the modern world where the vast numbers of domestic animals, required to feed the ever-increasing human population, are treated as animate vegetables, all bred to look identical and reared in rows of cages, to be harvested when required. Considering the cruelty this inflicts on the animals, it is ironic that in western societies we seem to be on a parallel course, incarcerating ourselves in batteries of small clean buildings, protected from physical threats, and with a greatly reduced perception of the living world and its other inhabitants.

REFERENCES

Bökönyi, S. (1989) 'Definitions of animal domestication', in J. Clutton-Brock (ed.) *The Walking Larder: Patterns of Domestication, Pastoralism, and Predation*, London: Unwin Hyman.

Clutton-Brock, J. (1979) 'The mammalian remains from the Jericho Tell', *Proceedings of the Prehistoric Society* 45: 135–58.

—— (1987) *A Natural History of Domesticated Mammals*, Cambridge: Cambridge University Press; London: British Museum (Natural History).

—— (ed.) (1989) *The Walking Larder: Patterns of Domestication, Pastoralism, and Predation*, London: Unwin Hyman.

—— (1992) 'The process of domestication', in *Mammal Review* 22 (2): 79–85.

—— (1992) *Horse Power: a History of the Horse and the Donkey in Human Societies*, London: Natural History Museum and Cambridge, Mass.: Harvard University Press.

——(1993) 'The animal that walks by itself', in *1994 Yearbook of Science and the Future*, Chicago: Encyclopedia Britannica Inc.: 156–77.

Cohen, M. N. (1977) *The Food Crisis in Prehistory*, New Haven: Yale University Press.

Coppinger, L. and Coppinger, R. P. (1982) 'Livestock-guarding dogs that wear sheep's clothing', *Smithsonian*, April: 64–73.

Darwin, C. (1845) *Journal of Researches during the Voyage of HMS 'Beagle'*, London: John Murray.

—— (1868) *The Variation of Animals and Plants under Domestication*, 2 vols, London: John Murray.

Forster, E. S. and Heffner, E. H. (trans.) (1968) *Lucius Junius Moderatus Columella on Agriculture*, vol. II, Loeb Classical Library 407, London: Heinemann.

Garrard, A. N. (1984) 'The selection of south-west Asian animal domesticates', in J. Clutton-Brock and G. Grigson (eds) *Animals and Archaeology: Early Herders and their Flocks*, Oxford: BAR International Series 202.

Hale, E. B. (1962) 'Domestication and the evolution of behaviour', in E. Hafez (ed.) *The Behaviour of Domestic Animals*, London: Baillière, Tindall & Cox.

Hall, R. L. and Sharp, H. S. (eds) (1978) *Wolf and Man: Evolution in Parallel*, New York and London: Academic Press.

Harris, D. R. (1989) 'An evolutionary continuum of people–plant interaction', in D. R. Harris and G. C. Hillman (eds) *Foraging and Farming: the Evolution of Plant Exploitation*, London: Unwin Hyman.

Hemmer, H. (1990) *Domestication: the Decline of Environmental Appreciation*, Cambridge: Cambridge University Press.

Higgs, E. S. (ed.) (1972) *Papers in Economic Prehistory*, Cambridge: Cambridge University Press.

Hooper, W. D. and Ash, H. B. (trans.) (1967) *Marcus Porcius Cato on Agriculture. Marcus Terentius Varro on Agriculture*, Loeb Classical Library 283, London: Heinemann.

Ingold, T. (1980) *Hunters, Pastoralists and Ranchers*, Cambridge: Cambridge University Press.

Kerr, S. G. C., Wood-Gush, D. G. M., Moser, H. and Whittemore, C. T. (1988) 'Enrichment of the production environment and the enhancement of welfare through the use of the Edinburgh Family Pen System of Pig Production', *Research and Development in Agriculture* 5 (3): 171–86.

Khazanov, A. M. (1984) *Nomads and the Outside World*, trans. J. Crookenden, Cambridge: Cambridge University Press.

Lee, R. B. and Devore, I. (eds) (1968) *Man the Hunter*, Chicago: Aldine.

Lorenz, K. (1954) *Man Meets Dog*, London: Methuen.

Maekawa, K. (1980) 'Animal and human castration in Sumer Part II: human castration in the Ur III period', *Zinbun* 16 (Kyoto University): 1–55.

Nitechi, M. H. and Nitechi, D. V. (eds) (1986) *The Evolution of Human Hunting*, New York and London: Plenum Press.

Rindos, D. (1989) 'Darwinism and its role in the explanation of domestication', in D. R. Harris and G. C. Hillman (eds) *Foraging and Farming: the Evolution of Plant Exploitation*, London: Unwin Hyman.

Steward, J. H. (1968) 'Causal factors and processes in the evolution of pre-farming societies', in R. B. Lee and I. Devore (eds) *Man the Hunter*, Chicago: Aldine.

Tani, Y. (1989) 'The geographical distribution and function of sheep flock leaders: a cultural aspect of the man–domesticated animal relationship in southwestern Eurasia', in J. Clutton-Brock (ed.) *The Walking Larder: Patterns of Domestication, Pastoralism and Predation*, London: Unwin Hyman.

Tchernov, E. and Horwitz, L. K. (1991) 'Body size diminution under domestication: unconscious selection in primeval domesticates', *Journal of Anthropological Archaeology* 10: 54–75.

Thomas, E. Marshall (1990) 'The old way', *New Yorker* 15 October: 78–110.

Uerpmann, H.-P. (1987) *The Ancient Distribution of Ungulate Mammals in the Middle East*, Wiesbaden: Dr Ludwig Reichert.

Wood-Gush, D. G. M. (1985) 'Pigs back to nature', *Ark* January: 20–2.

Zeuner, F. E. (1963) *A History of Domesticated Animals*, London: Hutchinson.

3

ANIMALS IN THE ANCIENT WORLD

Calvin W. Schwabe

INTRODUCTION

A strikingly common feature among early Old World civilizations was the pervasive importance of other species of animal life, both wild and domestic. Beyond the forms of utility that some species acquired before or after domestication, pre-literate peoples in antiquity apparently perceived an additional closeness or interrelatedness to particular animals. They admired or feared – were seemingly awestruck by – certain characteristics which some species possessed in common with themselves, but in greater and more impressive measure. These special qualities included physical and behavioural ones, such as size, bravery, speed, grace, cunning, strength and libido. Some animal species also became important by association with aspects of the unknown, such as with phenomena associated with life versus death.[1] Among different peoples this perceived closeness of human and other species led to varied forms of prominence for these species within evolving cosmologies, including their actual worship.

This chapter will explore this distinctive and less familiar aspect of man–animal relations in antiquity. Though common to the distant past of many present-day peoples, it is a phenomenon virtually unknown to us today except through survival in myths and fables (or, with respect to cattle, in modern expressions of Hinduism).[2]

Despite the wealth of evidence that these relationships were especially prominent, there has been a tendency among modern scholars of *particular* ancient civilizations (who are themselves products of today's values and mindsets) to treat such apparently profound animal relationships in the past as *simply* metaphorical. And, since metaphors are regarded as obviously exaggerated (or purely poetic) comparisons today, this tendency underestimates the importance of the considerable *fusion* in ancient minds not only of such notions as metaphor, symbol, simile, analogue and identity/sameness,[3] but also of such activities/institutions as religion, animal husbandry and healing,[4] which are now totally distinct (see Table 3.1).

Table 3.1 Different social contexts and the roles of animals

Societal types (Riggs)	I Folk	II Agrarian	III Industrial
'Optical Analogs' (Riggs)	'Fused'	'Prismatic'	'Diffracted'
Modern equivalents	Economically undeveloped	Economically developing	Economically developed
Type-economy	Pastoral	Village-based, mixed plant-animal agriculture	Industrial with increasingly intensive monocultural agriculture
Social characteristics	Slight division of labour (age, sex; priests, warrior-herders); no differentiation among institutions, (e.g. religion, healing, animal husbandry); close linkages among values, loyalties, functions with respect to families & larger social structures	Considerable division of labour & differentiation of institutions; slightly separated conceptions of values, loyalties, functions at the different levels of social structure	Extreme division of labour & differentiation of institutions (e.g. 'disciplines' like sociology, political science, religion, philosophy); compartmentalization/ fragmentation of values & loyalties in individual lives at different levels of social structure
Animal roles	Species & individual animals completely integrated culturally & economically within social fabric	Individual animals fulfil multiple utilitarian purposes central to the family & wider economy	Species & individual animals with highly specialized functions & relations as direct food providers, close personal companions, providers of aesthetic & recreational pleasure

Source: adapted from Schwabe (1985b), employing concepts and terminology from Riggs (1957, 1973).

KINGS, GODS AND HEAVENLY BODIES AS BULLS

Here I shall concentrate on the most profound and widespread of such interspecific 'identifications' in antiquity, that between the bovine and human species. Wild bulls (the aurochs *Bos primigenius*), possibly the largest, strongest, bravest and most successfully libidinous animals with which the founding peoples of most ancient civilizations were familiar, became their pre-eminent models both for male power[5] *and* fertility, especially as applied to their chiefs or incipient kings. These related phenomena of power (e.g. dominion, bravery) and fertility (e.g. life, libido) also became associated over time with heavenly bodies and with weather, particularly with thunder, lightning and rain[6] (and, in at least the Minoan civilization, with earthquakes as well).

Thus, as exemplars *par excellence* of both 'dominion' and the mysteries of 'life', wild aurochs bulls (and hence their mothers and consorts, cows)[7] became central to the conceptions and practices of several ancient religions through which the special relations of chief/king to god(s), people and the physical universe were defined and solidified. As a result – and in contrast to dogs, sheep and goats, which many present-day scholars believe virtually domesticated themselves – cattle were probably domesticated later, and more intentionally, for just such religio-political or cosmological reasons.[8]

It may also be that these important and partially related aspects of man–bull rivalry and emulation, which were so characteristic of several major ancient civilizations over a very broad geographical expanse of Asia, Africa and Europe (see Figure 3.1), were so ancient as to have developed before some of the major linguistic groups of modern man separated, as suggested for the Proto-Indo-Europeans by Vendryes (1918).[9]

Alternatively they may have originated some time later as more or less identical and quite rational responses of different peoples to commonly shared ecological determinants, as argued by Lincoln (1981) for the emergence of a societally similar cattle-culture pastoralism in or at the margins of the Old World's natural grasslands amongst diverse and apparently separated peoples.[10] In either case, all of these cattle beliefs and practices probably *appeared* rational or at least practical in the eyes of their creators. It is also possible, though unlikely, that these striking notions shared by many ancient Old World civilizations could have been the result of very early diffusion from one of them.

Whatever the actual case, there are good reasons to believe that bull and man were originally viewed in a much more practically analogical than purely metaphorical relationship to one another. And we might posit further that some key requisites of civilization actually 'gelled' *only* when some of these highly cattle-oriented peoples entered and dominated certain fertile riverine deltas and floodplains where other sedentary peoples were already practising simple digging stick agriculture.[11] I will return to that idea in a moment, but let us first consider how important and complex these relationships between human and bovine *species* became.

Though a number of surviving geographical names were derived in antiquity from cattle or from particular bulls or cows,[12] a far more striking and profound consequence of such tendencies to associate 'places' with cattle was the frequent identification of the two most prominent heavenly bodies (and some constellations of stars) with bulls, or parts of bulls, the whole sky with a cow and, then sometimes, to deify them all.[13] At the same time, the kings of

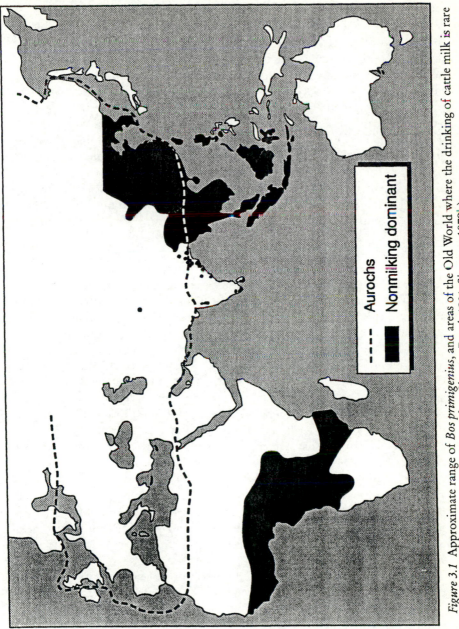

Figure 3.1 Approximate range of *Bos primigenius*, and areas of the Old World where the drinking of cattle milk is rare (after Clutton-Brock 1981; Simoons 1979b).

Aurochs

Nonmilking dominant

ancient civilizations also became commonly and inextricably associated with bull, sun and moon. An important point to note is that these associations usually involved the identification of kings, certain gods and heavenly bodies *as bulls*. It was not the converse, whereby bulls were regarded as gods, or kings related to heavenly bodies. Thus the bull was clearly the main point of reference, the familiar model to which these others were compared.[14]

'Bull-leaping' as a demonstration of bravery and strength (possible symbolic representation for recreational or other purposes of the original pitting of kings or other powerful men against wild bulls in the bull hunt) was practised in more than one ancient civilization. Boundary-marking (and associated fertility) representations of the bull or the bull-plough combination were also shared in antiquity. Each of these was a manifestation of the early and preponderant association of bull with the idea of dominion.

Related evidence suggests that cattle sheds were precursors of some civilizations' temples, and bull-cow statuary and other art, especially bovine heads (bucrania), received architectural prominence in the fully evolved temples of a number of otherwise distinct civilizations. Prehistoric examples suggest linkages between portions of all of this and the much older cave art of earlier hunters' cults (Mellaart 1967).

Cattle domestication itself must have been accompanied by the development of three surgical techniques necessary (even today) to control the powerful and unpredictable domestic bull. Thus, castration, nose-ringing and cutting off the sharp tips or all of the horns, are themselves evidence that – in contrast to dogs, sheep and goats – cattle did not domesticate themselves. Most ancient peoples seemed reluctant to dehorn or blunt the horns of bulls if it could be avoided, as has been the case everywhere until recently.[15] Castration of cattle was probably originally purely a behaviour- (i.e. aggression-) modifying operation since semen was regarded by several ancient civilizations to originate as the white marrow of bones. Eventually Aristotle doubted it and Galen actually established the testes as its production site.

In fact this belief that semen arose from bones as marrow and was channelled to the penis via the spine's 'marrow' (the spinal cord) was possibly the earliest physiological theory formulated (Schwabe *et al.* 1982; Schwabe 1986). It apparently originated before the advent of major civilizations from priests who frequently presided over the ritual dissection of bulls. The bull's penis actually is connected to its spine by the two cord-like, white unstriated retractor penis muscles, a connection of organs early priest-sacrificers must surely have noticed.

By far the greatest consequence of domestication of cattle was the contribution of yoked domestic bulls to the emergence of major Old World civilizations. They provided humans with their first (and for a very long time their *only* significant) source of power for plant food production greater than that of their own muscles (Schwabe 1978a). Thus, the ox was the key to human socioeconomic evolution from primitive digging-stick agriculture to more energy-intensive systems which produced true surpluses of grains. These changes took place mostly within certain fertile riverine valleys. This satisfying of food needs, while providing surpluses for trade, did not require participation of the entire population, as had digging-stick agriculture (or subsistence-level purely pastoral systems).[16] The changes introduced by the yoked ox and plough provided some people with leisure and release from the labours of food-providing. Associated with this was the emergence of the first social division of labour and more differentiated sociocultural institutions (see Table 3.1).

The notion of cattle as *primary* wealth (and as the apparent inspiration eventually for metal coinage) probably preceded a similar perception of surplus grain. Cattle wealth was a widespread idea tied to both the earlier religious power/fertility and subsequent 'harnessed power/fertility' roles cattle served.[17] As a consequence, cattle and stored grain were both prominent in the evolution of some of the first symbols for writing, a device for recording this wealth.[18]

Again, an important point to note with respect to these profound man–cattle relationships in antiquity is that – except for some unusual *individual* living bulls who received recognition as gods incarnate – these interactions were at the *species* level and apparently seldom depended upon any widespread 'bonding' between individual people and individual bulls (or cows). However there is also evidence of affectionate relationships between individual men and their domestic cattle in antiquity. For example, the existence in some civilizations of living bull gods such as the Egyptian Apis (Plate 3.1) and the survival of songs sung to their cattle by Egyptian cowmen (see Pritchard 1969: 469). The Egyptian word *ka*, a man's (or bull's) 'animating principle' or 'double', also means 'bovine animal' and is represented in hieroglyphic form as human arms upraised in imitation of a bull's horns. This suggests an original 'brother bond' between individual men and individual bulls in antiquity.[19]

THE EXAMPLE OF EGYPT

Although popularly associated with the Minoan civilization of Crete, 'bull-leaping' or bull-dancing was also prominent in ancient Egypt.[20] Like bull-baiting and bull-fighting practices in modern Spain and other countries, it probably arose and was practised as a ritual form of prowess-demonstrating and bravery-testing among leaders of the earlier wild bull hunt. Wild bull hunting by monarchs is well described and portrayed in Egypt up until the time of Amenhotep III in the Middle Kingdom (mid-2nd millennium BC), when the wild bull apparently became extinct (Epstein 1971, I: 235). Only later, perhaps, did such rituals become popular spectator recreation in which hostages or slaves sometimes substituted for the king, or for local heroes or youths.

Several forms of Egyptian evidence exist for cattle constituting the first (or one of the first) forms of primary wealth among individuals (e.g. the king), the temple community and the ancient state. Cattle-raiding expeditions by the earliest Egyptian kings into adjacent areas, Nubia especially, are well documented (Adams 1977). While some modern scholars have assumed that the large numbers of cattle said to have been taken were exaggerated, there is no evidence that this was so. That large numbers of cattle, even by modern ranching standards, were still possessed by particular temples at a later time is also recorded. It was surely reflective of a large cattle population and its significance as primary wealth that the annual cattle census of the Egyptians became such a very important national event.

In any case, cattle were certainly numerous in Old Kingdom Egypt, and probably before, and the taking and keeping of cattle purely as wealth by the Egyptians probably preceded the hoarding of gold or pretty stones for the same purpose. One urban anthropologist and Nile Valley specialist, Richard Lobban (1989), has even advanced the interesting hypothesis that it was this cattle wealth, acquired especially from foreign raids, that provided the capital to finance the monumental construction so characteristic of the Egyptian civilization. Lobban also contends that intensive plant cultivation may have developed in the delta (following its capture by the king of Upper Egypt) less from the necessity at first of producing more food for a still small human population, than to produce fodder for maintaining this expanding cattle herd as the surrounding grasslands dried. As Lobban points out, *berseen*, a fodder plant for livestock feeding, is still Egypt's major crop.

The Egyptian association of the heavens and its prominent bodies with cattle was possibly much older than this conquest of the fertile delta lands by peoples of Upper Egypt.[21] A rock drawing ascribed to prehistoric times in Upper Egypt is of a bovine animal with a solar symbol (Winkler 1937). And already in their oldest religious literature, the funerary Pyramid Texts, the king is referred to as the 'sun bull' and identified with the god Re. Specific utterances in the Pyramid Texts refer to this 'Bull of Re' as the male counterpart of the cow goddess Hathor, and to the king as 'Bull of Heaven' taking the place of Re. Elsewhere in these same texts Re is specifically equated with the 'Great *Wild* Bull'. These identifications persisted over very long expanses of time. From the Middle and New Kingdoms, additional references emerge to the then sun god Atum as a bull.

Also in Egypt some specific *living* bull gods emerged who were also associated with sun.[22] Perhaps the earliest example is Mnevis, who is already called 'Bull of Heliopolis', a 'sun bull', the 'Herald of Re' in the Pyramid Texts. He was also called 'Living sun god' and frequently depicted with the sun disc between his horns. Similar living bull gods included Montu, Buchis and Kamutef. From the Middle Kingdom onward, Montu was named bull and associated with the sun (Plate 3.5). During later times he too was connected with Re, and eventually became a universal sun god. Buchis was called 'Living soul of Re' from Dynasty 30, while Kamutef bred daily with his cow mother Hathor to be reborn as the sun calf.

Hathor, the cow goddess whose cult goes back to pre-Dynastic times (according to a range of evidence reviewed by Van Lepp 1990), was portrayed frequently with a sun-disc between her horns and was associated in other ways with Re. More specifically, Hathor, and another cow goddess Nut, were referred to and portrayed as the sky (Plate 3.2). During later times she was described as a celestial goddess who carries and then rejuvenates her son, the solar-disc which, as we recall, was also identified with the king.

Especially interesting in this connection is Egyptian evidence that the drinking of cow milk by ancient peoples, especially as portrayed by the adult pharaoh (shown kneeling at the side of the cow goddess sucking directly from her teat in Plate 3.3), was associated with early beliefs in the cow mother of humankind (Schwabe 1984a) (see Figure 3.1).[23]

Additionally, the moon God Khonsu was called bull (the crescent moon's horns were especially likened to the heavenly bull in several ancient civilizations), and the Ursa Major constellation was to the ancient Egyptians the bull's forelimb. Egyptologist Andrew Gordon and I believe that this association had profound importance with respect to one of the Egyptians' earliest attempts to distinguish biologically between life and death.[24] That is, muscle fascicles and intact muscles of the amputated forelimb, so commonly portrayed as the first part removed from sacrificial bulls, can be stimulated to contract for a considerable period after the animal's death. It was this observation that the forelimb seemingly contained an 'animating principle' that led the priest-dissectors to touch it to the dead pharaoh's mouth in the revivification ceremony of Opening-of-the-Mouth.

While Henri Frankfort (1948: 170), as well as a number of earlier scholars, drew attention to the importance of this strong interpenetration of solar and bovine images in ancient Egypt, its implications have been slighted by most modern scholars. My own evolving explanation for this fusion of images and concepts is that it derives originally from anatomical, physiological, behavioural and social observations by Egyptians of wild and (later) domestic cattle. These led to analogies drawn for people (the human 'herd' and its chief), gods, and finally heavenly bodies, in sum the derivation of an inclusive cattle-culture cosmology.[25] To restate, the basis for comparisons is clear. Sun and king were likened to/identified with the bull. The wild bull was the brave, powerful, libidinous bovine leader of his herd whom the Egyptian king so earnestly wished to emulate. For millennia he bore the title 'mighty bull', and, not surprisingly, Egyptians referred to themselves as 'cattle of Re', the divine sun bull which the king became in his rebirth after death.[26]

These associations are also apparent orthographically in other epithets for pharaoh. One such is 'victorious bull', *k3 nht*, written as a bull shown with the *ka*, a sign of two upraised human arms, together with a human penis. In other words, in this representation of pharaoh, the horns and penis, both sources of the bull's dominion, have evolved into human representations of the mighty bull's organs, the sources of his power. Another probably earlier orthographic example was an anatomical derivation of the king's most frequent epithet *ankh, djed, w3s* ('life, stability, dominion') from the bull's reproductive system as it was understood by the Egyptians (Plates 3.4 and 3.5; Schwabe *et al.* 1982; Schwabe and Gordon 1988, 1989; Gordon and Schwabe 1989). An even more striking, extremely early example of these bovine attributes of pharaoh and their source is his portrayal as a goring bull in the well-known palette of the first pharaoh Menes-Narmer (4th millennium BC; Plate 3.6).

MAN AS BULL IN OTHER CIVILIZATIONS

Throughout the Fertile Crescent (Mesopotamia, the coastal strip of Phoenicia-Canaan and the northern rim of city states connecting these two 'horns'), bovine emulations and associations also were prominent in antiquity.[27] Several gods from the Mesopotamian civilizations of antiquity were called bull, including some members of the Sumerian pantheon. Examples were Anu, the 'Bull of Heaven', the 'almighty Wild Bull',[28] husband to the cow goddess Ninhursag, who personified the sky and could send the celestial bull to earth; Enlil, the god of air and water[29] who was described as follows: 'overpowering ox . . . at thy word which created the world, O lord of lands . . . O Enlil, Father of Sumer . . . overpowering ox' (Farnell 1911: 56; see also Pritchard 1969: 576). Later, the Akkadian crescent moon god Shin, represented with bull's horns, was also called 'Young Bullock of Enlil'; and Amarut(k) (Marduk), 'young bull of the sun'.

Ninhursag, sometimes wife or mother of the chief god(s), was paramount among Mesopotamian cow goddesses, several others of which were assimilated to her at various times.[30] About her an active cult with a living herd was centred at the Temple of el-'Obeid (Plate 3.7). As with the Egyptian pharaoh and Hathor, Sumerian kings claimed to be the cow goddess's children, 'fed with the holy milk of Ninhursag'. She was also called 'Mother of the Gods' and associated with the birth of mankind.[31] Her symbol, the bicornuate uterus of the cow, was used on boundary stones (Barb 1953, pl. 27; boundary stones were also associated elsewhere in antiquity with the penis).

There are indications, too, that the commonly portrayed Mesopotamian reed cattle house was the prototype of more permanent and grand temple architecture (Plate 3.7). One of the clearest examples is the famous frieze from the Temple of Ninhursag from el-'Obeid, now in the British Museum, of priests in front of a reed cattle shed milking cows and making butter.

In the Phoenician-Canaanite horn of the Fertile Crescent, the senior god El was also called 'bull' and shown in surviving portrayals as a man with bull's horns. His son Baal, grandson Aleyin and granddaughter Anat were also called bulls and cow, respectively. Baal and two of his manifestations, Hadad and Dagon, were represented as bulls or as men standing on the backs of bulls. Related biblical references exist, as with Aaron and the golden calf at Sinai and the persistence of Baal-worship in Judaea (Bodenheimer 1960).

On Crete, Zeus was the earthshaker bull[32] born within the bowels of the earth in the Dictean cave, while the Cretan demi-god Minotaur, was born of the mating of the Minoan queen Pasiphae with a bull.[33] Among the Indo-European Greeks more generally, their father god Zeus Pater (cf. Roman Jupiter [Jovis Pater], Indian Dyaus Pitar), who sometimes bore an epithet *helios tauropolos*, could assume bull form even after his otherwise complete anthropomorphization, as for example when he carried Europa on his back from Phoenicia to Crete (Fraser 1972).

Bulls were also central to the festival honouring Poseidon called the Taureia. But perhaps the most complex and persistently bovine of Greek gods was Dionysus.[34] He was often represented as a bull or with bull's horns. Dionysus was worshipped in theophagic communion rites by 'ecstatic and frenzied worshippers . . . tearing at the raw flesh of a bull that was thought to be the actual embodiment of the god. By eating this flesh, the worshipper believed he received a little of the god's power and character' (Young 1979: 14). It is interesting to note here the common belief that Dionysus was originally from Egypt.[35]

Artemis, a Greek fecundity goddess, was also called *tauropolos* at some sites of her worship. A herd of sacred cattle was maintained at the Temple of Eleusis, near Athens, dedicated to Demeter, goddess of fertility, also earth mother. Similarly, Hera and Zeus' lover Io had strong bovine associations (see Cook 1964).

Turning to other Indo-European civilizations, the scriptures of the Persians clearly indicate the central importance of pre-existing bull worship to their religion. Examples from the sacred Zend Avesta include: 'Hail bounteous Bull! Hail to thee, beneficent Bull . . . to the body of the Bull, to the Soul of the Bull; to thy soul, to thee, O beneficent Bull.' This primeval bull's soul went to heaven where he sits as Goshurun (protector of animals) in the sphere of the sun, while his semen went to the moon: 'To the Moon that keeps in it the seed of the Bull, to the only created Bull, to the Bull of many species.' The latter referred to the belief that this primeval bull's semen gave rise to all 272 kinds of animal.

Goshurun's female counterpart was Drvaspa: 'To the body of the Cow, to the soul of the Cow, to the powerful Drvaspa, made by Mazda and holy.' Mithra, lord of pastures, was another bull god, who cast his 'health-bringing eye' upon the 'abode of cattle, the dwelling of cattle'. The importance of cattle generally in ancient Persian civilization is summed up in another passage from the Zend Avesta: 'In the ox is our strength, in the ox is our need, in the ox is our speech, in the ox is our victory, in the ox is our food, in the ox is our clothing, in the ox is our tillage, that makes food grow for us.'[36]

Among the creators of the ancient Indus Valley civilization,[37] a plethora of similar beliefs and practices abounded. The relative familiarity of many of them to us today is due, of course, to their unique survivals in multiple forms within modern expressions of the Hindu faith.[38] These are the only really important examples of cattle cultures surviving from ancient civilizations to the present day. The origins of current beliefs about cattle and man in India are the subject of an active academic debate.[39] I shall not even attempt to chronicle their specifics beyond a quotation or two to illustrate similarities to other already cited examples. From the Rig Veda we learn how the father god Dyaus Pitar, the 'bull with the thousand horns', bred Prithivi, the earth cow, to produce the gods and all other animals. Similarly, when cosmic force was released at creation it was in the form of cows as rain clouds from which the sun also arose. Thus the cow and its father/husband the bull were the sources of all.

Regardless of the outcome of the current debate about how and why cow protection (*ahimsa*) in modern Hinduism may have originated, abundant evidence from India corroborates the overall thesis advanced here about very close interspecific identifications between man and cattle among the earliest creators of civilizations. This originally religious association of our two species led to the development of widespread cattle-culture pastoralism as well as to plough-based plant cultivation which relied on ox power. This provided the food surpluses and wealth which were the keys to civilization.[40]

Finally, it seems that the Romans added little that was original or very significant to pre-existing cattle culture. But they do indicate how, as time went on, these earliest relationships between the human and bovine species dimmed in memory and were replaced by more comprehensible (to us) utilitarian relationships. In Roman legend and myth the boundaries of the city state of Rome were said to have been laid out by cattle, as was the case for the laying out of Thebes, the capital of the Greek 'cattle land' Boeotia, by Cadmus).[41] Moreover, Romulus and Remus were said to have been suckled by the wolf outside the temple of the cow goddess Rumina.

In the subsequent records of the Roman civilization (as in the Greek) we can begin to see how such ancient notions began to fade in importance before the dawn of the first Christian millennium. In Marcus Terrentius Varro's detailed work on agriculture, including animal husbandry, which dates from the first century BC (Hooper 1935) we can read such statements as: 'the ancient Greeks, according to Timaeus, called bulls *itali*, and the name Italy was bestowed because of the number and beauty of its cattle',[42] 'When the city was founded the position of walls and gates was marked out by a bull', 'If the flock had not been held in high honor among the ancients, the astronomers, in laying out the heavens, would not have called by their names the signs of the zodiac . . . the names of the Ram and the Bull,[43] placing them ahead of Apollo and Hercules', 'up to this day a fine is assessed after the ancient fashion in oxen and sheep; the oldest copper coins are marked with cattle', 'the very word for money is derived from them, for cattle are the basis of all wealth', 'the ancients made it a capital offense to kill one'.

Thus, by Varro's time, though Romans still remembered some of these ancient cattle associations of their own and of Greece, bulls and cows, like other farm and draught animals, had simply become utilitarian possessions, albeit ones of the greatest value to the economy.[44] By this time, much of their prior prestige value to sovereigns had been taken over by horses or mules, species which had played no role in the *creation* of ancient civilizations.

In summary, companion, as well as utilitarian, functions of animals were completely overshadowed at civilizations' creation by the religio-political functions of a few animal species. For some time after that, some of the most all-embracing and absolutely fundamental relationships of power, fertility and sex were still envisaged between the human and bovine *species*.[45] The very fact of this central common feature among the several peoples who created civilizations supports its ancient origins in man's evolution, before major groups divided and dispersed, and probably long before cattle were first domesticated.

OTHER SPECIES ASSOCIATIONS IN EARLY CIVILIZATIONS

In more restricted senses, or in more specific contexts, special cultural relationships also existed in ancient times between *Homo sapiens* and other animals. For example, in a few civilizations the lion shared, in comparatively minor ways, the power role of the bull. But some other species associations, especially with the dog and snake, were profound and, as with cattle, were shared by more than one ancient civilization. Although it may seem odd to us now, dog and snake associations in antiquity were similar in that both originally seem to have been with death. They then evolved in parallel ways. The snake killed people and the wild canine killed and ate them (as it also scavenged bodies dead from other causes). In the Egyptian god Anubis we see some of the earliest and most persistent of these canine roles.

Clearly the earliest Egyptians feared dismemberment after death and it is probable that Anubis' prominent funerary roles (Plate 3.8) evolved from such fears. Among some modern Nilotes, for example, the Turkana and Nandi, the dead (or dying) are deliberately put out for canids (or hyenas) to eat and for some of these peoples the 'soul' of the deceased must pass through such an animal to achieve afterlife (see discussion in Schwabe 1978b: 58–9). Exceptions are sometimes made for chiefs or other important elders whose bodies are buried deeply or beneath stone cairns precisely to prevent their being consumed: they have an alternative route to the afterlife. Early Egyptian funerary texts clearly indicate the expectation, and fear, of such dismemberment after death, especially for the pharaoh, and this could explain the origin of early mud-brick mastabas and then pyramids to protect them.

The Israelites feared dismemberment of their dead by semi-domesticated pariah dogs, as indicated in such biblical verses as 1st Kings, 14: 11: 'Him that dieth of Jeroboam in the city shall the dogs eat'; 21: 23: 'The dogs shall eat Jezebel by the wall of Jezreel'; Psalm 22: 'Deliver . . . my darling from the power of the dog'; and: 'thou hast brought me into the dust of death. For dogs have compassed me.'

Similarly in Mesopotamia we find many related beliefs and practices, for example dogs as harbingers of death. There, as well as in Egypt and Greece, these earliest associations of dogs with death and dismemberment, including the foretelling of death, seemed to have evolved gradually into beliefs that the dog could also ward off death, prevent death, and hence cure (Leach 1961). The Mesopotamian healing goddess Gula was shown with her healing companion the dog (Plate 3.9). By the same token, dogs were kept as co-therapists in Greek healing temples.[46]

The Zoroastrian Persians seem to have evolved the most positive ideas from such commonly observed facts about the canine species and death. Originally, a deceased person needed to be eaten by a dog for the soul to enjoy afterlife but later the body had only to be rent by a dog. Later still it was sufficient simply to be gazed upon by a dog. As a consequence of this among these Persians all dogs received unusual respect, protection and care.

In antiquity snakes evolved remarkably similar associations to those of dogs. These 'limbless spinal columns'[47] are mentioned almost as frequently as are cattle in the Egyptian funerary literature. Moreover, between them, cattle and snakes seem to have stimulated early Egyptians to develop the earliest biomedical theories about life and death. Snakes' spines (vertebral columns) were regarded as playing a reciprocal role to the spines of bulls (in the case of snakes, as sources of poison, the fluid of death, while the bull's spine was considered the source of semen, the fluid of life).[48] Therefore, rebirth (re-creation) of the pharaoh following death was sometimes portrayed as a journey along the same route as that taken by semen in procreation, that is the deceased was portrayed being pulled by priests through the spinal cord of a bull (or, rather perversely, by the route of semen's negative analogue snake poison,[49] by pulling him through the spine of a snake). Not surprisingly, the pharaoh wore both the snake's head (*uraeus*) on his brow (top of his own spine) and the bull's tail attached to the rear of his kilt.

In other ancient civilizations these associations between snakes and death also evolved towards the perception of snakes as healing companions. This was apparent in Mesopotamia in portrayals of snakes, as dogs, with the healing goddess Gula. Also, like dogs, snakes were kept in Greek healing temples and the caduceus symbol of healing may well have had similar origins. The Late Greek god Hermanubis, an amalgam of the Egyptians' Anubis and Hermes, carried the caduceus. Interestingly, among the cattle culture Dinka Nilotes of the southern Sudan, snakes (both poisonous and constrictors) command special respect and solicitude. They are regarded as *jok*, a local spirit or 'god' to be placated. To kill one accidentally causes great social turmoil and snakes are allowed to enter huts unmolested; indeed milk and butter are put out to attract and placate them. It is possible that similar approaches (deliberately putting out food) for the man-killing, man-eating wild canid, originally to bribe or placate him, contributed to this species's domestication.

Other complex and widespread animal associations arose in antiquity. In early Mesopotamia, evidence suggests that small ruminants began to fulfil an important *surrogate* religious role as substitute cattle, particularly when cattle were scarce.[50] But only in rare instances such as Middle Kingdom Egypt did ram gods like Amun actually replace or augment bulls as principal gods. There, too, we have the living ram god of Mendes and the fertility connections, again especially prominent in later times, of another ram god Khumn.[51] But even among Amun's powerful priesthood, the bull still remained the central animal of sacrifice and of many associated beliefs and practices.

Other quite different associations with sheep, especially lambs, began to arise within certain civilizations (or neighbouring pastoral communities) of the Fertile Crescent. For example, analogies abound linking kings with shepherds and ordinary people with sheep – i.e. emulation by the king of the shepherd's compassion and gentleness towards his flock. The Bible is replete, of course, with similar ovine allusions and other imagery, mostly of this gentle, innocent, humane God-as-shepherd, people-as-sheep type. In fact the Bible provides one chief source of how pervasive and important sheep–man relationships became to some ancient peoples. Such importance probably originated among peoples who then – as now – lacked cattle wealth and the power and prestige associated with it. While sheep-keeping may have been, as the Bible suggests, the paradigm for encouraging humane conduct between people, sheep seem to have played no seminal role in the creation of civilization as such. Nevertheless, some biblical texts can be read with little difficulty as a kind of shepherds' handbook, a religiously enhanced stockman's almanac for living the good pastoral life.

The horse entered most ancient civilizations too late to stimulate seminal religious or other cultural associations. But once introduced, its importance was profound, especially when it was understood that it could be ridden or that it could pull war chariots. Numerous Ugaritic, Hittite, Greek, Indian and other hippological texts suggest, however, that the horse may well have played the same religio-political roles as did cattle. Mythological accounts exist among ancient peoples, such as those shared in Greek, Mesopotamian (Kassite) and Indian portrayals and/or stories about centaurs (or their analogues), but these all seem to originate with legends about later invaders of the original civilizations. Nevertheless, there are a few early examples of Indo-European chimera gods, some of them centaurs which are half horse, half man, such as the Greek god Cheiron.[52]

But it is clear that, as horse-keeping pastoral people invaded, conquered and absorbed (or were absorbed by) some of these oldest civilizations, horses did provide the new rulers of these cattle-rich states with a source of speed and stamina far in excess of man alone or his powerful but plodding cattle. They provided some of these original city state civilizations with the means to engage in long-range overland trade and foreign conquest. Horses became as profoundly important to these 'ageing' ancient civilizations as cattle had been to their creators. Gradually, however, while the horse as property also took over some of the power-prestige functions of cattle, religions themselves became progressively more abstract and celestial, less autochthonous or tied to certain animal characteristics. Except among the horse-possessing, cattle-raiding nomads who eventually overran many of the great early civilizations, horses never became as integrated into their religious beliefs or general culture as cattle. Persia is a possible exception, as were some successive ancient Indian civilizations following the initial civilization of the Indus Valley.[53]

At the same time individual horses and, occasionally, mules came to be highly prized as very close *companions* by important men. Some acquired a special reputation for loyalty and affection, which was often reciprocated. Examples include Alexander's love for his horse Bucephalus and Cyrus' for his favourite horse which drowned under him in Mesopotamia's Diyala River (causing, it is said, his engineers to wreak revenge by dividing it into 365 channels which then flowed out into the desert and died!). Evidently among mounted soldiers, as among rulers, individual horses were regarded as partners and companions in ways similar to the relationship which developed between individual men and their dogs.

SUMMARY

At the dawn of Old World civilizations there was widespread recognition that certain animal *species* shared important characteristics with humans but in exaggerated forms. This frequently inspired admiration or fear, which prompted various feelings of kinship, identification and awe, with a desire to emulate, placate or even, in extreme instances, to worship such animals. Among the most culturally and historically significant of these shared attributes were those representing power/dominion and libido/fertility. These were linked in various ways, and together helped to define the institution of kingship and solidify emerging cosmologies dealing with the overall relationships of humankind to the heavenly bodies, earth and gods. Amongst these relationships, bovine and solar images became pre-eminent.

Certain animal species also enjoyed prominence through their associations with the concepts of creation, procreation and rebirth and man's efforts to comprehend the significance of life and death. As civilizations emerged no species was so intimately intertwined with humankind as cattle: bulls and cows. With the eventual yoking of the ox to the plough, man–cattle relationships took on even greater significance. By providing humankind with the first source of power for plant cultivation greater than that of their own muscles, cattle proved the key to surplus grain production and, hence, to the development of civilization.

Other especially prominent relationships existed in antiquity between people and dogs and snakes, especially in relation to death and its consequences.

Such man–animal relationships, which originally represented or bordered upon identification, gradually evolved to become less central and real. They became more peripheral and symbolic, and/or purely utilitarian or social as civilizations aged. Such changes occurred more slowly in some civilizations (such as the Egyptian and Indian) than others and survivals from antiquity still persist to a considerable measure in India.[54]

Similar religio-political roles for the horse may have existed among other pastoral peoples who did not themselves create ancient civilizations, but solid evidence for this is relatively scarce. However, once the horse did enter early city states, its stamina and speed, far in excess of those of people, proved to be the key to emergence of the large landed empires developed by some ancient civilizations.

Sheep, or the sheep–man relationships which their domestication prompted, may have had an early and seminal influence upon man's admiration and striving for other qualities which we now regard as humane – compassion, trust and caring.

NOTES

1 Individuals from the 'western tradition' will be most familiar with such an early perspective *vis-à-vis* animals not only in what is revealed in surviving portions of Greek mythology, and references by ancient authors to other myths since lost, but also in fables collected by the Greek Aesop, who lived from about 620 to 560 BC and the Roman Aelian, of late second and early third century AD (see also Lawson 1964). Bodenheimer (1960) is a useful zoological source about animals and man in the ancient Near East generally and Paton (1925) gives many Egyptian textual sources.

2 As well as among various pre-literate present-day African pastoralists, notably the Nilotes of East Africa.

3 Dulling, for example, recognition of the roles the gradually increasing ability to differentiate between such notions played in beginning stages of evolution of the approach to unknowns we now regard as science. This has been my own special interest in this subject, an interest based upon conclusions which more or less parallel ones reached by Lloyd (1966, 1990).

4 As evidenced, for example, from studies of modern pre-literate cattle-culture peoples of the Nile basin.

5 A present-day example of adolescent boys being taught to assume the role of bull of the herd has been described among West Africa's Fulani by Lott and Hart (1979).

6 All these relationships merged at some point. Thus thunder was sometimes understood as the heavenly bull's libidinous bellow, lightning his ejaculation and rain his semen fertilizing the earth.

7 Walsh (1989) would reverse this ordering, finding earliest evidence to be of associations among a feminine birth goddess (with lunar cycle for menses), the horned cow and the horned (crescent) moon and its cycle. That would be

consistent with Hornblower's (1943) belief that the male role in reproduction was not understood until herding animals (especially cattle) were confined, then domesticated. Neither Walsh (personal communication), nor I, have seen evidence to the contrary and it is likely that the original bull associations *per se* were with power/dominion only and then later acquired the fertility aspect.

8 As suggested first, but more generally, by Eduard Hahn (1896). One of Hahn's more ardent modern supporters was Carl Sauer (1952) who argued that most contemporaries of Hahn resisted his views then because he stressed the role of sex in evolution of religions and religion over materialistic rationalism as an instigator of man's apparent inventiveness. Some of the circumstances surrounding evolution of just such a scenario as Hahn postulated were illustrated through the excavations by Mellaart (1967) at Çatal Hüyük near the Taurus Mountains of Anatolia. However, with respect to the general implications for early civilizations of such cattle-culture possibilities, these are still being largely overlooked. Since most students of ancient civilizations have tended, understandably, to be highly specialized and to consider development of single civilizations quite independently, important common features and their likely origins may easily be neglected. This is especially so if these are not readily comprehensible from our present-day perspective of possibilities (mindset). Therefore, some phenomena, such as identifications between other animals and man, have tended to be trivialized by scholars and their possible importance missed. This seems very much the case with cattle and man in antiquity. As Walsh (1989: 15) notes: 'animal domestication and contemporary ancient religions are topics that are usually treated as discrete phenomena despite the fact that animals were, and remain, of seminal importance in the belief systems of many societies'. The major philological demands upon scholars of these ancient records, which so compartmentalize their individual fields, also continue to act as formidable barriers to inputs into work on particular civilizations of heuristic contributions possible only from other specialized, even distant, disciplines. A notable exception with respect to cattle and religion among modern scholars interested in ancient civilizations has been Henri Frankfort (1948: 162ff.). And only a few other investigators from any relevant discipline, most notably Cook (1964), Von Lengerken and Von Lengerken (1955), Conrad (1957), Mourant and Zeuner (1963) and Walsh (1989), have yet focused even more broadly upon the general subject of man–cattle extensive relationships in antiquity. Simoons (1968), as well as the fairly extensive literature on present-day Nilotic peoples, gives especially important insights into ancient mindset and process.

9 He considered that shared anatomo-pathological vocabularies among speakers of a wide range of Indo-European languages probably resulted from information gained by the earliest Indo-European priests during dissection of religiously important animals.

0 With respect to the more commented upon instance of such cattle-culture survivals in India, the principal proponent of this theory of purely rational ecological determinants has been Harris (1966).

1 Or that these same peoples had already evolved both a small ruminant pastoral system and simple digging-stick agriculture and simply had to await domesticated cattle for the ingredients of civilization to gel. In that connection, Louis Grivetti (1980) has suggested from observations among present-day goat-herders (who are also hunter-gatherers) in southwestern Africa that the idea of 'gardens' may have originated in antiquity when herded goats or similar animals corralled for their protection at night deposited with their faeces in that confined well-fertilized place seeds of a variety of plants (including some highly scattered plants prized by gatherers). Especially when these corrals were moved, as they were periodically,

these concentrated seeds germinated and the seedlings survived and thus there grew man's first gardens! In fact, these observed agro-pastoralists of the Kalahari now transplant such desired plants from these natural goat-created 'gardens' to their own household compounds, and then tend them. This idea prompts speculation about the huge accumulations of cattle dung described from Neolithic India by Allchin (1963).

12 Among instances of Greek origin are the Anatolian Taurus mountains, Taurean (Crimean) peninsula, Greek Boeotia and Euboia, Bosporus (literally, 'Ox Ford'), Italy.

13 Other important chthonic gods, too, were sometimes more or less equated with bulls.

14 While present-day Nilotic Dinka liken practically everything, including 'Spiritual Force', to particular qualities of bulls and cows (Schwabe 1987), elders and priests interviewed vociferously denied that they 'worshipped' cattle. It should be noted that few Dinka have not had some exposure to the religions of outsiders (and are somewhat defensive or secretive about their own beliefs). However, even the strongest analogies may be quite different from identity; for example, the biblical assertion that man was created in God's image.

15 But the practice appears to have become an early legal recourse for victims of cattle that frequently gored, as evidenced by one rendering (Pritchard 1969: 163) of a passage in the fragmentary Mesopotamian legal code of the city state of Eshnunna (older than the intact Old Babylonian legal code of Hammurabi).

16 The Sudan's several million Dinka are a major modern example of a pastoral cattle-culture society who also practise digging-stick agriculture but have yet to yoke the ox to the plough.

17 Earliest coinage in some ancient civilizations suggests that precious metals were at least partially a wealth surrogate for cattle since cattle were actually portrayed on some of the first coins. And, among early speakers of at least the Indo-European phylum of languages, the proto-Indo-European word *pek'u for cattle is preserved not only in pecuaria in Spanish for animal industry, but in the English pecuniary and impecunious and similar wealth words originally meaning the possession or non-possession of cattle. Similarly, the word chattel relates etymologically to cattle and capital in the wealth sense originally referred to head of cattle. (Similarly, many related words in Sanskrit have cattle origins. As to the context of their origins, 'to fight' in Sanskrit meant literally 'to raid for cattle' and the word for 'leader' is literally 'lord of cattle'.) Even the origins of such modern English financial terms such as stock, stock market, watered stock, etc., though much more recent, are similar. The early Indo-European prophet Zoroaster indicated this wealth significance of cattle and attendant responsibilities scripturally, as for example, in: 'Give him welfare in cattle, three times a day raise thyself up and go take care of the beneficent cattle.'

18 As to writing symbols which evolved at the dawn of at least several ancient traditions, at least the first three numbers (counters) in Egyptian hieroglyphs, Sumerian cuneiform, Roman numerals, Chinese ideograms (and surviving cursive scripts like modern Arabic or our own numerals) are simply the requisite number of short straight marks in a row. But probably the first symbol for the things 'to be counted' (i.e. wealth), as evidenced by its becoming the first letter in alphabetic writing systems, was the horned bovine head (i.e. capital), drawn, for example, in cuneiform as ∀, on its side with its horns curved in Greek as α and still in our own alphabet, on its back as A.

19 Further hints of such more personal and intimate relationships are still to be found among Dinka and other Nilotic cattle-culture pastoralists – peoples whose ancestors are also believed to have lived near the upper Nile since antiquity (Ehret

1982). Each young male at puberty is given a special 'name' or 'song' bull to which he is bonded as a brother and to which he talks and composes sung verse.

20 It was also portrayed in the Indus Valley civilization.

21 Some of these subsequent points are from a study in progress by Andrew Gordon and the author which is currently available for comment as a working paper (1989).

22 Apis, the best known and longest persisting living bull god, was associated instead with (or was the 'double' of) the important ancient chthonic god Ptah.

23 The drinking of cow's milk by human babies – *and by human adults* – has been so taken for granted for so long in many (but surely not all) societies (Simoons 1979b) that its origins and the profundity of the relations between man and cow it originally signified now totally escape our inquiry. Yet nothing less than carriage to term within one's mother's body so identifies the mother–child bond of dependence and protective love that is basic to the existence and continuity of one's line than nursing from one's mother's teats. How biologically unique among relationships of one animal species to another is the fact that our species *Homo sapiens* sought the aid of another species to wet-nurse its young, to enter into this most intimate of relationships, for the cow in particular to become in effect foster mother to man. How great a contrast is the great pharaoh (king-god) drinking from the cow goddess's teat with the purely *biological* process among all mammalian species wherein milk secretion and milk drinking is confined to the immediate postpartum period of greatest infant dependence. *Adult* men, like the adults of all other mammalian species, have long ceased such dependence upon their *own* natural mothers and most cultures make much of a boy's severing this and other dependent bonds to his natural mother. Only the profoundest cultural needs, therefore, initially caused adult man to continue to drink the cow's milk through life (Schwabe 1984a).

24 An hypothesis initially sketched in Schwabe (1986) and developed in detail in Schwabe *et al.* (1989). For some present-day Dinka parallels see Schwabe (1987).

25 Belief in a similar cosmology can still be found today among some Nilotic pastoralists.

26 Ancient man had yet to conclude that one correct explanation for a phenomenon precluded alternative explanations. Rather, alternative explanations were seen as reinforcing and complementing one another.

27 However, if cattle once played the central ritual functions in religious sacrifice among most of these peoples, and probably continued to do so to some extent for some time in Phoenicia-Canaan, even early historic records suggest that sheep were already playing some of these ritual roles too, possibly, of course, first as surrogates for cattle, which were no longer sufficiently numerous. This species shift also occurred among many present-day Nilotic cattle-culturalists after the late 1890s African rinderpest pandemic decimated their cattle population. However, sheep/goat sacrifices among these modern pastoral peoples such as the Dinka are still referred to by them as 'bulls'!

28 As late as the Assyrian kings Sargon II and his grandson Naram-Sin, rulers of Mesopotamia still called themselves 'Wild Bull' and wore the horned headdress of their office.

29 The word for 'water' in Sumerian also meant 'semen' (as it sometimes did in Egyptian). Enlil's ejaculation filled the Tigris (Kramer 1963: 179).

30 Examples included Ninsuna, Gula and Ishtar (see Walsh 1989, for a more complete list). Ninhursag was also associated with Innana, the consort of the 'Wild Bull' or 'Divine Shepherd' god Dumuzi (Tammuz).

31 Some scholars have directed attention to many parallels between Ninhursag and the Egyptians' Hathor.

32 In Homer we read 'in bulls does the earthshaker delight'.

33 The supposedly original temple on Athens' acropolis, the *Bukolion* (cattle barn) was also the reputed site of the ritual mating of its queen archon with a bull representing Dionysus.

34 E. R. Dodds (1960 *passim*, esp. p. 194, notes on 920–2): 'a bull thou seem'st that leadeth on before; and horns upon thine head have sprouted forth. How, *wast* thou brute? – bull art thou verily now!' and on Dionysus as 'the bull who leads the herd'; see also Plutarch's hymn (Q. Gr. 36, 299) to Dionysus by the women of Elis: 'Come hither, Dionysus, to thy holy temple by the sea; come with the Graces to thy temple, rushing with bull's foot, O goodly bull, O goodly bull' and designation of his priests as 'cattleherds'.

35 Herodotus 2.42 2, 49.2, see Dodds (1960), 126–6, notes on 406–8.

36 'Ox' is used here as singular of cattle.

37 For much interesting material in the context of this conference, see Leshnik and Sontheimer (1975).

38 For example, the early origins of *goshalas* or 'old cattle homes' still present in India are detailed by Lodrick (1981). A modern Indian scriptural defence of cattle protection there against common western perceptions (as well as against some western scholarship *vis-à-vis* cattle and ancient India) is Anon. (1971).

39 Keys to this extensive literature and ongoing debate may be found in recent works of Harris (1966), Heston (1971), Odend'hal (1972), Simoons (1979a) and Lodrick (1981). For some modern Hindu religio-political arguments see Gandhi (1954) and Anon (1971).

40 In part I think the protagonists in today's Indian sacred cow debate, both Indian and foreign (of two camps) are mostly talking past one another, often advancing extreme or too-embracing scenarios, sometimes from pre-existing ideological beliefs, and sometimes anachronistically mixing historical events with current concepts and practices, all without regard to ancient parallels outside of India. My conclusion is that, while the religious ideas about bull-chief-gods-men came first, these ideas were only irrational when perceived from the modern western mindset, not the ancient, and that other rational forces (even from a modern perspective) – and surely including ecological ones – importantly influenced events during the roughly 3,000 years between the time cattle were first domesticated and the time when the complexes of actions and their natural consequences we identify as civilizations fully emerged.

41 For details on boundary-marking and dominion see Schwabe and Gordon (1988) and our further work in progress (Schwabe and Gordon 1989).

42 He also mentions Italy being named for the bull Italus chased from Sicily by Hercules.

43 It is of interest that all ancient Old World civilizations arose in the astrologically designated Age of Taurus.

44 For how some of these very important utilitarian roles of oxen (and horses) in agriculture and transport arose in the ancient world see Littauer and Crouwel (1979).

45 Among many present-day cultural derivatives are such terms in English as 'strong as an ox', 'take the bull by the horns', 'to bully someone', 'to be horny' and 'to be cowed'.

46 Compare also, in the New Testament, a dog licking Lazarus' wounds. Examples of much of this same type of lore survive in more recent times; for example folk beliefs today that a dog licking its, or our, wounds is a helpful thing.

47 Aelian (*On Animals* I, 51): 'The spine of the dead man, they say, transforms the [its] putrefying marrow [cord] into a snake.'

48 For evidence of beliefs among Egyptians that bone marrow, especially of the spine (the spinal chord was considered 'marrow') was semen and the widely shared nature of this belief outside Egypt in antiquity see Schwabe *et al.* (1982).

49 Thus the Egyptian word *mtwt* meant both semen and (snake) poison.
50 As mentioned, this surrogate religious role of sheep and goats is seen increasingly among modern Nilotes who, nevertheless, still refer to the ovine or caprine sacrifice as 'bull'.
51 Comparative examples from Greece are given by Cook (1964, I).
52 And surely among much later Indo-European invaders of northern Europe, the horse played a central religious role. Ostensibly it was to help stamp out Odin worship, for example, that Pope Gregory II in 732 forbade the eating of horsemeat since it was a practice central to sacrifice and communion rituals among such peoples. Of course, just as the ox gave man the source of power for the agrarian revolution and the emergence of civilization, the horse provided man with speed and stamina far in excess of that of his own muscles. This was, in turn, the key to communication, transport and control that helped small city states to grow into and rule the first large landed empires. Some of the more interesting recent studies of horses in antiquity are those of Cohen and Sivan (1983) on the Ugaritic hippiatric texts (from that Pheonician city state) and of Mack-Fisher (1990) proposing, from the study of these and other ancient equine veterinary texts, that the obscure Latin word *veterinarius* derives via Carthage (perhaps in the Carthagian city of Gades, modern Cadiz) from the ancient Ugaritic (semitic) *btr*, an official of the Ugaritic queen responsible for horse health and care.
53 An account of the utilitarian and companion roles of the horse in ancient Greece is that of Anderson (1961).
54 These are also prominently preserved in many respects among the cattle-culture Nilotic pastoralists of the Nile Basin today (e.g. the Dinka, Nuer, Turkana, Maasai) who never did develop 'civilization'.

REFERENCES

Adams, W. (1977) *Nubia: Corridor to Africa*, Princeton, New Jersey: Princeton University Press.
Allchin, F. (1963) *Neolithic Cattle-Keepers of South India: a Study of the Deccan Ashmounds*, Cambridge: Cambridge University Press.
Anderson, J. (1961) *Ancient Greek Horsemanship*, Berkeley, Calif.: University of California Press.
Anon. (1971) *A Review of 'Beef in Ancient India'*, Gorakhpur, India: Gita Press.
Barb, A. (1953) 'Diva matrix', *Journal of the Warburg and Courtauld Institutes* 16: 193–238.
Bodenheimer, F. (1960) *Animal and Man in Bible Lands*, Leiden: Brill.
Clutton-Brock, J. (1981) *Domesticated Animals from Early Times*, Austin: University of Texas Press.
Cohen, C. and Sivan, D. (1983) *The Ugaritic Hippiatric Texts: a Critical Edition*, American Oriental Series 9, New Haven: American Oriental Society.
Conrad, J. (1957) *The Horn and the Sword: the History of the Bull as Symbol of Power and Fertility*, New York: Dutton.
Cook, A. (1964) *Zeus: a Study in Ancient Religion*, vol. I, New York: Biblo & Tannen. First published 1914.
Dodds, E. (1960) *Euripides Bacchae*, Oxford: Clarendon Press.
Ehret, C. (1982) 'Population movement and culture contact in the southern Sudan, c. 3000 BC to AD 1000: a preliminary linguistic overview', in J. Mack and R. Robertshaw (eds) *Culture History in the Southern Sudan*, Nairobi: British Institute in East Africa Memoir 8.

Epstein, H. (1971) *The Origin of the Domesticated Animals of Africa*, 2 vols, New York: Africana.

Farnell, L. (1911) *Greece and Babylon*, Edinburgh: T. & T. Clark.

Frankfort, H. (1948) *Kingship and the Gods*, Chicago: University of Chicago Press.

—— (1955) *Stratified Cylinder Seals of the Diyals Region*, Chicago: University of Chicago Oriental Institute.

Fraser, P. (1972) *Ptolemaic Alexandria*, Oxford: Clarendon Press.

Gandhi, M. (1954) *How to Serve the Cow*, Ahmedabad: Navajivan.

Gordon, A. and Schwabe, C. W. (1989) *The Egyptian 'w3s' Scepter and its Modern Analogues: Uses as Symbols of (Divine) Power or Authority*, Working Paper 52, Agricultural History Center, University of California, Davis.

Grivetti, L. (1980) 'Goat kraal gardens and plant domestication: thoughts on ancient and modern food production', *Ecology of Food and Nutrition* 10: 5–7.

Hahn, E. (1896) *Die Haustiere und ihre Beziehungen zur Wirtschaft des Menschen*, Leipzig: Duncker & Humblot.

Harris, M. (1966) 'The cultural ecology of India's sacred cattle', *Current Anthropology* 7: 51–66.

Heston, A. (1971) 'An approach to the sacred cow of India', *Current Anthropology* 12: 191–210.

Hooper, W. (trans.) (1935) *Marcus Porcius Cato on Agriculture. Marcus Terrentius Varro on Agriculture*, Loeb Classical Library, Cambridge, Mass.: Harvard University Press.

Hornblower, G. (1943) 'The Egyptian fertility rite: postscript', *Man* 43: 31.

Kramer, S. (1963) *The Sumerians*, Chicago: University of Chicago Press.

Lawson, J. (1964) *Modern Greek Folklore and Ancient Greek Religion*, New Hyde Park, New York: University Books. First Published 1910.

Leach, M. (1961) *God Had a Dog: Folklore of the Dog*, New Brunswick, New Jersey: Rutgers University Press.

Leshnik, L. and Sontheimer, G.-D. (eds) (1975) *Pastoralists and Nomads in South Asia*, Wiesbaden: Otto Harrassowitz.

Lincoln, B. (1981) *Priests, Warriors, and Cattle: a Study in the Ecology of Religions*, Berkeley: University of California Press.

Littauer, M. and Crouwel, J. (1979) *Wheeled Vehicles and Ridden Animals in the Ancient Near East*, Leiden: Brill.

Lloyd, E. (1966) *Polarity and Analogy: Two Types of Argumentation in Early Greek Thought*, Cambridge: Cambridge University Press.

—— (1990) *Demystifying Mentalities*, Cambridge: Cambridge University Press.

Lobban, R. (1989) 'Cattle and the rise of the Egyptian state', *Anthrozöos* 2: 194–201.

Lodrick, D. (1981) *Sacred Cows, Sacred Places. Origins and Survivals of Animal Homes in India*, Berkeley: University of California Press.

Lott, D. and Hart, B. (1979) 'Applied ethology in a nomadic cattle culture', *Applied Animal Ethology* 5: 309–19.

Mack-Fisher, L. (1990) 'From Ugarit to Gades: Mediterranean veterinary medicine', *Maarav* 5–6: 207–20.

Mellaart, J. (1967) *Çatal Hüyük*, New York: McGraw-Hill.

Mourant, A. and Zeuner, F. (eds) (1963) *Man and Cattle*, London: Royal Anthropological Institute of Great Britain and Ireland Occasional Paper 18.

Odend'hal, S. (1972) 'Energetics of Indian cattle in their environment', *Human Ecology* 1: 3–22.

Paton, D. (1925) *Animals in Ancient Egypt*, Princeton, New Jersey: Princeton University Press.

Pritchard, J. (ed.) (1969) *Ancient Near Eastern Texts Relating to the Old Testament*, 3rd edn, Princeton, New Jersey: Princeton University Press.

Riggs, F. (1957) 'Industria and agraria – toward a typology of comparative administration', in W. Siffin (ed.) *Toward the Comparative Study of Public Administration*, Bloomington: Indiana University Press.

—— (1973) *Prismatic Society Revisited*, Morristown, New Jersey: General Learning Press.

Sauer, C. (1952) *Animal Origins and Dispersals*, Cambridge, Mass.: MIT Press.

Schwabe, C. (1978a) 'The holy cow – provider or parasite? A problem for humanists', *Southern Humanities Review* 13: 251–78.

—— (1978b) *Cattle, Priests and Progress in Medicine*, Minneapolis: University of Minnesota Press.

——(1984a) 'Drinking cow's milk: the most intense man–animal bond', in R. Anderson, B. Hart and L. Hart (eds) *The Pet Connection*, Minneapolis: Center to Study Human–Animal Relationships and Environments, pp. 50–7.

—— (1984b) *Veterinary Medicine and Human Health*, 3rd edn, Baltimore: Williams & Wilkins.

—— (1986) 'Bull semen and muscle ATP: some evidence of the dawn of medical science in ancient Egypt', *Canadian Journal of Veterinary Research* 50: 145–53.

—— (1987) 'Dinka "spirits", cattle and communion', *Journal of Cultural Geography* 7: 117–26.

Schwabe, C. and Gordon, A. (1988) 'The Egyptian *w3s*-scepter and its modern analogues: uses in animal husbandry, agriculture and surveying', *Agricultural History* 62: 61–89.

—— (1989) *The Egyptian 'w3s'-Scepter: a Possible Biological Origin as a Dried Bull's Penis in Relation to an Ancient Egyptian Theory on Bones as the Source of Semen*, Working Paper 53, Agricultural History Center, University of California, Davis.

Schwabe, C., Adams, J. and Hodge, C. (1982) 'Egyptian beliefs about the bull's spine: an anatomical origin for ankh', *Anthropological Linguistics* 24: 445–79.

Schwabe, C., Gordon, A., Ashmore, C. and Ortmayer, H. (1989) *'Live Flesh': Rudiments of Muscle Physiology in Ancient Egypt*, Working Paper 54, Agricultural History Center, University of California, Davis.

Simoons, F. (1968) *A Ceremonial Ox of India*, Madison: University of Wisconsin Press.

—— (1979a) 'Questions in the sacred-cow controversy (with comments by many others)', *Current Anthropology* 20: 467–93.

—— (1979b) 'Dairying, milk use and lactose malabsorption in Eurasia: a problem in culture history', *Anthropos* 74: 61–80.

Van Lepp, J. (1990) 'Predynastic origins of Hathor', paper presented at the 1990 meeting of the American Research Center in Egypt, Berkeley.

Vendryes, J. (1918) 'Les correspondances de vocabulaire entre l'indo-iranien et l'italo-celtique', *Mémoires de Société de Linguistique de Paris* 20: 265–85.

Von Lengerken, H. and von Lengerken, E. (1955) *Ur, Hausrind und Mensch*, Berlin: Deutsche Academie der Landwirtschaftswissenschaften.

Walsh, K. (1989) 'Cattle of the moon: religion and ritual in the domestication and early history of *Bos primigenius* in the Mediterranean region', PhD dissertation, University of California, Berkeley.

Winkler, H. (1937) *Volker und Volkerbewegungen im vergeschichlichen Oberägypten im Lichte neuer Felsbilderfunde*, Stuttgart.

Young, F. (1979) *The Use of Sacrificial Ideas in Greek Christian Writers from the New Testament to John Chrysostom*, Cambridge, Mass.: Philadelphia Patristic Foundation.

Zeuner, F. (1963) *A History of Domesticated Animals*, New York: Harper & Row.

4

ANIMALS IN MEDIEVAL PERCEPTIONS
The image of the ubiquitous other

Esther Cohen

In the early years of the eleventh century, a poor southern French knight decided to undertake a pilgrimage to Rome. Owning no mount, he borrowed a mule from his brother. On the way, the mule died near the monastery of Conques. Distraught with the magnitude of the catastrophe, the knight railed against fate, which not only prevented him from completing his pilgrimage, but made it impossible for him even to reimburse the mule's original owner. But being near Conques, he addressed his specific complaints to the local saint, Saint Foy (Faith), who promptly brought the mule back to life (Bouillet 1897).

The story of the resuscitated mule, incorporated into the collection of Saint Foy's miracles, epitomizes various aspects of the relationship between humans and animals in the early Middle Ages. On the one hand, there was the painful scarcity of domestic animals, which not only forced a knight to ride a mule (horses being too expensive), but also turned the death of a domestic beast into a major catastrophe. Bearing in mind that miracle tales were disseminated as propaganda for the saint's powers, it says a great deal concerning the importance eleventh-century people attached to the life of a mule that the saint's power should be evinced in its resuscitation. On the other hand, the close familiarity of humans and animals made people treat their beasts in a manner inconceivable in more clearly categorized societies. That a man should implore a saint to revive a beast, that the saint should accede to this request, and above all, that the event should serve to enhance the saint's glory in everybody's eyes is clear evidence of a very great intimacy indeed between human and animal.

Nobody has ever attempted even an estimate of the animal population of Europe in the Middle Ages. It is, of course, an impossible task. While evaluations of the number of domestic animals do exist (Duby 1968), it is impossible to determine the number of wild beasts, to say nothing of lice and other vermin infesting human bodies and habitation. Historians assume that the paucity of domestic animals in the early Middle Ages was offset by an increase in abundance of wildlife, mainly because of the demographic contraction and the reversion to forest of previously cultivated land (Ortalli

1985). The subsequent recovery of populations and the land reclamation of the eleventh to thirteenth centuries presumably brought about a concomitant expansion of domestic fauna and a contraction of wildlife. The numerous laws protecting hunting rights and criminalizing poaching clearly indicate the value attached by lords and peasants alike to hunting and the ever-increasing scarcity of venison (Birrell 1982).

Clearly, though, the animal population of Europe exceeded by far the human, and was undoubtedly ubiquitous. Far from being confined to the countryside, domestic animals also lived in the greatest urban centers, being essential to domestic economy. Town records constantly complained about pigs running loose in the streets, biting unsupervised babies (Coyecque 1891). The growth of the domestic animal population in the later Middle Ages only increased the familiarity in which human and animal cohabited.

ANIMALS IN MEDIEVAL CULTURE

For a society as intimately connected with the animal world as the medieval, there was no such thing as generic 'animals'. It is said that the Eskimos have sixteen different words for snow of different types. Medieval French has almost as many different words for horse, each signifying a different animal with a different function. Generalizations only function at a distance from the object of study, and medieval society as a whole lived very close to the animal world indeed, much too close for generalizations.

One must therefore speak of specific animals, but one cannot cover the entire fauna of Europe in one chapter. What I intend to do is to speak not of animals, but of the use people made in their perceptions of animals and animal symbolism. For very often, when human beings wanted to express a concept, they dressed it in animal symbolism. They spoke of the lamb or the lion when they meant Christ or a king. Time and again they used animals to symbolize human traits – in literature, in pageants, in public rituals and in criminal trials. In each case, the specific animal used epitomized specific characteristics attributed to the human protagonist of the situation. This sort of 'animal vocabulary' could only exist and function in a society in close daily contact with animals. The variations between different attitudes were largely dictated by the coexistence of specific social groups with various animals. Clerics wrote of the pelican as a symbol of charity, noblemen judged their peers' position by their horses and hounds, town authorities complained of loose dogs and pigs in the streets, and peasants shared their real and imaginary lives with chickens, pigs, goats or sheep. A society in which animals were omnipresent naturally had many views of animals.

Perhaps the most common perception of animals in western learned culture was based upon the story of creation. Nature was created prior to the human race, as preparation for its existence. Humanity was the crown of creation, destined to rule over nature and use it for its own ends (see Plate 4.1).

Consequently, whatever taxonomy there was of the natural world, it was purely functional and anthropocentric. The thirteen-century encyclopedist Bartholomeus Anglicus provides perhaps the most succinct summary of this view: 'All types of animals, domestic and wild beasts as well as reptiles, were created for the best use of man.' Certain animals, such as deer and cattle, were given to people for eating; others, such as the horse, the donkey, the ox and the camel, to help them; again others, like the monkey, the songbirds and the peacock, to amuse them. A fourth category, containing fleas, lice and the like, was created to remind people of their fragility, and a fifth, comprised of such as the bear, the lion and the serpent, existed in order to frighten them and remind them of God's power. Finally, many animals were created so that their bodies could be used to alleviate human sickness, for the lion's hairs cured hemorrhoids, and the bear's eye was good for quartan fever (Bartholomeus 1601: 985–6).

This functional view of nature also implied a hierarchy, in which humans stood above animals. Humanity was measured in the distance from the animal, and the lower a person sank, the closer he or she was to the animal world. The search for perfect humanity consisted in distancing oneself as far as possible from the animal. Human soul, destined for an afterlife and capable of salvation or damnation, was something that animals did not possess. Nor did animals have the gift of reason or thought. The animal was therefore not only inferior to the human in a hierarchy of government. It was also farther removed from divinity. The Aristotelian teaching, attributing a rational soul to man alone, fitted in well with the Christian tradition.

The hierarchical view was reinforced in the thirteenth century by a strong taxonomical trend. The scholastic authors of the great *summae* were embarking upon a major attempt not only to codify but also to classify all human knowledge and experience under specific categories. By the same token, the physical and metaphysical world were also organized in clear-cut classifications. In this sense, there was little difference between types of angels, stones or laws. All must be firmly classified and placed within one major hierarchy.

The approach was not limited to scholastic philosophers. When Bartholomeus Anglicus wrote his compendium, his aims were more modest. Indeed, he also refrained from using the philosophical term *summa*. Still, the aim was the same: to summarize all that he knew of man, or nature, or morality, or theology, and to do so within clearly predefined categories. Animals, therefore, were clearly distinguished as different from human beings, any attempt to breach the impassable theological and physical barriers awakening all the associations of impurity commonly attendant upon such blurring of boundaries (Douglas 1966). The animal kingdom, in learned tradition, was thus inferior to human beings and unalterably different.

While this trend became significant with the revival of Aristotelian studies in the thirteenth century, it was based upon a long tradition of learned bestiaries going back to the seventh century.[1] All of these relied originally

61

upon the *Physiologus* of Smyrna, a second-century list of animals (Orlandi 1985; McCulloch 1962). While they attempted no classification, they did list and describe animals.

There was a clear distinction within the learned tradition between the overall view of the animal kingdom, opposed to the essence of humanity, and the perception of individual animals, all of them possessing symbolic and transcendent characteristics. The latter enjoyed a special proximity to human beings by virtue of their embodiment of specific human and metaphysical traits. In the *Physiologus* and in the bestiary tradition every animal possessed specific moral and symbolic qualities beyond its physical attributes, but derived from them. The otter, for example, was reputed to hate and attack the sleeping crocodile. Since the crocodile resembled the devil, the otter was perceived as the type and image of the Saviour (Seel 1967: 23). Preachers used such traits either as a warning or as an example. The dove, faithful to her mate and inconsolable at his death, was presented as a model for widows exhorted not to remarry (Zink 1976: 405).

The bestiary tradition incorporated many elements of popular lore. Though the theological significance of each animal was undoubtedly of learned origin, the principle that dictated an individualized attitude towards each animal may well have come from popular origins. Certainly the preachers relying upon the individual symbolism of each animal in their exhortations were deliberately trying, in their use of *exempla*, to bridge the gap between their theories and their audiences: 'There is a kind of frog which, when placed in a dog's mouth, silences it. Similarly, gifts placed in the hands of a judge silence him and make him avoid true judgment' (Welter 1973: 133). Animals in the *exempla* literature were also indices of piety. Etienne de Bourbon tells of storks who deserted their nest on top of an excommunicated man's house, returning only when the excommunication was lifted (Lecoy de la Marche 1877: 255).

The use of animal symbolism here had nothing theological about it. It was merely an effort to bridge the distance between two perceptual schemes by using familiar examples. At the same time, the preachers yielded nothing when it came to the confusing of categories. Etienne de Bourbon conducted an energetic campaign to extirpate the cult of the hound Saint Guinefort, popularly canonized for having saved its master's baby from death and mistakenly martyred by the same master. Caesarius of Heisterbach, a popular author of *exempla*, warned that a dog baptized as part of a children's game immediately became rabid (Schmitt 1979: 15–17; Caesarius 1851: 2:249).

The *exempla* literature was probably one of the means by which animal lore flowed from learned to popular strata and vice versa, merging into one tradition. Perhaps the clearest example of such a merging is the fifteenth-century *Livre du roy Modus et de la reyne Racio*, in which Queen Reason posits a taxonomy of the animal world which is strong evidence of everyday familiarity. Animals, quite simply, are divided into sweet [-smelling] beasts and stinking beasts. Nevertheless, smell in this context means more than the purely olfactory sensation produced by proximity to a byre, for example. The hart heads the list of sweet beasts mainly because of its role in religious symbolism and in saints' legends. The pig heads the list of smelly beasts not only because of the physical facts, but due also to its symbolic associations. Predatory animals, such as the wolf and the fox, are also considered smelly (Anon. 1486).

Late medieval popular culture was more than familiar with the specific characteristics and properties of each animal. More than that, it often attributed transcendent characteristics to the live animals that surrounded the humans of the time, even to the point of heretically assuming that animals had souls. Saint Guinefort and the baptized dog are only two cases out of many. In Germany clerics complained more than once about peasants showing the host to sick horses, in order to cure them. The 'Mass for horses' was common, especially in Bavaria (Rothkrug 1979; Zika 1988). In all fairness, the attribution of spiritual qualities to animals was not limited to the popular sphere. The 'Feast of the donkey', in which a live ass was brought into church before parading in town, was celebrated in France every January 1st, as thirteenth-century missals indicate (Heers 1983: 136–41). In Germany, a donkey took place of honor in the Palm Sunday procession (Scribner 1987: 26).

Even when people avoided the error of imbuing the animal kingdom with spirituality, they still persisted in attributing human qualities to animals. Hunting dogs stood for pride and arrogance, pigs for gluttony, lions and cocks for courage (Schmitt 1979: 87–8; Sainéan 1972, I: 61–6). But it was not enough to know that the lion symbolized courage; it was necessary to find a way of transmitting this courage to human beings. True, wearing a belt of lion's pelt, or carrying on one's person the lion's eye or heart would achieve this end, but lions were notoriously scarce and dangerous. The far more common dunghill cock was equally useful. In fact, lions were known to fear cocks (Hambroer 1966). It was thus possible for people lacking courage to infuse this quality into their spirits by carrying a cock, or some parts of a cock's carcass. Women used to carry the womb of a barren bitch, or expose their genitals to the smoke generated by burning the hoof of a mule (sterile by its very nature) as contraceptive measures (Laurent 1989: 33–4). Any quality sought could be achieved by the use of the appropriate organs from the proper animals. These beliefs were all incorporated in an anonymous text, attributed to the man who was probably the greatest zoologist of the Middle Ages, Albertus Magnus. The *Grand et petit Albert* contains a 'Treatise concerning the marvels of the world' which is a thorough exposition of the use of animal organs by analogy to human characteristics. Another treatise within this collection explains the various uses of animal urine in popular medicine (Husson 1978).

Animals not only embodied specific human traits: they often came to symbolize specific types of human being. The anthropomorphic tradition of the beast epics in which animals stood for human roles was part of a rich folkloristic stratum of animal lore common to the entire Indo-European world (Bédier 1969). Here the lion ceased to be a symbol of courage and became king of the beasts, parallel to and parody of the human ruler. The wolf, the camel, and most of all the fox, evolved as full 'human' personalities in the beast epic. Notably, the central characters of these tales were not the domestic animals familiar to late medieval peasants from everyday life. The pig, the hare and the plebeian dog (as opposed to the aristocratic hound) play a very minor role in the beast epics. Wolves and foxes were probably far more familiar than lions and camels, but they lived beyond the control of the domestic sphere. The very fact that they did not share in everyday life made them convenient subjects for allegorical representation. Everyday familiarity bred if not necessarily contempt, certainly too much detailed knowledge of domestic beasts for the dissociation necessary for an allegorical perception to take place. The less familiar the actual animal was to popular audiences, the easier it was to imbue it with symbolic and human characteristics.

Animals in fables acted in all human spheres, and in a manner hardly complimentary to humans. The anthropomorphic perception of animals is central especially to the Renard beast epics (Jordogne 1975). There the wily fox appears in several human roles. The legal motif plays an important role in these epics. The trial of Renard before King Lion for raping the she-wolf (see Plate 4.2) is central to all versions of the tale. Various branches of the tale follow different legal procedures: the German *Reinhardt Fuchs* is a satire of imperial justice, while the northern French *Roman de Renart* and the Flemish *Van den Vos Reynaerde* adhere strictly to local feudal law (Krause 1983; Dievoet 1975). The motifs, however, concern fairly universal issues: lineage loyalty, vendetta, fraud and honour.

Though animals were undoubtedly inferior to man in the hierarchy of creation, the perceptual animal kingdom of the later Middle Ages was a much wider land than the modern, post-Linnaean one. In it dwelt cheek by jowl not only domestic and wild animals, but also fabulous beasts, such as the basilisk and the unicorn, and creatures both human and animal, or neither. All bestiaries listed the fabulous beasts in precisely the same manner as the donkey or the lion. The human and the animal merged in that borderland between the settled and the wild, reality and fantasy, to create the fabulous and the monstrous. The far reaches of the earth, according to late medieval travelers, were inhabited by fantastic monsters, part human, part animal, notorious for their ferocity, cruelty and savagery (Kappler 1980: 147–57). Later medieval literature also populated the known geography of the west with mermaids, women-serpents, werewolves and child-swans, all beings who magically crossed the barriers between categories of being (Poirion 1982: 29–30, 110–15). Some of them, like Mélusine, the serpent-woman, were beneficient and maternal (Le Goff 1977: 307–31; Gaignebet 1974: 87–103), while others, like werewolves, were extremely dangerous.

Not all of these monsters impinged upon daily life, though trials of werewolves were not unknown (Otten 1986: 69–76). However, their presence in contemporary imagination did affect the attitude towards any human beings too closely associated with animals. When the gypsies appeared in the West, their uncanny closeness to horses was one of the reasons for their rejection and stigmatization (Egmond 1988). The same unnatural closeness had earlier been attributed to the Tartars, and both groups were also closely associated with the devil. The animal as such possessed no demonic qualities: it was the breach of the barrier between human and animal that endowed both sides with demonic qualities (Smith 1978: 96–113). Werewolves, more frightening than any animal precisely because they underwent a metamorphosis from human to animal and back, embodied this belief.

The human being who became most closely identified with the animal world was the person deprived of reason. This particular perception of madness was closely tied to the belief in the existence of wild men and women – hairy, frightening, semi-humans who lived in wild places (Kappler 1980: 157–64; Bernheimer 1952). Some of them belonged to a special race of such monsters, but others were merely temporarily deranged inhabitants of civilization. From Nebuchadnezzar to Chrétien de Troyes's Yvain, kings and heroes repeatedly lost their reason, fled to the forest or ate grass, and became for some time wild men (Gervase of Tilbury 1707: 1003; Bernheimer 1952: 8–17; Le Goff 1985: 107–31).

Paradoxically, the assumption of animal qualities could be viewed either as punishment or as sin. Audiences could sympathize with the fictional plight of someone bewitched into lupine form or held by temporary madness, but any real-life encounter with hybrid forms got short shrift. Werewolves, when caught, were tried and executed. Monsters born in civilization were promptly exterminated, and people who had committed bestiality were burnt at the stake together with the animal. Others, charged with animal metamorphosis by means of witchcraft, suffered the same fate (Otten 1986: 99–134; Russell and Russell 1978; Smith 1894; Damhouder 1562: 282–3; cf. Clark 1986).

ANIMALS IN MEDIEVAL PUBLIC RITUAL

Given the rich spectrum of animal symbolism in medieval culture, the use and inclusion of animals, both real and figurative, within public rituals was an obvious development. Most urban pageants and processions in the later Middle Ages displayed animals in symbolic and literary guises. When Philip the Fair knighted his sons in 1313, all orders of society competed in adding their contributions to royal magnificence. The guilds of Paris erected, in the space of two days, a new wooden bridge over the Seine exhibiting a series of pageants. Here, in the procession mounted by the weavers, Renard the Fox appeared in the guise first of a doctor and later of a chanter, sandwiched between Herod and Caiaphas on one side and Adam and Eve on the other. Except for Hersent the she-wolf, Renard was the only non-biblical personage in the pageant. The tanners, not to be outdone, included a whole biography of Renard, shown not only as a poultry-stealing fox, but also as a bishop, archbishop, and even as a pope (Geffroi de Paris 1968: 137–8). Other crafts apparently had other animals in their own processions, 'in which the specific animals depicted fulfilled specific functions' (Jean de Saint-Victor 1968: 656–7; Favier 1978: 61). Here the chronicler describing the feast summed up in one sentence the role of literary animals both in public ritual and within the cultural context.

Nor were animals in public rituals limited to the popular sphere. Few ceremonies could qualify as more elitist and intellectual than the pageant planned for the solemn entry of Isabel of Bavaria, bride of Charles VI, in 1389. It was put on by the confraternity of legal clerks, speaking for all the jurists of Paris at the time. The pageant presented, quite literally, a *lit de justice* – a royally furnished chamber, in which Saint Anne (always a symbol of justice) rested. Into this chamber came, from an adjoining garden, a white hart from one side, a lion and an eagle from the other. Twelve maidens with unsheathed swords protected the bed and the hart from the other two animals. The white hart, associated in the bestiaries with Christ, had by the late fourteenth century come to symbolize both justice and the person of the king (Bryant 1986: 178–80).

Live animals were also part of public processions. Animal processions took place in several cities of France and the Low Countries. Sculptures describing such processions could be found in Strasbourg and in Aix-en-Provence (Berkenhoff 1937: 72–3). Late medieval Ypres institutionalized the 'Cat feast' on the second Wednesday of Lent, which is still celebrated today. Originally, the 'feast' consisted of a procession, followed by the throwing of cats from a tower. The whole city participated in the event (Viaene 1939). The cat-burning ceremony, celebrated in Paris each year on the eve of Saint-John's day as part of the traditional bonfires, was even more cruel. Again, it was a city-wide celebration. The pyre was erected in the Place de Grève, and one or two dozen cats in bags were hung on it. On one occasion, a fox was added. The king and nobility watched from specially erected galleries, and the cat-burning was followed by a public feast at the king's expense. Similar cat-burning feasts were also held on Saint John's eve in Metz and Saint Chamand (Franklin 1928: 508–9; Darnton 1984: 83–4).

Was the maltreatment of the cats merely public sadism? The fact that it invariably took place within a public ritual, procession or execution indicates otherwise. Animals, especially domestic ones, were sometimes the mirror image of the human community and the bearer of its guilt. The idea that the public death of an innocent animal can cleanse the community is age-old, and is described in the Bible, specifically in two ritual practices. Whenever a dead man was found and his killer could not be traced, the elders of the community were to behead a heifer which had never been put to the yoke on the spot and wash their hands over her body, declaring their community clean of the spilled blood (Deuteronomy 21: 1–9). Once a year, at the ritual atonement of the entire people's sins, the high priest was to take two goats, sacrifice one and place upon the other's head the sins of the whole people. The scapegoat, carrying those sins, was then sent into the wilderness (Leviticus 16: 5–22) (Plate 4.4).

Biblical rituals had little significance in medieval culture, except when transmuted into Christian perceptions. Christianity had so far internalized this feeling as to name Christ dying for people's sins, *Agnus Dei*. Nor was this purely a figure of speech, for paintings of the mystical lamb, depicted as a flesh-and-blood lamb, were a commonplace of late medieval iconography. Sacrificial victims were invariably perceived in animal terms. The dying animal always had to be pure and blameless, and its public ritual death cleansed the guilty community. Very little indeed of this solemn ritual remained in the public killing of cats, except for the fact that it was timed to coincide with periods of cleansing, either the Christian cleansing of Lent, or the bonfires lighted on Saint John's eve, a leftover of the summer solstice celebrations (Vaultier 1965: 73–9).

The public efficacy of the ritual was based upon a layer of folkloristic belief. The animal procession of 1313 took place on Pentecost, which fell that year on 6 June, only two weeks away from Saint John's feast. Though named for a saint, this festival was full of folkloric traditions considerably predating Christianity (Cohen 1941, II: 86). Herbs gathered on the eve of Saint John's were useful for a variety of magical purposes, from poisoning to verifying pregnancies (Jannet 1855: 154; Vaultier 1965: Muchembled 1985: 84–5). But the saint also associated the human and the animal in some curious ways. He was the patron of epileptics, those who suffered from 'Saint John's disease'. In some parts of northern France in the fourteenth century it was believed that three successive acts of bestiality would cure epilepsy (Vaultier 1965: 77–8). Saint John, and by extension his day, were thus associated with the merging of the human and the animal. The bonfires of Saint John's and the idea of animal sacrifice were joined in the public cat-burning ceremony.

Renard is another story. In the first place, here was no flesh-and-blood fox, but a human being dressed as an animal dressed as a human being – doctor, chanter, bishop, even pope. Renard was no scapegoat, but the personification of specific, essentially human characteristics, imposed by popular imagination upon the characters of the beast epics. Unlike the hapless cats, he did not suffer for his or anyone else's misdeeds. On the contrary, he got away with them. Public rituals articulated both the aspect of animals in their own form assuming human guilt and punishment and animals aping humans and getting away with it.[2]

Both the symbolic and the sacrificial animal appeared at carnival time – that very special time during the year when all barriers fell and all categories were inverted. Again, carnival was connected with very specific animals, who were also sometimes sacrificed at the end of the ceremony, or with people dressing up as specific animals. Foremost among these were the animals denoting virility (or, for that matter, cuckolding) – the cock and the horned hart. Many confraternities of fools dressed up in the costume of a cock, and a 'king cock' also symbolized the king of the carnival (Gaignebet 1974: 133–5). Other carnival animals had to do with rituals of shame and punishment, such as the ass (used for parading battered husbands, see Plate 4.3) or the horse. But on many occasions the symbolism of carnival animals was far more specific than that. During the famous carnival in Romans (1580), which ended in riot and bloodshed, the bourgeois of the town used the cock, the eagle and the partridge in their parade and costumes. The artisans, relying upon older popular traditions, expressed their collective consciousness in parading as a bear (symbol of spring), a sheep, a hare, a capon (not exactly a cock!), and of course, an ass. The 'higher' classes deliberately chose to identify with aerial animals of strong sexual and virile associations, while the poor were identified by terrestrial animals, some of them castrated (the capon), and others of no particular sexual association (Le Roy Ladurie 1979: 240–1).

The animals in carnival situations deserve a separate study. I would merely like to connect once more what we know about the importance of carnival and its animal imagery. Carnival was a time of inversions, but inversions, as we know, serve largely to strengthen pre-existent categories by the very attempt to ridicule them (Babcock 1978: 14). The assumption by human beings of an animal guise in public rituals was not necessarily a humiliation. It depended not only upon the animal chosen, but also upon the situation. At a time of total (though temporary) structural breakdown, the choice of an animal disguise was a statement of identity, not a loss of identity. But this sort of symbolic identity could only function in a society which possessed a rich and permanent vocabulary of animal associations and symbolism. The animal in itself was not as important for the ritual as its associations.

Animals, collectively and individually, meant different things to different socio-intellectual groups. Broadly speaking, clerical culture attempted to distance the human from the animal as far as possible, using the latter only to symbolize abstract concepts and characteristics, not people. Lay culture, whether courtly or popular, consistently attributed to animals not symbolic values, but rather human traits, actions, modes of thought and feeling. Furthermore, the value of specific animals to human beings often lay precisely in this similarity of characteristics. Whenever animals appeared in public rituals it was in the role of human substitutes. Domestic animals were mostly scapegoats, the archetypal animal figure to assume human guilt. The beasts of the wild, by contrast, personified human shortcomings. In symbolic terms, it made perfect sense for the blameless cats and cocks to suffer, while the guilty fox remained unscathed, for he was too culpable to carry any but his own blame.

ANIMALS AS BEARERS OF GUILT

If animals could carry the burden of communal human guilt, they could obviously also symbolize in public ceremonies personal guilt. Indeed, animals often surface in late medieval punitive rituals in a very similar role. It was not a common practice, but in specific cases concerning certain types of crime malefactors were associated during their punishment with animals symbolizing their guilt. The placing of a human being in the position of an animal within the legal context was an infamy. But more so – the association with specific animals in a public punishment of any kind was meant to elucidate the nature of the crime committed.

This phenomenon was most clearly seen in the backwards ride. On occasion, criminals were not carried to execution in a cart, but riding backwards upon a donkey, a ram (for licentious women), or a sick horse. What changed the 'ordinary' infamy of execution into an extraordinary occasion was the addition of an animal as a beast of burden. Often the sources stressed the scatological aspect of this ride, when the rider was forced either to hold on to the animal's tail or lower his face into its anal cleft. But even when the ride was simply backwards, it carried an association of infamy. People guilty only of offending public norms usually suffered no worse than the ride, as did husbands whose wives had beaten them, but many traitors ended their backwards ride at the gallows (see Plate 4.3). The specific beast of burden chosen for the ceremony had a symbolic role to play in the ritual as well. Riding backwards was not limited to the kind of popular justice meted out to beaten husbands or domineering wives. It was an aggravated form of pre-execution disgrace and punishment going back to early medieval times, and not necessarily limited to western culture (Mellinkoff 1973).

The animal motif was also closely tied to another form of aggravated infamy, the upside-down hanging. In the High Middle Ages this punishment existed as an especially infamous death reserved for vassals who had killed their lords. The murderer of Count Thietmar of Hamburg (1048) was put to death in this way when caught by the dead count's son (Adam of Bremen 1917: 149; Ström 1942: 128). One of the murderers of Count Charles the Good of Flanders in 1127, according to one source, died in this manner. Interestingly, an eyewitness to the events of 1127 in Flanders mentions no such death, while a hearsay witness, residing in Paris, did add this detail. The historicity of the execution is therefore highly doubtful, but the fact that a chronicler saw fit to 'punish' the murderer of his lord in such a manner is indicative of his own views and those of his time (Suger of Saint-Denis 1964: 248–9; Galbert of Bruges 1967: 250–4).

In the later Middle Ages the custom of hanging a man upside-down with two dogs, or sometimes even wolves, on either side was reserved for Jews (Kisch 1954). Whether originally Jewish or not, the inverted execution was firmly perceived as both Jewish and animal by this era. When the Basle authorities exhorted a condemned Jew 'not to die like an animal' but to convert, they were putting into words a parallel that any spectator to the ceremony could see (Glanz 1943: 4). When Shakespeare's Gratiano accused Shylock of being the transmigrated soul of a wolf executed by hanging for homicide, he was making a similar connection.[3] The Jew was a creature of doubtful humanity, closely associated with the animal world and with specific, symbolic animals in it (Cohen 1989a).

The idea that the boundary between the human and the animal was far from absolute, in conjunction with the hierarchical view, lay at the foundation of the legal symbolism of animals. In so far as one approximated a culprit to animals symbolically, one degraded and punished him. Furthermore, the specific choice of the animal employed, with all of its attendant cultural associations, could either aggravate the punishment (if the animal was a particularly infamous one) or elucidate to the public the nature of the crime by way of association with that animal's characteristic traits. Thus, in the realm of legal symbolism the roles of animals are fairly clearly defined. Both English and Icelandic law identified the outlaw and criminal with the wolf (Berkenhoff 1937: 64; Bracton 1879, II: 314–15, 338–9). In executions associated with an extraordinary degree of infamy, dogs were hanged on either side of the criminal.

The most famous animal-associated execution was also in punishment for a reversal of hierarchical structures. Already the Theodosian Code had ordained that parricides should suffer the *poena culei*: to be sewn into a sack together with a cock, a serpent, a monkey and a dog. The penalty remained not only in Roman law, but appeared also in the thirteenth-century northern German customary law collection, the *Sachsenspiegel*, and was fairly common in early modern Germany (Egmond 1989; Bukowska-Gorgoni 1979). A fourteenth-century glossator of the *Sachsenspiegel*, Johann von Buch, explained the specific meaning of each animal:

> The dog indicates that such a man has never shown honor to his parents, like the dog, who is blind the first nine days. The cock signifies the man's crime and unbridled presumption wreaked on his father or child. The adder signifies the misfortune of such parents. For of their procreation it is said that when they would mate, the male puts his head into the female's mouth, whereby she conceives, and thereupon she bites off the male's head from lust. Then when she gives birth to her young she, in turn, must die through them: for when they are about to be born, they bite their way out of the mother's body, of which she dies in that hour. The monkey signifies the likeness of man or the image of death without deed. For as the monkey is like a man in many things and yet is no man, so was this one similar to a man but in deed and heart was not a man because he could act so inhumanely against his own flesh and blood.
>
> (Kisch 1954: 78–9)

Legal symbolism perceived the animal in punitive law as the hierarchical opposite of the human being. But the use of animal imagery and associations in rituals of infamy and executions in the later Middle Ages was applied also to far less heinous offences. As a rule, it was used in relation to offenders who had transcended the boundaries of the normative: the vassal who had broken faith, the public servant who had failed to fulfil his duty, the husband who had allowed his wife to reverse the natural order by beating him.

Most often animal imagery was used in those cases which the law could not formally penalize, but the community felt compelled to punish. Such cases were obviously rarely recorded in formal proceedings. The backwards ride upon an ass of the battered husband was known as a common form of *charivari*, or ritual public derision, but it had never achieved the dignity of a legal procedure (Vaultier 1965: 40–2; Mellinkoff 1973: 172–3). A similar semi-judicial ritual of shame was the carrying of a saddle. The earliest mentions of this punishment all refer to rebellious vassals who, in order to gain their lords' pardon, undertook a specified journey barefoot, carrying a horse's saddle upon their back, all the way to their lord's seat. By the fourteenth century this type of humiliation was translated, in an extraordinary case, into more plebian and graphic terms. A royal official in a small northern French town who had refused to participate in a lynching party was placed between the shafts of a cart in the manner of a horse and made to drag the cart along a prescribed journey (Cohen 1989b).

GUILTY ANIMALS BEFORE THE LAW

Given the long tradition of anthropomorphism in western culture, the criminal trials of noxious animals were a logical conclusion. It must be stressed that the practice was emphatically not typical of medieval jurisprudence, nor did it die out at the end of the Middle Ages. It was common throughout Europe until the eighteenth century. These trials were firmly embedded not only within the history of European jurisprudence, but even more within the perception of animals and their role in human society. Animals were subject to people and created for their utility. But animals were also mirror images of humanity and human guilt. Consequently, an animal who had reversed the order of nature by harming a human being (see Plates 4.5 and 4.6) could most certainly not be excused from punishment merely on the grounds that it lacked reason and intent and could therefore not assume guilt (Cohen 1986; Mason 1988).

The trials of animals deserve attention within a study of human justice precisely because, as in all other rituals, animals mirrored the human world. The trial protocols and sentences reveal in their phrasing a deeply embedded anthropomorphic attitude, coupled with the uncomfortable awareness of the very basic differences between human and animal culprits. These protocols stem from two different sources: the laconic, formula-like sentences of lay courts, and the long, semi-philosophical debates of early modern ecclesiastical tribunals.

The lay sentences invariably stressed that the verdict had been reached after due deliberation, consultation with experts in customary law, and proper procedure: 'also [having taken] counsel with wise men and practitioners of law, and also considering in this case the usage and custom of the land of Burgundy ...'; 'according to the duty of justice, following consultations in the said procedure ... I have just consulted with these good men, and here is our sentence, which I have had inscribed upon this paper' (Berkenhoff 1937: 121, 124). Furthermore, as in the case of a human killer, the sentences took trouble to imply, though they did not openly say so in their phrasing, malicious intent. A sow tried for biting a child to death was 'taken en flagrant délit, having committed and perpetrated ... murder and homicide'. Another had 'killed and murdered' its victim, and yet another one had displayed 'cruelty and ferocity' in killing a child (Berkenhoff 1937: 120; Evans 1987: 288, 309).

Nevertheless, a perception lingered that the killing of a human being by an animal was not quite the same thing as the killing of one person by another. It was indeed a breach of the hierarchy of the universe, an unnatural act. This perception probably lay at the roots of the inverted hanging of animals, especially pigs, practiced in Burgundy and northern France. It was, as we have noted, a sign of special infamy. The feeling also remained embedded in the language of the sentences. A sow was punished 'due to the heinousness of the crime', a bull sentenced 'in detestation of the said crime of homicide', and a pig 'in detestation and horror of the said deed' (Berkenhoff 1937: 123; Evans 1987: 311, 307). The last sentence added immediately after the visceral reaction of horror the words 'and in order to make an example and guard justice'. The same insistence upon justice was echoed in other sentences: 'in the said case we wish to proceed as justice and reason desire and require' (Evans 1987: 306). The verdicts both juxtaposed and identified the preservation of the universal hierarchy with the maintenance of justice. Justice assumed the proportions of suprahuman, universal law, beyond the simple mechanisms of human relationships.

While the protocols of lay courts simply stated these issues in a succinct manner, ecclesiastical courts debated them at length. The arguments tended to centre on two questions. The first, and most basic, was the right of the animals to survive in nature. Animals, argued the defense, were created before human beings and thus enjoyed prior rights in the vegetable kingdom. Moreover, though lacking reason, animals did fulfil a preordained role within creation, and their consumption of vegetation is no more than a fulfilment of God's plan. In fact, they were well within their rights according to divine law. If this consumption reached the proportions of a scourge, it was undoubtedly no more than God's punishment for people's sins. Was it either just or useful to punish God's emissaries, asked the defense? To the contrary, an attempt to stop them would be tantamount to opposing God. It would be better to pray, repent, give alms and pay tithes more faithfully, they suggested.

The counter-arguments invariably centred on the hierarchy of creation. On cosmogonic grounds, both animal and vegetable kingdoms were created for the utility of mankind, and any beast contravening this order by consuming people's food and causing them famine automatically went against God's will. Once again, both divine and natural law were cited, this time to support the opposite point of view. Man's creation as last of all only indicated his supreme position and the subordination of all the rest to him. Furthermore, numerous precedents, both biblical and hagiographical, could be adduced to support the intervention of human beings against animals, plants, or even objects. David had cursed the mountains of Gilboa, Christ had cursed the barren fig tree, and Saint Bernard had done the same to the flies that interrupted his sermon. Thus a holy man, or even simply a man imbued with God's power by reason of his office, could invoke heavenly wrath upon an animal or plant that had not fulfilled its role in relation to human beings. The fact that even a fig tree that had done no worse than refrain from bearing fruit could incur a curse indicated that those creatures actually noxious to man could all the more be punished (Boglioni 1985: 970–1).

Indeed, ecclesiastical sentences, being part of an adversary procedure, did not aim to exterminate or punish, but to get rid of the pests and thus obtain relief for the plaintiffs. The very use of exorcism against animals does not imply destruction, but the removal of a noxious element. The sentences insist upon one point – the objects of the ritual should suit their existence to human convenience: 'wherever you go, be cursed so that you may decrease from day to day, till nothing is left of you except what is needed for the use of humans . . . whose shape He who will judge the living and the dead by fire has deigned to assume'; 'I exorcize you . . . that you should immediately retreat from these fields . . . nor should you further reside there, but should move to such places where you cannot harm any of God's servants' (Malleolus 1497: fo. 70ro; D'Eynatten 1626: 1201).

The results of the trials – whether the animals lost or won – made no difference to the underlying perception. The suggestion that the animals in question should be assigned a separate piece of land where they could live unmolested and unmolesting surfaces throughout the trials. In one case, it was a compromise suggested during the trial by the plaintiffs, and rejected by the animals' advocate only because the land in question was unsuitable for his clients. In another, the court itself decided upon this solution. The net result was that, whether willingly or under ecclesiastical coercion, the animals would be removed from the cultivated land to a wild place.

Throughout these trials runs the strong feeling that if animals be subject to human justice, they were just as much deserving of a full measure of justice. The very appointment of a procurator for them or the suggestion that they be assigned a separate piece of land reflected the same attitude. The most extreme example of this attitude comes from Stelvio in Switzerland, where the expulsion sentence of the fieldmice allowed the pregnant and infant rodents a longer term before vacating the fields (Evans 1987: 112–13, 259–60).

The clearest difference between the elitist, ecclesiastical view and the more pragmatic lay position is a measure of the distance between different human groups and the animals they were judging. As far as the church was concerned, all noxious beasts were subject to justice, regardless of their specific nature. Peasants and townsmen who sued specific homicidal animals, however, made a clear distinction between the different type of animal. Dog, horse, cow and pig were certainly not all one in their eyes. This difference is most clearly seen in one of the few law texts prescribing animal trials. The *Coustumes et stilles de Bourgoigne*, composed some time between 1270 and 1360, determines that

> It is stated according to the law and custom of Burgundy that if an ox or a horse commit one or more homicides, they should not die, nor should they be tried and executed. Rather, they should be impounded by the lord in whose jurisdiction they had committed the crime, or by his men, to be confiscated and sold for the said lord's profit. But if another animal or a Jew do it, they should be hung by their rear legs.
>
> (Giraud 1846, II: 302)

The statement is curious enough on the face of it. This is the only customary law collection specifically to mention the upside-down hanging, which remained common in Burgundy, though it was fairly rare elsewhere.[4] More importantly, the Burgundy customal distinguishes between two categories: the horse or ox, which is impounded and sold, and all the rest of the animal world plus the Jews, who are executed. The distinction makes little sense on the purely practical level, and indeed was never honored in practice. In 1314 an ox was hung in Moisey-le-Temple, and in 1389 a horse suffered the same fate in Dijon (Berkenhoff 1937: 28, 32–3). Furthermore, no such distinction was ever made elsewhere in France or in the rest of Europe. One could perhaps dismiss it as a local peculiarity, were it not for the fact that animal trials probably originated in Burgundy. Even if practice blurred the finer distinctions, the fact that the authors of the customals took the trouble to record them says a great deal about their perception of animals and animal categories. In this case, since Jews are included as well, the custom may also shed light upon attitudes to some human categories.

Ostensibly, simple economic calculations would justify the distinction. Horses and oxen are expensive animals, and their execution would be a waste. The economic argument, however, is not very plausible. If this were the reason, cows would be included in the same category. Secondly, the most common perpetrators were pigs, who accounted for more than half of all recorded animal executions, and within the context of peasant economy the loss of a pig could be just as disastrous as that of a bigger animal. Most people were far more likely to own a pig, or another small animal, than a horse or an ox. Nor is it likely that the law was implicitly distinguishing between animals owned by people of different classes. Given the contemporary tendency of custom to prescribe in all fields explicitly different standards for people of different socio-judicial standing, such a distinction would have been openly stated.

The only possible explanation lies in the special role assumed by horses and oxen within peasant existence. Of all domestic beasts, these two are the most common draught animals. Furthermore, they serve while harnessed and controlled by humans, so that their subjection to man is the most clearly explicit of all animals. Most other domestic beasts serve humans by providing food or wool, not by their actions. Nor are they physically constrained to do people's will. One may harness a horse to the plough or the cart; one cannot force the cow to give milk, or the chicken to lay an egg. The hierarchical relationship between mankind and the beasts of service was maintained by daily actions, and needed no ritual reaffirmation in cases of breach. By contrast, humanity's relationship to the pig or the sheep did need such a symbolic formulation when the hierarchy was breached, largely because the relationship was hardly as clear-cut.

The place of the Jew within this scheme is a clear indicator of the symbolic importance of the execution. The Jew was an inferior human being who refused to accept a subordinate role within what should have been Christian society. Very much like the pig that had killed a child, a Jew who had killed a Christian had committed an act so heinous, so much contrary to proper hierarchical perceptions, that he had to be executed by means of the inverted hanging.

The animals brought to trial in both secular and ecclesiastical cases were real, flesh-and-blood animals. Unlike literary animals and public scapegoats they were not human substitutes, but real 'offenders'. Nevertheless, their trials were part of the same perceptual scheme that incorporated the human and the animal into one framework of justice. Whether one turned a man into an animal in a ritual of infamy in the course of a trial, or treated animals like human beings in the course of another trial, the result was the same. The order and balance of justice were restored, not just within one courtroom, but within the universe that comprised both human and animal. The application of 'human' legal rituals to animals was the opposite mirror image of the animalization of human beings.

In this sense, court procedure mirrored and integrated an entire spectrum of attitudes concerning animals. Time and again jurists stressed that animals possessed neither reason nor malicious intent, being equated in this way to perpetual minors. Nevertheless, the procedures applied to animals in both secular and ecclesiastical courts evince an ineradicable anthropomorphism. Try as they might, jurists in these trials could neither abolish them (even had they wished to) nor conceptualize a new way of treating animals in law. Animals were incorporated into human categories and human arguments, and 'thought of' as humans, precisely because they were litigants facing the law.

CONCLUSION

Why would any society use animals as its mirror image? Had animals been rare, exotic, unique, one could understand it. Had they made a sudden impact on human sensibilities at a certain point – as the discovery of America and the Indians did – one could understand it. But the presence of animals in medieval society was probably as much taken for granted as we take for granted the revolutions of Earth and the power of gravity. One could not envisage a world without animals. And to make the question even more complex, it was not the clerics in their rarefied atmosphere who did this. They merely established a hierarchy in the universe, relegated real animals to a subordinate position and used imaginary ones as allegories of the Christian ethos. It was precisely those people who spent every moment of the day in the ubiquitous presence of animals who employed them as scapegoats, mirror images and representations of human reality.

The only answer I can suggest lies in the realm of self-definition. Self-definition depends in every instance upon the existence of boundaries for the self, and of some 'other' beyond those boundaries. The only alterity, or 'otherness' late medieval people could see, feel and smell was the animal alterity. By placing animals in human positions, they made their own humanity stand out in sharper contrast. Renard could epitomize a whole host of human failings precisely because he was *not* human – he was the other.

The mirror-image other was very different indeed from the semi-human creature of fabulous journeys and faraway lands, or the wild men and monsters of wilderness legends. Those did not impinge in any way upon everyday reality, any more than sixteenth-century American Indians did upon early modern people. It was therefore highly unlikely that Mélusine, the serpent-woman, or a werewolf, would be found in a public procession. They were too close to the human model for comfort, and their mixed nature made them natural abominations in any case. But flesh-and-blood animals were both ubiquitous – and others. They were ideally suited as tools for human self-definition, and their enormous variety could be used to reflect the whole spectrum of humanity – all the way from the lamb to the ass and the pig and the dog.

NOTES

I would like to express my gratitude to Prof. Nurit Kenaan-Kedar for her help with references to illustrations.

1 Some of these, like Isidore of Seville (1911) and Hrabanus Maurus (1844–55) are simply sections within larger encyclopedic works which describe the whole world. Others, like Hugh of Saint Victor, (1844–55) and Hildegard of Bingen (1844–55) are more limited in scope. For a full listing of bestiaries, see McCulloch (1962).

2 Cf. Handoo (1990).

3   Thou almost mak'st me waver in my faith
To hold opinion with Pythagoras,
That souls of animals infuse themselves
Into the trunks of men: thy currish spirit
Governed a wolf, who, hang'd for human slaughter,
Even from the gallows did his fell soul fleet,
And, whilst thou lay'st in thy unhallow'd dam,
Infuse'd itself in thee.
          The Merchant of Venice, Act IV, scene i.

4 Evans (1987: 300); Gui Pape, the fifteenth-century Burgundian jurist, both testified to this practice and gave it his seal of approval (Pape 1667, q. 238: 254–5).

REFERENCES

Adam of Bremen (1917) *Gesta Hammaburgensis ecclesiae pontificum*, ed. B. Schmeidler, Hanover: Monumenta Germaniae Historica, Scriptores rerum germanicarum in usum scholarum.

Anon. (1486) *Livre du roy Modus et de la reyne Racio*, Chambéry.

Babcock, Barbara A. (ed.) (1978) *The Reversible World: Symbolic Inversion in Art and Society*, Ithaca, NY: Cornell University Press.

Bartholomeus Anglicus (1601) *De rerum proprietatibus*, Frankfurt: Minerva.

Bédier, Joseph (1969) *Les fabliaux: études de littérature populaire et d'histoire littéraire du moyen âge*, 6th edn, Paris: Champion.

Berkenhoff, Hans. A. (1937) *Tierstrafe, Tierbannung und rechtsrituelle Tiertötung im Mittelalter*, Strasburg: Heitz, Akademische Abhandiungen zur Kuturgeschichte 7 (4).

Bernheimer, Richard (1952) *Wild Men in the Middle Ages: A Study in Art, Sentiment and Demonology*, Cambridge, Mass.: Harvard University Press.

Birrell, Jean (1982) 'Who poached the king's deer?: A study in thirteenth-century crime', *Midland History* 7: 9–25.

Boglioni, Pierre (1985) 'Il santo e gli animali nell'alto medioevo', *L'Uomo di fronte al mondo animale nell'alto medioevo* (Settimane di studio del centro Italiano di Studi sull'alto medioevo, Spoleto), pp. 935–93.

Bouillet, Auguste (ed.) (1897) *Liber miraculorum sancte Fidis*, Paris: Picard.

Bracton, Henricus de (1879) *De legibus et consuetudinibus Angliae*, ed. Travers Twiss, 4 vols, London: Rolls Series.

Bryant, Lawrence (1986) *The King and the City in the Parisian Royal Entry Ceremony: Politics, Ritual and Art in the Renaissance*, Geneva: Slatkine.

Bukowska-Gorgoni, Christina (1979) 'Die Strafe des Sackens – Wahrheit und Legende', *Forschungen zur Rechtsarchäologie und rechtlichen Volkskunde* 2: 145–62.

Caesarius of Heisterbach (1851) *Dialogus miraculorum*, ed. Joseph Strange, 2 vols, Cologne: Lempertz.

Clark, Stuart (1968) 'Inversion, misrule and the meaning of witchcraft', *Past and Present* 87: 98–127.

Cohen, Esther (1986) 'Law, folklore and animal lore', *Past and Present* 110: 6:37.

—— (1989a) 'Symbols of culpability and the universal language of justice: the ritual of public executions in late medieval Europe', *History of European Ideas* 11: 407–16.

—— (1989b) 'Inversie en liminaliteit in de rechtspraktijk van de late middeleeuwen', *Theoretische Geschiedenis* 16: 433–43.

Cohen, Gustave (1941) *Le Théâtre comique au moyen-âge*, 2 vols, Paris: Rieder.

Coyecque, E. (1891) *L'Hôtel-Dieu de Paris au moyen âge*, 2 vols, Paris: Champion.

Damhouder, Jodocus (1562) *Praxis rerum criminalium*, Antwerp: J. Beller.

Darnton, Robert (1984) 'Workers revolt: the great cat massacre of the Rue Saint-Séverin', in *The Great Cat Massacre and Other Episodes in French Cultural History*, New York: Basic Books, pp. 75–106.

D'Eynatten, Maximilian (1626) *Manuale exorcismorum*, in *Thesaurus exorcismorum atque coniurationum terribilium*, Cologne.

Dievoet, Guido van (1975) 'Le *Roman de Renart* et *Van den Vos Reynaerde*, témoins fidèles de la procédure pénale aux XIIe et XIIIe siècles?', in E. Rombauts and A. Welkenhuysen (eds) *Aspects of the Medieval Animal Epic*, Louvain: Louvain University Press, pp. 43–52.

Douglas, Mary (1966) *Purity and Danger*, London: Routledge.

Duby, Georges (1968) *Rural Economy and Country Life in the Medieval West*, trans. C. Postan, London: Edward Arnold.

Egmond, Florike (1988) 'Gypsies: crime, stigmatization and ambiguity. The case of the northern Netherlands, 1450–1780', paper presented at the Third International Conference of the International Association for the History of Crime and Criminal Justice, Paris.

—— (1989) 'Bijzondere beesten. Diersymboliek en strafvoltrekkingen', paper presented at the Alterity Symposium, Amsterdam, October.

Evans, Edward P. (1987) *The Criminal Prosecution and Capital Punishment of Animals*, London: Faber. First published 1906, Heineman.

Favier, Jean (1978) *Philippe le Bel*, Paris: Fayard.

Franklin, Alfred (1928) *Paris et les parisiens au seizième siècle*, Paris: Emile-Paul.

Gaignebet, Claude (1974) *Le Carnaval*, Paris: Payot.

Gaignebet, Claude and Lajoux, J. D. (1985) *Art profane et religion populaire au moyen âge*, Paris: Presses Universitaires de France.

Galbert of Bruges (1967) *The Murder of Charles the Good, Count of Flanders*, trans. and ed. J. B. Ross, New York: Harper & Row.

Geffroi de Paris (1968) 'Chronique rimée', in *Recueil des historiens des Gaules et de la France* 24 vols, Paris: Imprimerie Nationale, 22: 89–166.

Gervase of Tilbury (1707) *Otia imperialia ad Ottonem IV imperatorem*, in G. W. Leibnitz (ed.) *Scriptores rerum Brunsvicensium*, 3 vols, Hanover: Förster, 1: 881–1004.

Giraud, C. (ed.) (1846) *Essai sur l'histoire du droit français au moyen âge*, 2 vols, Paris: Videcoq.

Glanz, Rudolf (1943) 'The "Jewish Execution" in medieval Germany', *Jewish Social Studies* 5: 3–26.

Hambroer, Johannes (1966) 'Der Hahn als Löwenschreck im Mittelalter', *Zeitschrift für Religions- und Geistesgeschichte* 18: 237–54.

Handoo, Jawaharlal (1990) 'Cultural attitudes to birds and animals in folklore', in Roy Willis (ed.) *Signifying Animals: Human Meaning in the Natural World*, London, pp. 37–42.

Heers, Jacques (1983) *Fêtes des fous et carnavals*, Paris: Fayard.

Hildegard of Bingen (1844–55) *Physica, seu subtilitatum diversarum naturarum creaturarum libri novem*, in J.-P Migne, *Patrologiae Latinae cursus completus*, 221 vols, Paris, 197: 1117–351.

Hrabanus Maurus (1844–55) *De universo*, in *MPL*, 111: 9–612.

Hugh of Saint Victor (pseud.) (1844–55) *De bestiis et aliis rebus*, in J.-P. Migne, *Patrologiae Latinae cursus completus*, 177: 9–164.

Husson, Bernard (ed.) (1978) *Le grand et petit Albert*, Paris.

Isidore of Seville (1911) *Etymologiae sive originum libri XX*, ed. W. M. Lindsay, Oxford: Clarendon.

Jannet, P. (ed.) (1855) *Les Evangiles des quenouilles*, Paris: Bibliothèque Elzevirienne.

Jean de Saint-Victor (1968) *Memoriale historiarum*, in *Recueil des historiens des Gaules et de la France*, 21: 630–89.

Jordogne, O. (1975) 'L'anthropomorphisme croissant dans le *Roman de Renart*', in *Aspects of the Medieval Animal Epic*, pp. 25–42.

Kappler, Claude (1980) *Monstres, démons et merveilles à la fin du moyen âge*, Paris.

Kisch, Guido (1954) 'The Jewish execution in medieval Germany', in *Studi in memoria di Paolo Koschaker*, 2 vols, Milan: Giuffre, 2: 65–93.

Krause, Sigrid (1983) 'Le *Reinhart Fuchs*, satire de la justice et du droit', in Danielle Buschinger and André Crépin (eds) *Comique, satire et parodie dans la tradition renardienne et les fabliaux*, Goppingen, pp. 139–51.

Laurent, Sylvie (1989) *Naître au moyen âge. De la conception à la naissance: La grossesse et l'accouchement (XIIe–XVe siècle)*, Paris: Léopard d'Oro.

Le Goff, Jacques (1977) 'Mélusine maternelle et défricheuse', in *Pour un autre moyen âge*, Paris: Gallimard, pp. 307–31.

—— (1985) 'Lévy-Strauss in Brocéliande: a brief analysis of a courtly romance', in *The Medieval Imagination*, trans. Arthur Goldhammer, Chicago: University of Chicago Press, pp. 107–31.

Le Roy Ladurie, Emmanuel (1979) *Le Carnaval de Romans*, Paris: Gallimard.

Lecoy de la Marche, Antoine (1877) *Anecdotes historiques, légendes et apologues tirés du recueil inédit d'Etienne de Bourbon, dominicain du XIIIe siècle*, Paris: Renouard.

McCulloch, Florence (1962) *Medieval Latin and French Bestiaries*, Chapel Hill: University of North Carolina Press.

Malleolus, Felix (1497) 'Tractatus secundus de exorcismis', in his *Variae oblationes, opuscula et tractatus*, Basle.

Mason, Peter (1988) 'The excommunication of caterpillars: ethno-anthropological remarks on the trial and punishment of animals', *Social Science Information* 27: 265–73.

Mellinkoff, Ruth (1973) 'Riding backwards: theme of humiliation and symbol of evil', *Viator* 4: 154–66.

Muchembled, Robert (1985) *Popular Culture and Elite Culture in France, 1400–1750*, Baton Rouge: La, Louisiana State University Press.

Orlandi, Giovanni (1985) 'La tradizione del "Physiologus" e i prodromi del bestiario latino', in *L'Uomo di fronte al mondo animale*, pp. 1057–106.

Ortalli, Gherardo (1985) 'Gli animali nella vita quotidiana dell'alto medioevo: Termini di un rapporto', in *L'Uomo di fronte al mondo animale*, pp. 1389–443.

Otten, Charlotte F. (ed.) (1986) *A Lycanthropy Reader: Werewolves in Western Culture*, Syracuse, NY: Syracuse University Press.

Pape, Gui (1667) *Guidonis Papae decisiones*, Geneva.

Poirion, Daniel (1982) *Le merveilleux dans la littérature française du moyen âge*, Paris: PUF.

Rothkrug, Lionel (1979) 'Popular religion and holy shrines: their influence on the origins of the German Reformation', in James Obelkevich (ed.) *Religion and the People, 800–1700*, Chapel Hill: University of North Carolina Press, pp. 20–86.

Russell, W. M. S. and Russell, Claire (1978) 'The social biology of werewolves', in J. R. Porter and W. M. S. Russell (eds) *Animals in Folklore*, Ipswich: Brewer, pp. 143–82.

Sainéan, Lazar (1972) *Les sources indigènes de l'etymologie française*, 3 vols, Paris: Slatkine. First published 1925.

Schmitt, J.-C. (1979) *Le saint lévrier. Guinefort, guérisseur d'enfants depuis le XIII siècle*, Paris: Flammarion.

Scribner, Robert W. (1987) 'Ritual and popular belief in Catholic Germany at the time of the Reformation', in *Popular Culture and Popular Movements in Reformation Germany*, London: Hambledon, pp. 17–47.

Seel, Otto (ed.) (1967) *Der Physiologus*, Zurich.

Smith, Kathryn C. (1978) 'The role of animals in witchcraft and popular magic', in J. R. Porter and W. M. S. Russell (eds) *Animals in Folklore*, Ipswich: Brewer, pp. 96–113.

Smith, K. F. (1894) 'A historical study of the werewolf in literature', *Publications of the Modern Language Association* 9: 1–42.

Ström, Folke (1942) *On the Sacral Origin of the Germanic Death Penalties*, Stockholm: Ohlssons.

Suger of Saint-Denis (1964) *Vie de Louis VI de Gros*, ed. and trans. H. Waquet, Paris: Belles-Lettres.

Vaultier, Roger (1965) *Le folklore pendant la guerre de Cent Ans d'aprés les lettres de rémission du trésor des chartes*, Paris: Guénégaud.

Viaene, H. (1939) 'Kattedag te leper', *Biekorf*, 45: 47–52.

Welter, J-Th. (1973) *La Tabula exemplorum secundum ordinem alphabeti*, Geneva: Slatkine. First published Toulouse, 1927.

Zika, Charles (1988) 'Hosts, processions and pilgrimages: controlling the sacred in fifteenth-century Germany', *Past and Present* 118: 25–54.

Zink, Michael (1976) *La prédication en langue romane avant 1300*, Paris: Champion.

Plate 1.1 Images of the wild man: natives of Tierra del Fuego, studied and drawn by Robert FitzRoy, Captain of HMS *Beagle*. (Source: King *et al.*, 1839.)

Plate 1.2 The animal presents itself to the hunter. The moment of encounter between an Inuit hunter and a caribou, drawn by Davidialuk, an Inuit artist from Povungnituk in northern Quebec. (Source: Saladin d'Anglure 1979.)

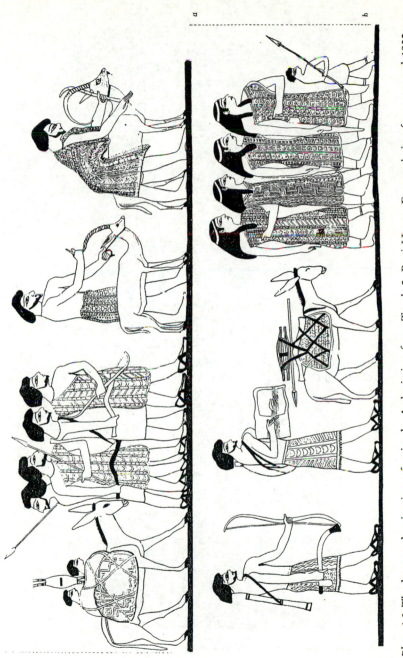

Plate 1.3 The human domination of animals. A depiction from Tomb 3, Beni Hasan, Egypt, dating from around 1900 BC. (Source: P.E. Newberry, *Archaeological Survey of Egypt.*)

Plate 2.1 A wolf and one of its domesticated descendants, a Pekinese dog.

Plate 2.2 The Durham Ox engraved by Whessell after Boultbee. More than 2,000 copies of this engraving were sold within a year of publication in 1802. (Supplied by the Rural History Centre, University of Reading.)

Plate 2.3 Thirteenth-century illustration of a bell-wether. (Source: Bodleian Library, Oxford, MS Douce 88.)

Plate 2.4 Assyrian relief of a eunuch leading a stallion (*c.* seventh century BC).

Plate 3.1 Mummified head and shoulders of an incarnation of the Egyptian bull god Apis (Agricultural Museum, Cairo).

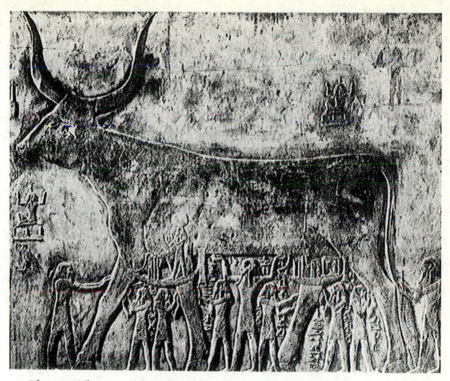

Plate 3.2 The Egyptian cow goddess Hathor as the sky supporting the world.

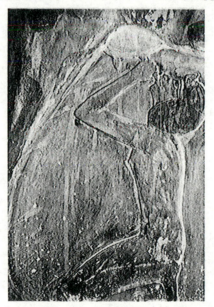

Plate 3.3 An Egyptian pharoah sucking the teat of Hathor.

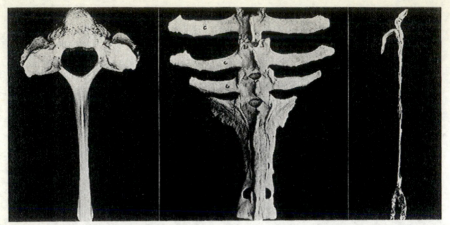

Plate 3.4 Probable anatomical origins of the most prominent Egyptian religious symbols/objects, *ankh, djed* and *w3s* in (from left to right) a bull's thoracic vertebra, his last three lumbar and sacral vertebrae and his dried penis (see Schwabe *et al.* 1982; Schwabe and Gordon 1989).

Plate 3.5 The Egyptian living bull god Montu (shown here as a hawk with the sun disc and bull's tail) with the *ankh, djed* and *w3s* combination of symbols/objects (i.e. the male bull's reproductive system) protruding from his groin like an erect penis. In the original for this drawing, on the chariot of Tuthmosis IV, Montu grasps in the same hand a scimitar, also a penis analogue, but it has been omitted here to make this portrayal clearer.

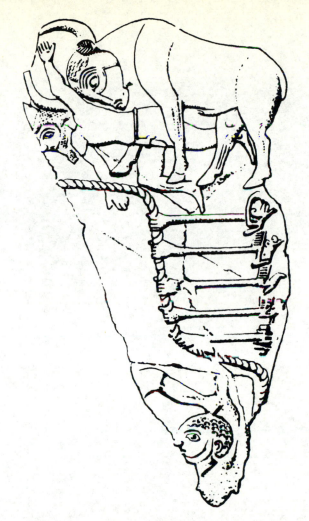

Plate 3.6 The first pharoah Menes-Narmer as a bull goring his enemies. (Source: Zeuner 1963, after Legge.)

Plate 3.7 A Mesopotamian reed calf-house or prototype temple. (Source: Frankfort 1955, courtesy of the Oriental Institute, University of Chicago.)

Plate 3.8 The Egyptian canine funerary god Anubis touching to the deceased's mouth an adze used to sever the sacrificial bull's 'living' forelimb (which was also touched to the mouth of the deceased). Scene in a noble's tomb, Thebes.

Plate 3.9 The mesopotamian healing goddess Gula (sometimes assimilated to the cow goddess Ninhurshag) with her healing companions the dog and snake (part of which is visible on the right).

Plate 4.1 God instructing the animals in the service of humanity (fourteenth-century relief, Orvieto cathedral).

Plate 4.2 Reynard the Fox on trial before King Lion for raping the she-wolf (woodcut by Reynaert den *Vos*, Antwerp, 1700).

Plate 4.3 Sixteenth-century woodcut of a carnival procession showing a wild man and a mock king and peasant astride a donkey. The backwards ride was often used to ridicule husbands who had been cuckolded by their wives (from Gaignebet and Lajoux 1985).

Plate 4.4 *The Scapegoat* by William Holman-Hunt (Manchester City Art Gallery).

Plate 4.5 Animals engaging in criminal acts. A pig devours a baby, a bull gores a man and a dog worries a sheep. (Illustration from Joducus Damhouder, *Praxis Rerum Criminalium*, 1562.)

Plate 4.6 The execution of a sow. In medieval Europe animals could not be excused from punishment merely because they lacked reason and intent.

Plate 5.1 Freiherr Samuel von Pufendorf (1632–94), a representative of the school of natural right, who taught that human beings had no legal obligations to animals and lived in a natural state of war with them (from Pufendorf 1744, vol. I, frontispiece. Niedersächsische Staats- und Universitätsbibliothek Göttingen).

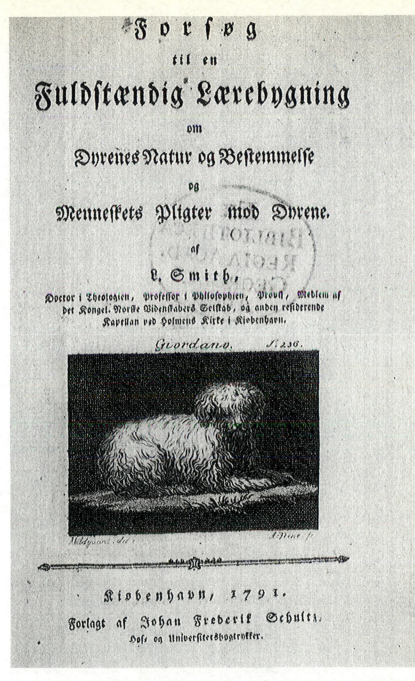

Forsøg

til en

Fuldstændig Lærebygning

om

Dyrenes Natur og Bestemmelse

og

Menneskets Pligter mod Dyrene.

af

L. Smith,

Doctor i Theologien, Professor i Philosophien, Provst, Medlem af
det Kongel. Norske Videnskabers Selskab, og anden residerende
Kapellan ved Holmens Kirke i Kiøbenhavn.

Giordano. S. 236.

Kiøbenhavn, 1791.

Forlagt af Johan Frederik Schultz,
Hof- og Universitetsbogtrykker.

Plate 5.2 Title page of the original Danish edition of the *Essay of a Complete Doctrine of the Nature and Destination of Animals and Man's Duties towards Animals* by the Danish clergyman Lauritz Smith (1754–94). It shows an engraving of the dog 'Giordano', the cleverness of which is described in an anecdote. The book is an example of eighteenth-century attempts to substantiate demands for kindness to animals with 'proofs' of animal intelligence (Niedersächsische Staats- und Universitätsbibliothek Göttingen).

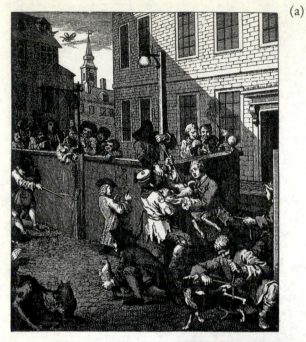

(a)

(b)

Plate 5.3 William Hogarth's series of engravings *The Four Stages of Cruelty* (1750) illustrating the widely held view that cruelty to animals leads to cruelty to human beings.

(c)

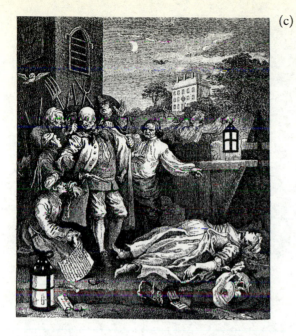

(d)

Plate 5.4 Jeremy Bentham (1748–1832). He belonged to those thinkers of the late eighteenth century who pleaded for the acknowledgement of animal rights, based on the idea that the capacity to suffer pain gives a moral status to animals (engraving by J. Posselwhite from an original picture by J. Watt, Wellcome Institute Library, London).

CRUELTY AND KINDNESS TO THE 'BRUTE CREATION'
Stability and change in the ethics of the man–animal relationship, 1600–1850*

Andreas-Holger Maehle

In the period from the seventeenth to the early nineteenth century ethical evaluations of human relationships with animals were influenced by various religious, philosophical and social factors. Contemporary views of animals were connected with such different areas as biblical exegesis and Christian morals, animal psychology, theory of moral rights and duties, vegetarianism, and love for pets. This chapter examines the role of these factors within the development of the discourse on the ethics of using animals. It looks at contemporary moral comments on slaughtering and meat-eating, care of domestic animals, hunting and blood sports, and vivisection.

PRECEPTS OF THE BIBLE AND OF CHRISTIAN MORALS

Throughout the period considered in this chapter a broad consensus regarding basic human rights over animals existed in western societies: because of God's grant of dominion according to Genesis 1:26–8 and Genesis 9:2–3, man was held to be allowed to use and kill animals for the satisfaction of his natural needs (Thomas 1983). The divine command that man should subdue all kinds of animals not only dominated the theological discussion of the subject, but also provided the basis for considerations concerning the theory of natural right. The same basic position can be found, for example, in such different sources as *Unerkannte Sünden der Welt* (1690) by the Lutheran clergyman and pietist Christian Gerber (1660–1731) and in the contemporary leading work on natural right and international law *De jure naturae et gentium* (1672) by Samuel von Pufendorf (1632–94). In the course of the eighteenth century the belief in a God-given right to make use of animals appears in writings of enlightened philosophers as well as in works of Protestant clergymen. The silence of the Roman Catholic church on this point is remarkable. Yet, following the doctrines of Augustine (354–430) and Thomas Aquinas (c. 1225–74), Catholics generally believed in a wide gap between rational human beings, endowed with immortal souls, and irrational animals (Passmore 1975). Because of this view, reflections on the moral right to utilize animals seem to have been quite superfluous.

Only a few thinkers who were influenced by doctrines of metempsychosis in Pythagoreanism and Brahmanism, such as the vegetarians Thomas Tryon (1634–1703) and John Oswald (d. 1793), did not fully acknowledge the biblical permission to make use of animals (Oswald 1791; Gharpure 1935). Occasionally, however, even orthodox authors discussing vegetarianism sometimes differentiated between the extent of the first grant of dominion to Adam and of the renewed one in the pact with Noah. Only the second one, according to Genesis 9:2–3, included the right to slaughter animals and to eat their meat. This grant, however, was a consequence of the Fall of man, which meant that the right over animals expressed here was only a right 'in statu corrupto', as Siegmund Jacob Apinus (1693–1732), professor of logic and metaphysics at the Nuremberg Gymnasium, put it in a dissertation dealing with the treatment of animals from the perspective of natural right (Apinus 1722: 9). John Hildrop (d. 1756), doctor of theology and rector of Wath-juxta-Ripon in Yorkshire, described the grant of meat-eating more specifically as a necessary consequence of the Flood: After Adam's sin God had subjected both man and animals to 'Vanity, Misery, and Death', but man had not yet been empowered to 'murder or abuse [animals], to kill or eat them'. Only after the Flood, which had so greatly corrupted and weakened nature that plants were no longer sufficient to maintain human beings, had God permitted humans to eat animals (Hildrop 1754: 229).

It was virtually undisputed among authors dealing with human relationships with the animal world that human beings were allowed to kill animals for food and clothing (Thomas 1983). Pufendorf (Plate 5.1) argued in favour of the right to kill animals by stating that it was impossible that God could have wished that man should keep himself alive by doing something wrong and sinful (Pufendorf 1744, I). In the middle of the eighteenth century the Leipzig philosopher Johann Heinrich Winkler (1703–70) wrote that man even had a duty to keep himself healthy by consuming meat (Winkler 1762, III). Concerning the right to kill harmful and dangerous animals there was also a consensus. As one Göttingen professor of philosophy put it in 1786: 'Either . . . the life of animals has to be sacrificed to the maintenance of human beings or the latter would have to be sacrificed to the former; not only in such cases where animals . . . are immediately dangerous to human beings, but also where they eat off or devastate indispensable human food, if man does not stop their spread' (Feder 1779–93, III: 309). Incontrovertibly, animal life had a lower value than human life, and this could be substantiated with the authority of the Bible. Franz Volkmar Reinhard (1753–1812), ecclesiastical councillor in

Dresden and preacher at the Court of Saxony, made this point perfectly clear in his *System der christlichen Moral* by quoting Matthew 6:26 and Matthew 10:31 (Reinhard 1816, V). In these passages Jesus Christ himself had given the assurance that human beings outvalued 'birds' or 'sparrows'.

Thus, from a theological perspective, there were no objections to the killing of animals for the purposes of nourishment, clothing and self-protection. Yet, from the seventeenth century onwards, wanton killing of harmless animals and every sort of cruelty to them increasingly came under attack (Thomas 1983). Essentially three main arguments can be distinguished. The first consisted in pointing to biblical passages, which could be interpreted as commands to treat animals carefully. Pufendorf, Gerber and Winkler in Germany argued in this way, as did John Hildrop and his contemporary Reverend Humphrey Primatt in England. Proverbs 12:10 ('A righteous man regardeth the life of his beast: but the tender mercies of the wicked are cruel') was cited by all of these authors. In addition, they regularly referred to the commandment that both man and his cattle should rest on the Sabbath (Exodus 20:10; Exodus 23:12; Deuteronomy 5:14); to the precept not to muzzle the ox, when it treads out the corn (Deuteronomy 25:4; 1. Epistle to the Corinthians 9:9); and to the exhortation not to take the dam with its young, when taking a bird's nest (Deuteronomy 22:6–7). All of these passages were seen as expressing a human duty to treat animals respectfully. The censure of Balaam who had beaten his ass (Numbers 22:28–30) was taken as unmistakable proof of divine care for animals. God's compassion for human beings *and* animals was exemplified again and again by quoting His sparing the town Nineveh, 'wherein are more than sixscore thousand persons that cannot discern between their right hand and their left hand; also much cattle' (Jonah 4:11). Occasionally in the eighteenth century whole sermons were preached on such biblical passages. In 1752, in the Leipzig Pauliner Kirche, the professor of philosophy and doctor of theology Christian Gottlieb Jöcher (1694–1758) exhorted people to treat animals carefully by preaching on Luke 14:5 (Winkler 1762, III), while in the church of Shiplake, Oxfordshire, the vicar James Granger (1723–76) spoke with the same intention about Proverbs 12:10 (Granger 1772).

A second, frequently adduced argument for the moral condemnation of cruelty to animals was God's grace and mercy towards all His creatures. Since animals were apparently endowed with the faculty to feel pleasure and pain – just like human beings – it was argued that animals also had a God-given 'right to happiness'. This would mean that friendliness to animals was imitating God's love for His creatures. Cruelty to animals sharply contrasted with God's will (Winkler 1762, III; Granger 1772; Dietler 1787; Young 1798; Reinhard 1816, V). Reverend Primatt even compared cruelty to animals with atheism and heresy (Primatt 1778).

The third reason why cruelty to animals was generally seen as reprehensible was the alleged danger of brutalization. Cruelty to animals would lead to callousness towards other human beings. Torturing animals was therefore regarded as an indirect offence against the Christian command of charity (Reinhard 1816, V). Man should rather practise treating cattle with kindness and friendliness in order to transfer these qualities to his human neighbour. This had already been demanded by the early Father of the Christian church, Tertullian (*c.* 155–222), as the pietist Gerber noted with apparent satisfaction (Gerber 1705–12, I). The same thought had earlier been expressed by Plutarch (*c.* 50–*c.* 125) in his vegetarian writing, *De esu carnium* (Dierauer 1977). After Tertullian the Neoplatonist Porphyrios (*c.* 232–304) had taken the same view in his work against the eating of meat *De abstinentia* (Porphyrios 1747). In the seventeenth century Pufendorf cited both these classics in this context (see Pufendorf 1744, I).

For James Granger, the argument of brutalization was important enough for him to put a corresponding motto on the title page, when he published his above-mentioned sermon (Granger 1772): 'Saevitia in Bruta est Tirocinium Crudelitatis in Homines' ('callousness against animals is training for cruelty against human beings'). Not surprisingly, he emphasized the importance of educating children to treat animals respectfully. Other theologians, such as Gerber, Primatt and the Danish Protestant clergyman Lauritz Smith (1754–94), substantiated this view with an example from the Roman rhetorician Quintilian (*c.* 30–*c.* 96). In his *Institutio oratoria* he cited the case of a boy who had been convicted by the judges of the Areopagus, because he had pulled out the eyes of living quails. The reason for the conviction was that it reflected 'a sign of a most pernicious way of thinking', which would lead him to harm human beings as an adult (Quintilian 1972–5, I).

Cases of tyrants in history, who had previously treated animals cruelly, were seen as additional proof of this theory of brutalization: for example, the young Roman Emperor Domitian, who used to torture flies (Sueton 1961, II); King Charles IX of France, who washed his hands in the blood of killed deer (Thuanus 1621, I) and who, on the night of Bartholomew 1572, shot the fleeing Huguenots from the windows of his castle just like a huntsman (Volckmann 1799); or King Louis XI of France, who was said to have become so cruel by torturing stags and caging birds that he finally had human beings executed for his entertainment or had them locked in iron cages for their whole life (Volckmann 1799). As an opposite example, of the kindly monarch who also shows mildness to animals, the Empress Maria Theresa was reported to have ordered straw to be laid out for the deer in the biting cold of winter 1755 (Winkler 1762, III).

In fact, the benevolent monarch, as opposed to the cruel tyrant, served as a kind of model for the ideal relationship that human beings should entertain towards animals in the mind of Christian thinkers. The view that man had been installed as God's steward on earth, as a responsible ruler over the creation entrusted to his care, was ultimately derived from Genesis 1:26–8 and often formed the final result of seventeenth- and eighteenth-century reflections upon human relations with the animal world (Thomas 1983; Guerrini 1989). Robert Boyle (1627–91) and Sir Matthew Hale (1609–76) have recently been quoted as prominent advocates of this concept of stewardship before 1700 (Passmore 1974; Oster 1989). It was still popular in the following century, and towards the time of the French Revolution it was combined with the ideal of brotherhood among all creatures (Thomas 1983). As the Mainz philosopher Wilhelm Dietler (d. 1797) put it:

> Man is the more clever brother on earth, therefore God has made him His steward here, so that he should rule over the other animals not like a tyrant, who believes that everything has been created for himself, but like a brotherly guardian, who guides his less intelligent brothers, so that they love him and will be happy with him.
>
> (Dietler 1787: 36–7)

In summary, treating animals carefully, respectfully and responsibly was the general conclusion drawn from the Christian concept of stewardship. Many authors elaborated catalogues, so to speak, of human duties towards animals based on this conclusion: animals should be slaughtered as quickly and painlessly as possible, cattle should be provided with adequate nourishment, domestic animals should be given a home and sufficient care, and animals used for work and transport should not be over-exerted except in emergencies. Harmless animals, which could not be utilized, should be allowed to enjoy their lives (Gerber 1705–12, I; Primatt 1778: Dietler 1787).

Several authors, while adducing the principles of the Bible and of Christian morals, did not forget to point to commands to treat animals carefully in other religions. Brahmanism, Zoroastrianism and Islam were repeatedly quoted as religions showing special kindness to animals. Pufendorf, for example, referred to a sect at Cambay in western India, that – due to their belief in metempsychosis – were reported to be vegetarians and to have hospitals for ill and injured birds (Pufendorf 1744, I). Though Reinhard rejected the Indian doctrine of transmigration of souls as superstition and argued that it favoured the propagation of harmful animals, he mentioned the duty to treat animals respectfully in Islam and believed that the 'benevolent interest in the existence, life and pleasure within the whole visible creation', as it had been present in Zoroastrianism, was revived by Christianity (Reinhard 1816, V: 125). In the seventeenth century Gerber had already emphasized that the Turks would severely punish anybody who killed an animal in an unmerciful way (Gerber 1705–12, I), and in the eighteenth century Primatt even dared to cite the kindness to animals among Mohammedans as a shaming example for Christians (Primatt 1778). It should be noted, however, that such remarks about other religions were rather marginal compared to comments based on biblical and Christian principles. Authors like John Oswald, who as a Scottish officer had become acquainted with Brahmanism in eastern India and who had become a champion of vegetarianism (Oswald 1791), must be seen as exceptions. It was only in the middle of the nineteenth century, with Arthur Schopenhauer's *Parerga and Paralipomena*, that criticism of the Jewish-Christian view of the man–animal relationship, based on Brahmanism and Buddhaism, became more widely known to the educated public (Schopenhauer 1947–50, VI). More important for moral judgements on the treatment of animals was the question of the existence and nature of animal souls, which was hotly debated in the seventeenth and eighteenth centuries.

THE PROBLEM OF ANIMAL SOULS AND ITS ETHICAL CONSEQUENCES

The Cartesian 'beast-machine'

In his influential *Discours de la méthode* of 1637 René Descartes (1596–1650) had stated that the bodies both of animals and human beings could be adequately compared with machines or automata. The bodily functions should be explainable by the laws of mechanics. Yet Descartes recognized two important features separating human beings from the animal world: their faculty of true speech and their rational, immaterial, imperishable souls. In contrast to the human body, the bodies of animals were supposed to operate without the guidance of a non-corporeal principle. An artificial machine perfectly imitating an animal would therefore be indistinguishable from the animal itself. According to Descartes, animals differed from man-made machines only in their degree of complexity. Being works by God's hand they were infinitely more complex and perfect than – but not fundamentally different from – artificial automata. The skilfulness of animals was seen as a result of their appropriate physical organization, not as a result of intellect (Descartes 1960).

The idea that animals were machines was not totally new in the seventeenth century. In his *Summa theologiae* Thomas Aquinas had already attempted to explain apparent animal sagacity as God-given instinct, and he had compared their faculties with those of watches made by man (Rosenfield 1940). Moreover, in the middle of the sixteenth century the concept of animals as machines had been propagated by the Spanish physician Gómez Pereira (Pereira 1749, I). To some extent Descartes's mechanistic view of animals can be seen as an extension of the mathematics and physics of Galileo and Kepler to the field of physiology (Rothschuh 1966). It has also been interpreted as a literary response to the way in which the sceptic philosophers Michel Eyquem de Montaigne (1533–92) and Pierre Charron (1541–1603) had seen animals (Boas 1933). Unlike Descartes, they had attributed the perfection of particular animal actions (for example, the construction of the swallow's nest or the organization of the 'bee-government') to animal intelligence, which might even exceed that of human beings. Accordingly these 'Theriophiles' (Boas) had been ready to ascribe a rational, though mortal, soul to animals.

86

Montaigne's 'theriophily', expressed particularly in his *Apologie de Raimond Sebond* (Montaigne 1924–41, III–IV), belonged to a genre of paradoxical literature with mainly satirical intentions: by demonstrating the (alleged) superiority of animals, human pride should be diminished. In the same vein the papal nuncio Hieronymus Rorarius had published two volumes in 1544 and 1547, arguing 'that animals make better use of their reason than man' (Rorarius 1666). Montaigne's disciple Charron, however, seems to have propounded his 'theriophily' seriously and was taken in that spirit by Descartes (Boas 1933).

As to the ethics of the treatment of animals, the crucial point in the Cartesian 'beast-machine' theory was the question of pain. Though Descartes himself had *not* held the view that animals were absolutely insensitive to pain (Cottingham 1978), some of his followers – the Oratorian Father Nicolas Malebranche (1638–1715) and the Jansenist Antoine Arnauld (1612–94) – had propagated this opinion. When the French writer Bernard le Bovier de Fontenelle (1657–1757) visited Malebranche, the latter is said to have kicked a pregnant bitch that had rolled at his feet and to have coolly responded to Fontenelle's cry of compassion with the laconic words: 'So what? Don't you know that it has no feeling at all?' (Sainte-Beuve 1840–59, II: 306). Nicolas Fontaine (1625–1709), secretary of several prominent Jansenist Fathers, reported the equally callous behaviour of solitaries of the monastery Port-Royal, who had been indoctrinated by Arnauld. They beat their dogs 'with the utmost indifference' and laughed about those who still maintained that animals could feel pain. Interpreting the cries of the dogs as the mere creaking of the animal 'clockwork', they vivisected them in order to study blood circulation (Fontaine 1738, II: 52), which had recently been discovered by William Harvey (1578–1657) and described in a modified way by Descartes in the *Discours*.

The idea of zealous Cartesians that animals were absolutely unfeeling machines gave rise to a philosophical debate on the nature of animals, which lasted until the end of the eighteenth century. The main topics of this discussion were the existence of animal souls, the question of rationality in animals, and their ability to use speech and to have feelings. From a theological point of view, the question of whether animal souls were immortal like human ones was a central problem. The development of this discussion has been studied in detail, particularly with respect to its consequences for contemporary views of human beings (Hastings 1936; Rosenfield 1940; Kirkinen 1960). The following section will take into account only some of those authors who connected their comments on the problem of animal souls with ethical conclusions concerning man's treatment of animals.

Animal souls and ethics

The debate on the problem of animal souls was dominated by criticism of the Cartesian 'beast-machine' theory. A good survey of the state of the discussion in the first half of the eighteenth century is provided by a series of rhetorical exercises on this subject under the direction of the Leipzig philosopher, Winkler, during the years 1741 to 1743 (Winkler 1742a, 1742b, 1743a, 1743b). These exercises dealt with the questions of whether animals had souls, whether such souls included intellect and reason, and whether they were immortal. It is quite clear that Winkler, from the very beginning, took an anti-Cartesian view, being convinced of the existence of more or less rational, thinking and imperishable animal souls. This opinion was also expressed in his textbook *Institutiones philosophiae universae* (Winkler 1762, I). In this work he drew ethical conclusions from his position on the question of animal souls. He argued that, since animals owned sensitive souls, no reason could be given why it should be permissible to torment them. Pain was imperfection *per se*. Only the aspect of perfection, however, would lead to real pleasure and happiness. This meant, in Winkler's view, that human beings should cause as little pain as possible when using or killing animals (Winkler 1762, III).

A similar connection between the question of animal souls and an appeal to treat animals carefully can be traced in the writings of John Hildrop. He believed in rational, immaterial and immortal animal souls and thought that the rough treatment of 'innocent unhappy Creatures' would mean 'a Breach of natural Justice' (Hildrop 1754: 230). The British clergyman Richard Dean (*c.* 1727–78) went a step further. Taking the same view on animal souls as his colleague Hildrop, he emphasized that sensibility and intelligence entitled animals to considerate treatment by man and added that their miseries gave them a claim 'to some Returns from a just and benevolent Being, in another State' (Dean 1768, II: 109). The argument based on the existence of animal souls was fully developed in the last decade of the eighteenth century. In 1791 the Danish clergyman Lauritz Smith published a comprehensive book on the nature and destination of animals and human duties towards them (Plate 5.2). It dealt mostly with the mental faculties of animals, although its declared purpose was not an exhaustive discussion of the question of animal souls, but to bring 'alleviation to the brute creation, which is groaning under its sufferings' (Smith 1793: XXI–XXII). Similarly, in 1799, the German lawyer Johann Friedrich Ludwig Volckmann (1757–1815) in *Menschenstolz und Thierqualen* tried to demonstrate in detail that animals possessed 'memory, phantasy, moral sense', and some degree of 'rationality', in order to convince his readers that such creatures had to be treated respectfully. Volckmann was explicit about the idea behind this argument: if man took less pride in himself and showed a higher esteem for the talents of animals, he would abstain from cruelty towards them (Volckmann 1799). Authors like Winkler, Hildrop, Dean, Smith and Volckmann tried to narrow the gap between human beings and animals as it existed in Roman Catholic as well as in Cartesian thinking. Their writings represented the beginnings of the idea of animal protection on the basis of animal psychology.

Another factor which pushed the debate in the same direction was the concept of the so-called 'Great Chain of Being', which was popular and widely accepted in the eighteenth century. The idea that all creatures were closely linked – like the segments of a chain – challenged the view of a gap between human beings and the realm of irrational animals (Lovejoy 1964; Thomas 1983). The metaphor of a chain was often used interchangeably with that of a 'scale' of all beings, which ascended from the lower to the higher animals and, via man, up to the angels. Though hierarchically structured – and thus essentially anthropocentric – it implied that there were only gradual differences between the creatures, which were supposed to be very small in neighbouring species. Some authors in the second half of the eighteenth century – e.g. Hildrop, Primatt, and the English writer and politician Soame Jenyns (1704–87) – applied this concept of a chain or scale of beings to the problem of animal souls. Following the principle of continuity inherent in the idea, they stressed that the sensitivity to pain in animals and their varying degree of intellect entitled them to considerate treatment (Hildrop 1754; Primatt 1778; Jenyns 1790, III).

A remarkable exception to this line of reasoning was the comment by the Halle professor of philosophy Georg Friedrich Meier (1718–77). Like his Leipzig colleague Winkler, he attacked the mechanistic views of Pereira and Descartes and argued for the existence of immortal animal souls. His main argument was that God must have given souls to animals in order to have the creation thought about and enjoyed from all possible perspectives. Man alone was unable to think and experience everything in the world. According to the continuous scale of all beings, Meier went on, animals possessed reason in different degrees, yet to a smaller extent than human beings. At this point the philosopher brought the doctrine of metempsychosis into the concept of the scale of beings: when an animal died, its soul could reach the next higher step in the following incarnation until it finally became a wholly rational human soul or pure 'spirit'. In contrast to the followers of the Pythagorean or Brahman doctrines of transmigration of souls, Meier's ethical conclusion was not extreme respect for animal life. On the contrary, he advocated the killing of animals, because this would mean that the rise of their souls was accelerated. He drew the unusual, but logical conclusion: 'there is no greater benefit that can happen to animals than to be killed' (Meier 1749: 118; Narr and Narr 1967).

The theories on animal souls and the concept of the 'Great Chain of Being' were strongly influenced by an anthropocentric view of the world, as is especially clear from this last example. Qualities common to both animals and human beings and the connections between them were pointed out again and again by eighteenth-century thinkers. But the superiority of human beings and their God-given right of dominion over the animal world was not seriously questioned. Some authors dealing with human relationships with animals did not limit their discussion to the theological and philosophical perspectives. Increasingly they asked how man should behave towards animals from the point of view of natural right.

ANDREAS-HOLGER MAEHLE

THE QUESTION OF ANIMAL RIGHTS

Creatures without rights

In the seventeenth century the school of natural right, represented by Hugo Grotius (1583–1645), Samuel von Pufendorf and Christian Thomasius (1655–1728), reinforced traditional Christian as well as Cartesian anthropocentrism. It was a doctrine of this school that law had developed within a community of rational beings for the purpose of regulating their social relations. Being regarded as irrational creatures, animals did not fall within the system of natural right (Juchem 1940). This point of view was expressed by Pufendorf in particular. He insisted that there were no legal or contractual obligations towards animals. Man had no duty to live in friendship and in community with animals, nor would animals be capable of keeping their obligations towards human beings if a pact existed. In Pufendorf's view the relationship with animals was a natural, permanent state of war. He substantiated this view by pointing to the behaviour of wild animals or formerly domesticated animals which had become wild again. The state of war between human beings and animals meant that martial law was effectively in force. It was therefore permitted to hurt or kill animals – just as an enemy – in one's own interest (Pufendorf 1744, I).

The doctrine of the representatives of the theory of natural right that there was no legal relationship between human beings and animals was not a new one. In antiquity Stoic philosophers had taken a similar view as a result of their strongly anthropocentric perspective. They had denied that animals were endowed with reason and had therefore advocated the unlimited right of man to make use of animals (Passmore 1975; Dierauer 1977). In the seventeenth and eighteenth centuries this position was known particularly through its tradition in Cicero's *De finibus bonorum et malorum*. Moreover, Augustine had adopted the Stoic point of view, emphasizing that Jesus Christ himself had been convinced that there was no legal community between human beings and the animal and vegetable creation. As in Stoic philosophy, animals had been characterized by Augustine as irrational beings, which were not connected with man, and the sufferings of which were not important. This opinion, repeated by Thomas Aquinas in the thirteenth century, had become basic to the position of the Roman Catholic church on the question (Passmore 1975; Sellert 1984). Philosophers of the seventeenth century, such as Thomas Hobbes (1588–1679) and Baruch de Spinoza (1632–77), had also provided arguments for the view that animals were creatures without rights. According to Hobbes the absence of rationality and speech in animals meant that they were unable to make a treaty with human beings (Sellert 1984). In Spinoza's opinion the rights of a particular being depended on its 'virtue and power'. This meant that human beings had far more rights over animals than animals over man. Correspondingly, he was convinced that man was allowed to make use of animals 'at will', all the more because their nature was different from that of human beings (Bregenzer 1894). The idea that animals had no rights at all provoked opposition, however, since it seemed to imply that man was free of any obligations towards them. The Nuremberg philosopher Apinus spoke of a 'great controversy among the scholars' concerning the question of 'whether one has duties towards animals' (Apinus 1722: 17). It seems that the central problem concerned the formulation of a strong argument for the more or less intuitive certainty that cruelty to and abuse of animals was reprehensible. In the course of the eighteenth century two main strategies of argumentation were developed here. Either *indirect* obligations towards animals were constructed on the basis of direct duties to God, to other human beings or to oneself; or animal rights were conceded by analogy to human rights, the consequence being *direct* obligations towards animals. Whereas the latter argument appeared after 1750, the former can be traced back to the early eighteenth century.

Indirect obligations towards animals

In his dissertation of 1722 Apinus introduced some important ideas concerning human rights over animals. He agreed with the doctrine that there was no contractual relationship involving direct human obligations to animals. But he stressed that animals were objects of human duties to God. These duties included the 'conservation of animals' ('brutorum conservatio') and respect for God's 'direction of animals to their purposes' ('directio brutorum ad suos fines'). The first principle meant that it was man's duty to care for domestic animals and to abstain from killing or hurting animals without necessity; and according to the second one, it was forbidden to mutilate an animal, for this would mean a disregard for its God-given design. So Apinus constructed indirect obligations to animals, which resulted from direct obligations to God. About thirty years later the Scottish philosopher David Hume (1711–76) brought forward another concept of indirect obligation in his *Enquiry Concerning the Principles of Morals*, first published in 1751. He too denied that man and animals could form a 'society', because this would presuppose 'a degree of equality'. Animals were far inferior to human beings, both physically and mentally, in Hume's view. Yet he stressed that man 'should be bound, by the laws of humanity, to give gentle usage to these creatures' (Hume 1964, IV: 185). Thus he advanced an obligation within the *human* community. Following a similar line of reasoning Immanuel Kant (1724–1804) finally stated in his *Die Metaphysik der Sitten* (1797) that a considerate treatment of animals was nothing else but 'man's duty to himself'. According to Kant a legal relationship including direct mutual obligations could exist only between rational – i.e. human – beings. There was, however, an indirect obligation to abstain from violence and cruelty to animals, because man's compassion for suffering human beings might be 'weakened and gradually obliterated' (Kant 1956, IV: 578–9; Patzig 1986). It is quite obvious that Kant's concept of human duties to animals was determined by the old, anthropocentric idea that cruelty to animals would result in cruelty to human beings. Animals suffering *as such* was not ethically relevant here, but only the effects of cruelty on human morality. William Hogarth (1697–1764) had illustrated this view in his series of moralizing engravings *The Four Stages of Cruelty* (Plate 5.3). From 1751 onwards the prints of these engravings popularized the lesson of Tom Nero, who starts as a juvenile tormentor of animals and ends as a murderer, who is hanged and finally dissected in the anatomical theatre (Kottenkamp 1857–8, II: Guratzsch 1987). Kant is said to have used these engravings by Hogarth to illustrate his view of the man–animal relationship in his lectures (Passmore 1975).

The concept of indirect obligation more or less restricted human rights over animals compared to Pufendorf's 'state of war' view of man's relationship to the animal world. Still, the basic doctrine of the school of natural right that animals were creatures without rights was never challenged by these concepts. Yet, in the second half of the eighteenth century, some thinkers broke with this doctrine and stated the existence of animal rights.

The rights of animals

In his *System of Moral Philosophy*, published posthumously in 1755, the Glasgow philosopher Francis Hutcheson (1694–1747) declared that animals 'have a *right* that no useless pain or misery should be inflicted on them'. Yet he stressed that they 'can have no right ... against mankind in any thing necessary for human support', thus not essentially differing from the traditional anthropocentric position (quoted in Thomas 1983: 179). Another early step towards the idea of moral rights of animals was made in 1769 by the Swiss scholar and naturalist Charles Bonnet (1720–93). In *La Palingénésie philosophique* he stated that a divine order existed in nature and that the purpose of this order consisted in the greatest possible happiness 'of sentient and of thinking beings'. Moral behaviour, he concluded, should aim at a maximum of conformity with this order. This meant that it was immoral to treat a sentient being like an insensible one or 'an animal like a pebble-stone'. Accordingly he enlarged the scope of natural right: 'Natural laws' should result not only from the interrelations of human beings, as the school of natural right had taught, but from man's relationship to *all* creatures (Bonnet 1779–83, VII: 405–7). Bonnet did not actually speak of animal rights as such, yet he expressed the idea that every sentient being had some sort of claim to happiness in its life:

He [i.e. 'a moral man'] will not regard it as a wholly indifferent action to crush a gnat, which has not done any harm to him and could not do so. As he knows that this gnat is a sentient being, which in its way enjoys the sweetness of existence, he will not kill it for his pleasure, out of a caprice or without consideration.

(Bonnet 1779–83, VII: 408)

Only seven years later, in 1776, Humphrey Primatt in England made the decisive second step towards an animal's right to happiness. He argued that the suffering of animals was worse than that of human beings, because animals had no hope of a future life. Moreover, as speechless creatures they were unable to accuse their tormentors, and as irrational beings they could not act immorally and therefore could not endure pain as punishment. For animals, Primatt concluded, present pain was the only evil and present happiness the only good. Because of this an animal, as long as it lived, had 'a right to happiness' (Primatt 1778: 39–40).

There are already some hints in Primatt's thoughts indicating that the faculty to suffer pain was to become the new criterion for the concession of rights. Indeed the old criterion of rationality was attacked by him. Primatt regarded the mental powers of a being as God-given just as its physical characteristics were. So they could be an object neither of pride nor of contempt. At this point he argued by analogy with racism – i.e. its reprehensibleness served as a model for the condemnation of cruelty to animals. Just as the white man had no right to treat a black man as a slave and in a tyrannical way because of the God-given colour of his skin, so an intelligent man was not allowed to oppress a fool. This meant, in Primatt's view, that man did not have a natural right to abuse or torture an animal, just because it did not possess the mental powers of a human being. The qualities of both human beings and animals came from God (Primatt 1778).

Primatt's argument foreshadowed the much better known plea for the acknowledgement of animal rights by the English theoretical jurist and philosopher Jeremy Bentham (1748–1832). The latter's famous dictum on animals 'the question is not, Can they *reason*? nor Can they *talk*? but, Can they *suffer*?' in his *Introduction to Principles of Morals and Legislation*, published in 1780, not only included the same essential message, but was formulated in a very similar context. Bentham (Plate 5.4) compared the status of animals in England with that of human slaves in other countries and argued for the existence of animal rights just as for the abolition of slavery. He pointed to the French *Code noir* of 1685, which regulated the status of slaves in the West Indies, forbidding the killing of slaves by their masters and entitling the royal authorities to protect slaves from maltreatment. According to Bentham, the French had thus recognized that the black colour of the skin was no reason why a human being should be abandoned without redress to the caprice of a tormentor. So he hoped that some day 'the number of the legs, the villosity of the skin, or the termination of the *os sacrum*' would be equally insufficient reasons for abandoning animals to a corresponding fate (Bentham 1968–84, II.1: 283).

For Bentham, generally regarded as the founder of Utilitarianism, the faculty to suffer pain together with the complementary faculty to feel pleasure was the central principle of his ideas. Supposing that nature had placed human beings 'under the governance of two sovereign masters, *pain* and *pleasure*', he defined utility as 'that property in any object, whereby it tends to produce benefit, advantage, pleasure, good, or happiness ... or ... to prevent the happening of mischief, pain, evil, or unhappiness to the party whose interest is considered' (Bentham 1968–84, II.1: 11–12). In the philosopher's view, animals had such interests of utility as well. He criticized the 'ancient jurists' who had degraded animals to mere things and had neglected their interests. Like Primatt, Bentham tried to demonstrate that rationality and speech were insufficient criteria for allocating rights. In his opinion a full-grown horse or an adult dog was much more rational and easier to communicate with than a newborn human baby (Bentham 1968–84).

A very similar argument had been put forward in Germany some two years earlier by the philosopher Wilhelm Dietler. In his booklet *Gerechtigkeit gegen Thiere* he criticized the traditional view that animals were creatures without rights as a 'very wooden philosophy'. The lack of rationality in animals and their inability to lodge their claims were not sufficient reasons to deny the existence of animal rights:

> Of course, if one concedes rights only to someone who is capable of taking legal steps against us, one has reason to deny them to animals, for they will hardly appear with us before court because of offences. But a minor child is unable to do this, either, and still one does not deny that it is illegal, unjust, to kill a child, to hurt it and so on, i.e. that the child has certain rights. Accordingly animals can have rights as well, which means that certain actions against them can be unjust and forbidden.
>
> (Dietler 1787: 28)

The thesis that animals had rights, formulated by Primatt, Bentham and Dietler, was an alternative to the concept of a merely indirect obligation towards animals as advocated by Apinus, Hume and Kant. So at the end of the eighteenth century one finds a dichotomy in the legal evaluation of the man–animal relationship: the alternatives were either an indirect duty towards animals as creatures without rights or an immediate obligation based on animal rights. Yet, if one compares the practical demands derived from these two positions, one finds that they did not differ much. For instance, a comparison between the conclusions of Kant and Bentham as exponents of the two concepts reveals an almost complete consensus: both of them accepted a speedy killing of animals in slaughtering or in the eradication of vermin; and they both repudiated cruelty to animals (Kant 1956, IV; Bentham 1968–84, II.1). In fact both concepts were occasionally used in a complementary way, as is evident from the example of the Danish clergyman Lauritz Smith. On the one hand – corresponding to the concept of indirect obligation – the danger of brutalization through cruelty to animals was an important aspect for him. On the other hand, he also emphasized that man had more than a 'mediate obligation' to animals resulting from his duties to God, to his neighbours and to himself (Smith 1793: 391). The argument that animals had no rights, because they had no idea about right and obligation, was not valid, for otherwise – and here Smith made the same point as Dietler – one would have no duties to the foetus, to children, or to mentally disordered persons either. Although Smith advocated the new concept of animal rights, he did not demand more than those authors who believed only in an indirect obligation to animals. His catalogue of duties included careful treatment for domestic animals, and quick and painless slaughtering or killing of harmful or dangerous animals. The same can be said about the English writer and farmer John Lawrence (1753–1839), who in 1796–8 published a *Philosophical and Practical Treatise on Horses* in two volumes, including a chapter entitled 'The Rights of Beasts'. He suggested here the creation of a 'jus animalium' (Lawrence 1810, I: 131), yet his practical demands were not different from those of earlier authors. It has to be asked whether these two concepts regarding the rights of animals were really more than a 'mere controversy about words', as Smith had put it (Smith 1793: 392). In the next sections the issue of cruelty and kindness to the 'brute creation' will be studied in the light of the actual treatment of animals in everyday life, blood sports and vivisection.

EARLY JURISDICTION ON CRUELTY TO ANIMALS

Before the nineteenth century there was no law regulating animal protection in any European country. Yet from the German and British jurisdiction before 1800 some condemnations because of cruelty to animals have been handed down. As early as 1684, in the Prussian principality of Sagan, a man was punished with two days' exposure at the pillory and an additional fine because he had severely maltreated his horse by blows and stabs (Bregenzer 1894). The basis for the judgment is not known in this case, but already in the sixteenth century an ordinance is said to have existed in Berlin, according to which torturers of animals should be exposed at the pillory (Sellert 1984).

Two sentences of the Leipzig Faculty of Law from 1765 and 1766 have been transmitted at first hand and are particularly revealing with respect to their motivations. The accused in the first case had cut off half of the tongue of his neighbour's cow with malice prepense ('invidiae causa'). He was sentenced to six weeks' imprisonment. Punishment was not only for the damage he had caused according to civil law, but his deed was punished as a crime being regarded as 'a malice to be avenged'. In the second case a postilion, who had run his horses to ground on a sandy street during stormy weather, was sentenced to twelve days' imprisonment, after he had spent several months in detention while awaiting his trial. In addition he had to reimburse the price of the horses to the postmaster. In the opinion it was said that his offence was judged as 'inhuman behaviour'.

The Leipzig jurist Karl Ferdinand Hommel (1722–81), who had been involved in both these verdicts, published both cases in a casuistic work on legal questions, 'which arise daily at court, yet are not decided by laws' (Hommel 1782–7, II). In his comments on these cases, Hommel dealt with the general legal problems of cruelty to animals. He did not share the opinion that human beings had no legal obligations to animals, regarding the definition of the term 'duty' by a corresponding legal claim ('jus exigendi') as insufficient. As did Dietler, Bentham and Lauritz Smith afterwards, he argued that under this presupposition there would be no obligations to the foetus and to the small child either, since they were also beings unable to make demands. The Leipzig jurist defined duty in a broader sense as 'an action, which the law of nature demands of us' (Hommel 1782–7, II: 38). On this basis he constructed – as did Apinus – an indirect obligation to animals derived from a direct duty to God. He substantiated the latter with the theological view that God wished the well-being of all His creatures and that He had created the world for the happiness and pleasure of all beings. Hommel's conclusions – reflected in both sentences – read as follows:

> So I state natural obligations of human beings towards animals and, as to written law, I do not hesitate to number cruelty against animals among those crimes which … are described as *crimina extraordinaria*, and which the judge avenges with an arbitrary punishment, though the law is silent on this point.
>
> (Hommel 1782–7, II: 39)

Furthermore, Hommel argued that cruelty to animals indicated pernicious views which should be persecuted in order to prevent more severe crimes. Those who had pleasure in maltreating animals would – if they only could and were allowed to – torture human beings in the same way. He pointed to Quintilian's example of the boy who tortured quails. Thus, according to Hommel, the obligation towards one's neighbour supplemented human duties to God.

The Leipzig cases show that the concept of indirect obligations to animals could well be sufficient reason to prosecute cruelty to animals as a criminal offence. Although Hommel partly argued like the later champions of animal rights (especially in his comparison with the duties towards children), he did not go so far as to speak of a direct duty to animals as owners of rights.

If cruelty to animals could be punished without allocating rights to them, it must be asked why certain thinkers demanded animal rights. A possible answer to this question lies in reports on some pertinent British cases around 1790. As in Germany, British courts of the late eighteenth century are known to have punished cruelty to animals. Magistrates and justices of the peace could avenge cruelty to cattle with fines. As the German officer Johann

Wilhelm von Archenholz (1743–1812) wrote in a report on his travels in England, it was not a rare event that someone was charged with cruelty to animals, and no leniency was shown in such cases (Archenholz 1785, I). Only in those cases, however, where malicious intentions of the accused towards the accusing owner of the maltreated animal could be demonstrated, was a condemnation possible. This is clear from the case of William Parker, in 1794, who had torn out the tongue of a living mare. The writer, John Lawrence, who cited this case, stated that the accused would have been acquitted if he had been the owner of the horse. There was a similar case of two butchers in Manchester in 1793. They had been sentenced to a fine of twenty shillings each, because they had cut off the hooves of sheep and then driven them through the streets. The conviction had been possible in this case because they were not the owners of the sheep. Lawrence adduced the case of another butcher in this context, who used to hang calves up alive, with the gambrel stuck through their sinews, and the rope thrust through their nostrils. The bleating of the animals had disturbed the neighbourhood. Yet legal proceedings against this butcher had been impossible, because the calves were his property (Lawrence 1810, I). Thomas Young (1722–1835), a fellow of Trinity College Cambridge, reported similar cases in his *Essay on Humanity to Animals*, published in 1798. During the last years, he wrote, several men had been brought to trial because they had cut or torn out the tongues of living horses. Yet the judgment had always been 'not guilty', since no base motives or revenge with respect to the owner of the horses could be proved.

Thus the treatment of animals by their *owners* was legally irrelevant. This was obviously the problem at which the contemporary demands for animal rights aimed. Lawrence, for instance, wrote:

> It results from such premises, that unless you make legal and formal recognition of the Rights of Beasts, you cannot punish cruelty and aggression, without trespassing upon right of property. Divest property of the usurped and fictitious addition to its right, and you have the means of protecting animals, and securing the dearest interests of morality.
>
> (Lawrence 1810, I: 133)

Referring to the last-named cases, Young who, like Bentham, derived the existence of animal rights from their faculty to experience pleasure and pain, demanded legal reform (Young 1798). Last but not least, Bentham himself in his comparison with the *Code noir* for the protection of human slaves, pointed exactly to the problem of maltreatment by owners. So it seems that the call for animal rights was not only a consequence of purely theoretical opposition to the older concept of indirect obligation. At least in England, this call was probably also an expression of growing dissatisfaction with contemporary jurisdiction in actual cases of cruelty to animals.

Seen as a whole, such cases of maltreatment of animals show that, until the end of the eighteenth century, jurisdiction was based on the concept of indirect obligations towards animals, which were regarded as beings without rights. Both concepts, however (i.e. that of indirect and of direct obligations), are reflected in the first laws for animal protection in the nineteenth century. The German states of Württemberg (1839), Hanover (1847), Prussia (1851), Anhalt-Bernburg (1852), Waldeck-Pyrmont (1855), Oldenburg (1858) and Baden (1863) made cruelty to animals punishable by law, only if it had happened publicly and caused offence to the spectators. In this way, these states followed the line of the concept of indirect obligation to animals based on man's direct duty towards other human beings. It was not the animal as such but human compassion that was protected by these laws. The first British Act of Parliament on animal protection (Martin's Act of 1822) against cruelty to horses and cattle, as well as the animal protection laws of Saxony (1838), Hessen-Darmstadt (1847) and Bavaria (1861), however, made malicious and wanton maltreatment of animals a punishable offence, even if it had not occurred in public. These laws seem to have been nearer to the concept of direct duties towards animals based on animal rights. To some extent the animal itself seems to have been protected here. Yet with respect to the penalties the two types of animal protection laws did not show significant differences. As in the eighteenth century, cruelty to animals continued to be punished with fines and several weeks' imprisonment (Crowe 1825; Bregenzer 1894; Juchem 1940; Hahn 1980).

THEORY AND PRACTICE OF THE TREATMENT OF ANIMALS

The changes described in theological and philosophical views of the man–animal relationship obviously reflect the development of a somewhat more friendly climate for animals in the eighteenth century. A number of contemporary intellectuals were certainly prepared to assume a less anthropocentric attitude than had prevailed in the sixteenth and seventeenth centuries (Harwood 1928; Thomas 1983). Yet it has to be stressed that such kindness to the 'brute creation' was still confined to an educated elite. In fact, even in the late eighteenth century, the position of authors pleading for the considerate treatment of animals still seems to have been rather a weak one. When in 1772 James Granger held his sermon on Proverbs 12:10, he is said to have aroused 'almost universal disgust to two considerable congregations', because his mention of dogs and horses was regarded as 'a prostitution of the dignity of the pulpit' (Granger 1772, postscript). The philosopher Dietler stated in the preface to *Gerechtigkeit gegen Thiere* (1787) that many people could not understand at all how it occurred to an author to write about such a topic. And Young feared to expose himself to ridicule by publishing his essay on humanity to animals. He was certain that, to many readers, this subject would appear 'whimsical and uninteresting' and its particulars 'ludicrous and mean'

(Young 1798: 1). Undoubtedly very rough treatment of animals dominated everyday life well into the nineteenth century, as can be inferred from the continuing complaints of humanitarian writers. Maltreatment of horses, cattle and other domesticated animals as well as cruelties in slaughtering seem to have been common (Young 1798; Crowe 1820; Dann 1838). Certain blood sports, such as bull-baiting, bull-running and cock-fighting, were still popular around 1800 among the lower classes, especially in Britain, as was hunting among the upper classes (Malcolmson 1973; Thomas 1983). From the sixteenth century onwards, animal experimentation had developed into a recognized method of medical research. Renaissance anatomists, such as Andreas Vesalius (1514–64) and Realdo Colombo (1516–59), revived and enlarged the vivisectional techniques of Galen of Pergamon (c. 130–210). The demonstration of the circulation of the blood by Harvey and the discovery of the lymphatic system by Gaspare Aselli (1581–1626), Jean Pecquet (1622–74), Thomas Bartholinus (1616–80) and Olof Rudbeck (1630–1702) in the seventeenth century were largely based on experiments on living animals and in turn caused widespread vivisectional activity. The same is true of the pioneer studies in experimental pharmacology and toxicology by the Swiss physician Johann Jakob Wepfer (1620–95) in the later seventeenth century, and the work on the sensibility and irritability of animal parts by Albrecht von Haller (1708–77) at Göttingen in the middle of the eighteenth century. One has to bear in mind that, throughout the period considered here, animals were generally not stupefied in experiments. Effective anaesthetic compounds, such as sulfuric ether and chloroform, were not introduced in either surgery or experimental medicine until the 1840s (Maehle and Tröhler 1990).

Typically enough, some eighteenth-century authors dealing with aspects of the morality of human relationships with animals have been identified as pet-lovers in their private lives. Jeremy Bentham is known as the owner of a tom-cat, which he called Sir John Langborn and, as the animal grew older and more sedate Reverend John Langborn, and finally Reverend Doctor John Langborn (Thomas 1983). The Danish clergyman Lauritz Smith also mentioned his clever poodle Udeis (Smith 1793). Alexander Pope, who in 1713 contributed an essay against cruelty to animals to the *Guardian* and who was very concerned about vivisection, was a dog-fancier, who grew up in a dog-loving family and in the course of his life was the owner of at least four dogs, each called Bounce. Two of these Bounces were immortalized in their master's poetry, and one of them was included in a portrait of Pope by Jonathan Richardson (Maehle 1990). Samuel Johnson, who in 1758 published a highly emotional denunciation of vivisection in his weekly paper the *Idler*, has often been quoted for his indulgence to his tom-cat Hodge, 'for whom he himself used to go out and buy oysters, lest the servants having that trouble should take a dislike to the poor creature,' as James Boswell remembered (Maehle 1990). John Lawrence may also be mentioned here: he was known as a horse-fancier (Lawrence 1810). Surely the practice of pet-keeping, which became increasingly popular during the seventeenth and eighteenth centuries (Thomas 1983), was not without influence on the ethical discourse on the treatment of animals. Moreover, it has to be remembered that some of the advocates of kindness to animals were vegetarians, who believed in the transmigration of souls.

Seen against these backgrounds, contemporary comments on the ethics of the man–animal relationship may appear as little more than 'straws in the wind' (Passmore 1975: 209). Yet it would not be appropriate to interpret them as mere expressions of individual over-sensitivity. In the seventeenth and eighteenth centuries the ground was evidently prepared for the rise of the humane movement of the nineteenth century. In the 1820s and 1830s the first important animal protection societies were founded. In 1824 the Society for the Prevention of Cruelty to Animals was established in London, known since 1840 as the Royal SPCA. In Germany the pioneer animal protection societies were those of Stuttgart, founded in 1837, Dresden and Nuremberg, both founded in 1839. The programmes of these societies included enforcement of the animal protection laws, mentioned above, and education of the general public (Harrison 1982; Ritvo 1987; Tröhler and Maehle 1990). As a consequence of the latter aim, a new genre of literature emerged in the first decades of the nineteenth century, comprising rather popularly written, sometimes inflammatory treatises against cruelty to animals. The authors of such writings repeated all the old arguments for a more careful treatment of animals that have been discussed in this chapter, i.e. those based on the Bible, on the fear of brutalization through cruelty to animals, on animal souls, and on the idea of moral obligations to animals (Crowe 1825; see also Ehrenstein 1840; Forster 1839; Gompertz 1852; Youatt 1839). The successes of the humane movement in Britain are well known: after the Act of 1822 to 'Prevent cruel and improper treatment of cattle', in 1835 a Cruelty to Animals Act established the illegality of blood sports involving the baiting of animals, the keeping of cock-pits and of places for dog-fights. Cock-fighting as such was prohibited by an Act of 1849 'for the more effectual Prevention of Cruelty to Animals' (Malcolmson 1973; Ritvo 1987). In 1876 Britain enacted the world's first law regulating experiments on living animals (French 1975).

It has been convincingly argued by modern historians of the animal protection and anti-vivisection movements in the nineteenth century that the former was also directed against elements of social disorder, particularly disorder associated with blood sports (Malcolmson 1973; Turner 1980; Ritvo 1987), and that the latter actually fought against a scientocratic and materialistic view of the world (French 1975; Rupke 1990). Yet the continuity of the modern humane movement with seventeenth- and eighteenth-century thought on the ethics of human relationships with animals should not be forgotten. Henry S. Salt (1851–1939), for example, who in 1891 founded the Humanitarian League in London (Hendrick 1977), explicitly took up again the late eighteenth-century concept of animal rights, quoting directly from the writings of Primatt, Bentham and Lawrence (Salt 1894). Even in current philosophical debates on the treatment of animals a remarkable revival of historical concepts can be observed. Peter Singer and Tom Regan have followed in Primatt's and Bentham's footsteps by making sentience the criterion which gives a moral status to animals. On this ground they condemn animal experimentation as well as 'factory farms' as an expression of unwarranted 'speciesism' and a violation of animal rights, respectively. Not surprisingly, both Singer and Regan also quote Salt as one of their intellectual forefathers (Singer 1975; Regan 1984). Conversely, anthropocentrism is still the common feature of arguments in favour of utilizing animals (Ullrich and Creutzfeldt 1985). Clearly the ethical debate on how to treat animals, as initiated by seventeenth- and eighteenth-century thinkers, is still with us and far from being closed.

REFERENCES

* This chapter mainly presents material from my Göttingen medico-historical inaugural dissertation: *Kritik und Verteidigung des Tierversuchs: Die änge der Diskussion im 17 und 18 Jahrhundert*, Stuttgart: Franz Steiner Verlag, 1992.

Alpinus, Siegmund Jacob (1722) *Dissertatio ex iure naturae an liceat brutorum corpora mutilare et speciatim Ob es recht sey daß man den Hunden die Ohren abschneide variis observationibus aucta et a nonullorum obiectionibus vindicata*, Altdorf: Literis Iod. Gvil. Kohlesii.

Archenholz, Johann Wilhelm von (1785) *England und Italien*, 2 vols, Leipzig: im Verlage der Dykischen Buchhandlung.

Bentham, Jeremy (1968–84) *An Introduction to the Principles of Morals and Legislation*, ed. J. H. Burns and H. L. A. Hart, in J. H. Burns (ed.) *The Collected Works of Jeremy Bentham*, 5 vols, London: Athlone Press, vol. II.1.

Boas, George (1933) *The Happy Beast in French Thought of the Seventeenth Century*, Baltimore: Johns Hopkins University Press.

Bonnet, Charles (1779–83) *Oeuvres d'histoire naturelle et de philosophie*, 8 vols, Neuchâtel: Samuel Fauche.

Bregenzer, Ignaz (1894) *Thier-Ethik. Darstellung der sittlichen und rechtlichen Beziehungen zwischen Mensch und Thier*, Bamberg: C. C. Buchner.

Cottingham, John (1978) '"A brute to the brutes?": Descartes' treatment of animals', *Philosophy* 53: 551–9.

Crowe, Henry (1820) *Zoophilos; or, Considerations on the Moral Treatment of Inferior Animals*, 2nd edn, Bath and London: Cruttwell/Longman, Hurst, Rees etc. First published 1819.

—— (1825) *Animadversions on Cruelty to the Brute Creation, Addressed Chiefly to the Lower Classes*, Bath: Printed by J. Browne.

Dann, Christian Adam (1838) *Bitte der armen Thiere, der unvernünftigen Geschöpfe, an ihre vernünftigen Mitgeschöpfe und Herrn die Menschen*, 2nd edn, Tübingen: Ludwig Friedrich Fues. First published 1822.

Dean, Richard (1768) *An Essay on the Future Life of Brute Creatures*, 2 vols, London: G. Kearsly.

Descartes, René (1960) *Discours de la Méthode pour bien conduire sa raison, et chercher la verité dans les sciences*, ed. Lüder Gäbe, Hamburg: Felix Meiner.

Dierauer, Urs (1977) *Tier und Mensch im Denken der Antike. Studien zur Tier-psychologie, Anthropologie und Ethik*, Amsterdam: B. R. Grüner B. V. (Studien zur antiken Philosophie, 6).

Dietler, Wilhelm (1787) *Gerechtigkeit gegen Thiere*, Mainz: Schillerschen Verlage.

Ehrenstein, H. W. von (1840) *Schild und Waffen gegen Thierquälerei. Ein Beitrag zu allgemeiner Förderung der Menschlichkeit*, Leipzig: B. G. Teubner.

Feder, Johann Georg Heinrich (1779–93) Untersuchungen über den menschlichen Willen, 4 vols, Lemgo: Meyersche Buchhandlung.

Fontaine, Nicolas (1738) *Mémoires pour Servir à l'Histoire de Port-Royal*, 2 vols, Cologne: Aux dépens de la Compagnie.

Forster, Thomas Ignatius Maria (1839) *Philozoia; or Moral Reflections on the Actual Condition of the Animal Kingdom, and on the Means of Improving the Same*, Brussels: Printed by Deltombe and Co., for W. Todd.

French, Richard D. (1975) *Antivivisection and Medical Science in Victorian Society*, Princeton/London: Princeton University Press.

Gerber, Christian (1705–12) *Unerkannte Sünden der Welt*, 3 vols, Dresden/Frankfurt: Christoph Hekels/Johann Jacob Wincklern.

Gharpure, Narhar Kashinath (1935) *Tierschutz, Vegetarismus und Konfession (eine religions-soziologische Untersuchung zum englischen 17. und 18. Jahrhundert)*, Munich: E. Hohenhaus.

Gompertz, Lewis (1852) *Fragments in Defence of Animals, and Essays on Morals, Soul, and Future State*, London: W. Horsell.

Granger, James (1772) *An Apology for the Brute Creation or Abuse of Animals Censured*, London: T. Davies.

Guerrini, Anita (1989) 'The ethics of animal experimentation in seventeenth-century England', *Journal of the History of Ideas* 50: 391–407.

Guratzsch, Herwig (ed.) (1987) *William Hogarth. Der Kupferstich als moralische Schaubühne*, Stuttgart: Gerd Hatje.

Hahn, Ute (1980) 'Die Entwicklung des Tierschutzgedankens in Religion und Geistesgeschichte', Veterinary thesis, Tierärztliche Hochschule, Hanover.

Harrison, Brian (1982) *Peaceable Kingdom. Stability and Change in Modern Britain*, Oxford: Clarendon Press.

Harwood, Dix (1928) 'Love for animals and how it developed in Great Britain', PhD thesis, Columbia University, New York.

Hastings, Hester (1936) *Man and Beast in French Thought of the Eighteenth Century*, Baltimore: Johns Hopkins University Press (Johns Hopkins Studies in Romance, Literatures and Languages, 27).

Hendrick, George (1977) *Henry Salt. Humanitarian Reformer and Man of Letters*. Urbana, Chicago and London: University of Illinois Press.

Hildrop, John (1754), 'Free thoughts upon the brute-creation' in J. Hildrop *The Miscellaneous Works*, 2 vols, London: John and James Rivington, vol. I, pp. 159–294.

Hommel, Karl Ferdinand (1782–7) *Rhapsodia quaestionum in foro quotidie obvenientium neque tamen legibus decisarum*, 7 vols, 4th edn, ed. Karl Gottlob Roessig, Bayreuth: Prostat apud Ioh. Andr. Lubecci Heredes.

Hume, David (1964) *The Philosophical Works*, 4 vols, ed. Thomas Hill Green and Thomas Hodge Grose, Aalen: Scientia. First published London, 1882–6.

Jenyns, Soame (1790) *The Works of Soame Jenyns, Esq.*, 4 vols, ed. Charles Nalson Cole, London: T. Cadell.

Juchem, Theodor Hans (1940) 'Die Entwicklung des Tierschutzes von der Mitte des 18. Jahrhunderts bis zum Reichsstrafgesetzbuch von 1871', Juridical thesis, University of Bonn.

Kant, Immanuel (1956) *Werke*, 6 vols, ed. Wilhelm Weischedel, Darmstadt: Wiss. Buchgesellschaft.

Kirkinen, Heikki (1960) *Les Origines de la conception moderne de l'homme-machine. Le problème de l'âme en France à la fin du regne de Louis XIV (1670–1715)*, Helsinki: Suomalainen Tiedeakatemia (Ann. Acad. Scient. Fennicae, ser. B, vol. CXXII).

Kottenkamp, Franz (ed.) (1857–8) *William Hogarth's Zeichnungen ... Mit der vollständigen Erklärung derselben von G. C. Lichtenberg*, 2 vols, Stuttgart: Rieger.

Lawrence, John (1810) *A Philosophical and Practical Treatise on Horses, and on the Moral Duties of Man towards the Brute Creation*, 2 vols, 3rd edn, London: Sherwood, Neely & Jones.

Lovejoy, Arthur O. (1964) *The Great Chain of Being. A Study of the History of an Idea*, Cambridge, Mass. and London: Harvard University Press.

Maehle, Andreas-Holger (1990) 'Literary responses to animal experimentation in seventeenth- and eighteenth-century Britain', *Medical History* 34: 27–51.

Maehle, Andreas-Holger and Tröhler, Ulrich (1990) 'Animal experimentation from antiquity to the end of the eighteenth century: attitudes and arguments', in N. A. Rupke (ed.) *Vivisection in Historical Perspective*, London: Routledge, pp. 14–47.

Malcolmson, Robert W. (1973) *Popular Recreations in English Society 1700–1850*, Cambridge: Cambridge University Press.

Meier, Georg Friedrich (1749) *Versuch eines neuen Lehrgebäudes von den Seelen der Thiere*, Halle: Carl Herrman Hemmerde.

Montaigne, Michel de (1924–41) *Oeuvres complètes*, 12 vols, ed. A. Armaingaud, Paris: Louis Conrad.

Narr, Dieter and Narr, Roland (1967) 'Menschenfreund und Tierfreund im 18. Jahrhundert', *Studium Generale* 20: 293–304.

Oster, Malcolm R. (1989) 'The "Beame of Diuinity": animal suffering in the early thought of Robert Boyle', *British Journal of the History of Science* 22: 151–79.

Oswald, John (1791) *The Cry of Nature; or an Appeal to Mercy and Justice, on behalf of the Persecuted Animals*, London: J. Johnson.

Passmore, John (1974) *Man's Responsibility for Nature. Ecological Problems and Western Traditions*, London: Duckworth.

—— (1975) 'The treatment of animals', *Journal of the History of Ideas* 36: 195–218.

Patzig, Günther (1986) 'Der wissenschaftliche Tierversuch unter ethischen Aspekten', in Wolfgang Hardegg and Gert Preiser (eds) *Tierversuche und medizinische Ethik. Beiträge zu einem Heidelberger Symposion*, Hildesheim: Olms/Weidmann (Frankfurter Beiträge zur Geschichte, Theorie und Ethik der Medizin, vol. III), pp. 68–84.

Pereira, Gómez (1749) *Antoniana Margarita, opus nempe physicis, medicis ac theologicis, non minus utile, quam necessarium*, 2 vols, 2nd edn, Madrid: Ex Typographia Antonii Marin.

Porphyrios (1747) *Traité ... touchant l'abstinence de la chair des animaux*, Paris: Chez de Bure.

Primatt, Humphrey (1778) *Ueber Barmherzigkeit und Grausamkeit gegen die thierische Schöpfung*, trans. from English edn of 1776, Halle: Johann Jacob Gebauer.

Pufendorf, Samuel Freiherr von (1744) *De jure naturae et gentium, libri octo*, 2 vols, ed. Gottfried Mascovius, Frankfurt/Leipzig: Ex Officina Knochiana. First published Frankfurt 1672.

Quintilian (1972–5) *Institutionis oratoriae libri XII*, 2 vols, ed. and trans. into German by Helmut Rahn, Darmstadt: Wiss. Buchgesellschaft.

Regan, Tom (1984) *The Case for Animal Rights*, London and Melbourne: Routledge & Kegan Paul.

Reinhard, Franz Volkmar (1816) *System de Christlichen Moral*, 5 vols, Vienna: Cath. Grässer & Härter.

Ritvo, Harriet (1987) *The Animal Estate: The English and Other Creatures in the Victorian Age*, Cambridge, Mass. and London: Harvard University Press.

Rorarius, Hieronymus (1666) *Quod animalia bruta ratione urantur melius homine. Libri duo*, Amsterdam: Apud Joannem Ravensteinium.

Rosenfield, Leonora Cohen (1940) *From Beast-Machine to Man-Machine. The Theme of Animal Soul in French Letters from Descartes to La Mettrie*, New York: Oxford University Press.

Rothschuh, Karl Eduard (1966) 'René Descartes und die Theorie der Lebenserscheinungen', *Sudhoffs Archiv* 50: 25–48.

Rupke, Nicolaas A. (ed.) (1990) *Vivisection in Historical Perspective*, 2nd edn, London and New York: Routledge (Wellcome Institute Series in the History of Medicine).

Sainte-Beuve, Charles A. (1840–59) *Port-Royal*, 5 vols, Paris: Eugène Renduel.

Salt, Henry S. (1894) *Animals' Rights Considered in Relation to Social Progress*, New York and London: Macmillan.

Schopenhauer, Arthur (1947–50) *Sämtliche Werke*, ed. Arthur Hübscher, 7 vols, 2nd edn, Wiesbaden: Brockhaus.

Sellert, Wolfgang (1984) 'Das Tier in der abendländischen Rechtsauffassung', in *Studium generale. Vorträge zum Thema: Mensch und Tier, WS 1982/83 Tierärztl. Hochschule Hannover*, Hanover: M. & H. Schaper, pp. 66–84.

Singer, Peter (1975) *Animal Liberation. A New Ethics for Our Treatment of Animals*, New York: New York Review.

Smith, Lauritz (1793) *Versuch eines vollständigen Lehrgebäudes der Natur und Bestimmung der Thiere und der Pflichten des Menschen gegen die Thiere*, Copenhagen: Christ. Gottlob Proft.

Sueton, C. (1961) *Kaiserbiographien – De Vita Caesarum*, 2 vols, ed. Adolf Stahr and Martin Vosseler, Munich: W. Goldmann.

Thomas, Keith (1983) *Man and the Natural World. A History of the Modern Sensibility*, New York: Pantheon Books.

Thuanus, Jakob August (1621) *Historische Beschreibung deren Namhafftigsten, Geistlichen und Weltlichen Geschichten*, 2 vols, Frankfurt am Main: In Verlegung Peter Kopffen.

Tröhler, Ulrich and Maehle, Andreas-Holger (1990) 'Anti-vivisection in nineteenth-century Germany and Switzerland: motives and methods', in N. A. Rupke (ed.) *Vivisection in Historical Perspective*, London and New York: Routledge, pp. 149–87.

Turner, James (1980) *Reckoning with the Beast: Animals, Pain and Humanity in the Victorian Mind*, Baltimore: London, Johns Hopkins University Press (Johns Hopkins University Studies in Historical and Political Science, 98th ser., 2).

Ullrich, Karl Julius and Detlev Creutzfeldt, Otto (eds) (1985) *Gesundheit und Tierschutz, Wissenschaftler melden sich zu Wort*, Düsseldorf and Vienna: Econ.

Volckmann, Johann Friedrich Ludwig (1799) *Menschenstolz und Thierqualen – eine Vertheidigung der seufzenden Creatur vor dem Richterstuhle der Menschlichkeit*, Helmstedt: C. G. Fleckeisen.

Winkler, Johann Heinrich (ed.) (1742a) *Die Frage, ob die Seelen der Thiere Verstand haben? in einer Gesellschaft guter Freunde untersucht*, Leipzig: Bernh. Christ. Breitkopf.

—— (ed.) (1742b) *Philosophische Untersuchung der Frage, Ob die Seelen einiger Thiere einem gewißen Grad der Vernunft haben, in einer Gesellschaft guter Freunde angestellet*, Leipzig: Bernh. Christ. Breitkopf.

—— (ed.) (1743a) *Die verschiedenen Meynungen einiger Weltweisen von der Existenz der Seelen der Thiere in einer Gesellschaft guter Freunde untersucht*, 3rd edn, Leipzig: Bernh. Christ. Breitkopf.

—— (ed.) (1743b) *Philosophische Untersuchung der Frage, Ob die Seelen der Thiere mit ihren Leibern sterben? in einer Gesellschaft guter Freunde angestellet*, Leipzig: Bernh. Christ. Breitkopf.

—— (1762) *Institutiones philosophiae universae usibus academicis accomodatae*, 3 vols, 3rd edn, Leipzig: In Officina Fritschia.

Youatt, William (1839) *The Obligation and Extent of Humanity to Brutes, principally considered with reference to Domesticated Animals*, London, Longman, Orme, Brown etc.

Young, Thomas (1798) *An Essay on Humanity to Animals*, London: T. Cadwell, Jun. & W. Davies.

6

ANIMALS IN NINETEENTH-CENTURY BRITAIN
Complicated attitudes and competing categories

Harriet Ritvo

At the beginning of the nineteenth century, the English would have been surprised to hear themselves praised for special kindness to animals. They were surrounded by evidence to the contrary. The streets of London were crowded with horses and dogs who served as draught animals and beasts of burden; human pedestrians often encountered herds of cattle and sheep being driven to the livestock market at Smithfield.[1] Many of these animals were obviously exhausted or in pain. Off the street, but not hard to find, were slaughterhouses and the knackers' yards where animals whose time had come were butchered with no special concern to minimize their final agony. And animals suffered in the cause of human pleasure as well as human profit. Popular amusements included cock-fighting, dog-fighting, rat-killing, bull-running and the baiting of wild animals; among elite amusements were numbered steeplechasing, fox-hunting, and occasionally, still, the pursuit of the noble stag.

Few people registered distress at the animal suffering that surrounded them. On the contrary, many took pride in the doughty national character revealed by its infliction. When, in 1800, the House of Commons considered the first animal protection bill ever presented to it, which sought only to abolish the sport of bull-baiting, few members bothered to attend the session, and some of those present made fun of the whole idea. According to *The Times*, which hailed the bill's defeat, the issue was beneath the dignity of Parliament. In the course of the debate the future prime minister George Canning defended bull-baiting on the grounds that 'the amusement inspired courage and produced a nobleness of sentiment and elevation of mind.'[2]

Such actions and attitudes drove those who deplored the mistreatment of animals to conclude that the English were especially inclined to inflict it. One patriotic journalist regretfully admitted in 1825 that, 'attached as we are to our native land . . . we are bound to confess, that the proverb is but too true, "that England is the hell of dumb animals"'; a decade later a well-known popular naturalist wrote that 'of all the nations of Europe, our own countrymen are, perhaps, the least inclined to treat the brute creation with tenderness'.[3] Abuse of animals was perceived to be widespread even among those who had no vocational occasion to beat oxen or overwork horses. Thus a country correspondent of the *Zoologist* complained in 1853 of 'the continual and wanton persecution of birds [and animals] in England, as contrasted with their kind treatment in Norway',[4] and even the passive indifference of many citizens was criticized as complicity. A humane clergyman named William Hamilton Drummond regretted that in a country where 'the duties of morality and religion have such eloquent advocates', so little attention was devoted to the abuse of animals. In 1832 a humanitarian periodical cited public apathy in the face of the horrors of the Smithfield market as evidence that 'Englishmen are really guilty of that love of cruelty which Hazlitt used to say was inherent in their character.'[5] The theme of English brutality was sounded well into the second half of the nineteenth century. In 1868, after referring the home secretary to an article on the subject in the *Daily Telegraph*, Queen Victoria herself opined that 'the English are inclined to be more cruel to animals than some other civilized nations are'.[6]

By the end of the century, however, a humanitarian crusader could celebrate the fact that

> to an increasing part of the race, especially in Anglo-Saxon countries, this sentiment of tenderness for those of the sentient lower creatures which are capable of recognising it . . . has become an element in the spiritual life so strong that the continual violation of social obligations to them is a cause of pain and revolt.

He was particularly cheered by the spectacle of squirrels begging confidently for food in public parks, rather than fleeing from anticipated torture, as had apparently been their custom at an earlier period. Indeed as early as the 1830s, despite the circumambient evidence to the contrary, the English humane movement had begun to claim kindness to animals as a native trait and to associate cruelty to animals with foreigners, especially those from southern, Catholic countries. Similar claims remained part of its stock rhetorical repertory throughout the Victorian period.[7]

Such confident assertions in the face of such incontrovertible facts can be hard to explain, particularly since the organized humane movement showed no inclination to gloss over manifestations of the darker side of the national character. Indeed, the mainstay of the movement – the (Royal) Society for the Prevention of Cruelty to Animals – spent much of its public relations energy detailing the widespread and gruesome cruelty that its force of special constables was paid to combat.[8] How could the English be distinguished at once for their cruelty and for their kindness to the brute creation? Or, to put it another way, how could the knowledgeable and experienced officers of the (R)SPCA offer such a confusing and self-contradictory account?

*

One possible explanation of this paradox is that the nineteenth century was an era of change in human–animal relations in Britain. In addition to the strong likelihood that any historical period will turn out to be an era of change, there is a lot of evidence to support this theory. On the legislative and popular education fronts, the Victorian humane movement proceeded from strength to strength. After several early defeats, the first animal protection legislation – Richard Martin's bill 'to prevent cruel and improper treatment of Cattle' – was enacted in 1822.[9] This first Act was quite focused – for example, both bulls and domestic pets were excluded from its provisions – but these and other omissions were subsequently remedied. The Society for the Prevention of Cruelty to Animals, founded in 1824 to fund the enforcement of the new law, which included no financial appropriation, struggled at first, but by 1832 it had attracted enough members to begin publishing rather elaborate annual reports, which documented a range of lobbying, prosecutorial and informational activities. In 1835 the SPCA acquired the first of many royal patrons (the Duchess of Kent and the then-Princess Victoria), and in 1840 Queen Victoria granted it permission to use the prefix 'Royal'.[10] By 1900 the RSPCA epitomized respectable philanthropy; it had become 'one of the standard charities remembered by British maiden ladies and others when making their wills'.[11] In this interpretation, the confidence of the humane movement reflected justified satisfaction with its impressive accomplishments, while the somewhat gory emphasis on continuing cruelty was designed to keep their supporters from resting on their laurels. The compulsive recounting of episodes of animal mutilation and torture that filled the pages of the RSPCA annual reports could also double as evidence of progress, since they were invariably success stories, at least from the enforcement point of view. That is, although most of the animals involved had suffered irredeemably, their abusers had all been reported, apprehended and brought to justice.

An alternative explanation of the apparent paradox might emphasize stasis, which is as strong a component of any history as change. That is, if we look around us today, we see great, indeed in some ways unprecedented, concern for animals, but it is far from clear that the sum of animal suffering is less than it was a century ago. Much of the reduction of suffering must be attributed to causes other than the spread of humanitarian attitudes or the enforcement of humanitarian laws. For example, there are many fewer suffering cab-horses, but that is more because of the invention of the internal combustion engine than because of any change of heart on the part of cabbies and bus drivers. If the march of time has healed some wounds, it has inflicted others. Animals suffer in our laboratories in numbers unimaginable to the most energetic nineteenth-century physiologists. It would be difficult to offer a single, consistent generalization about attitudes to animals in our own complicated societies, based on the humaneness (or the reverse) of the actual treatment they experience at our hands. Victorian society was no less complicated and diverse. That is to say, *mutatis mutandis*, that the reason why the RSPCA could offer apparently conflicting accounts of the mid-nineteenth-century English attitude toward cruelty to animals is that both (or all) of them were correct.

Similar paradoxes or complexities characterized the entire range of Victorian interactions with animals. Thus, the antivivisection movement, which coalesced in the third quarter of the nineteenth century, could be seen as the culmination of the increasing national concern for animal suffering exemplified by the steady growth of the RSPCA and other humane organizations. And in the political maneuvering that preceded the passage of the Cruelty to Animals Act of 1876, John Colam, the secretary of the RSPCA, offered elaborate, carefully reasoned testimony in favor of prohibiting all painful experimentation on living animals, and all experimentation, whether painful or not, simply for demonstration or training purposes. But the RSPCA found itself as little able to endorse the position of complete prohibition advocated by radical anti-vivisection organizations such as Frances Power Cobbe's Victoria Street Society for the Protection of Animals from Vivisection, as it was to stand behind the insistence of some members of the scientific community that no interference with research should be tolerated.[12]

Each of these extreme positions represented a widely held attitude to animals that was in conflict with the mainstream humanitarian position occupied by the RSPCA and its adherents. Like radical anti-vivisectionists, the RSPCA viewed experimental cruelty as a form of animal abuse, and it viewed the abuse of animals as symbolic of what was worst in human nature and therefore most dangerous in human society. But they disagreed on both the nature and the extent of the threat. The RSPCA feared social chaos and tended to focus on what it viewed as the disturbingly irrational behavior of the uneducated and insufficiently disciplined segments of society; the anti-vivisectionists feared what they viewed as the soullessness of modern culture, which was epitomized by the merciless intrusions of experimental physiologists. Many of them were sentimental reactionaries where the sufferings of individual animals, especially those belonging to pet species, were concerned. Among their most powerful weapons were the emotionalism and irrationality that, when expressed by members of the lower classes in the form of cruel sports and occupational practices, the essentially liberal RSPCA was committed to eradicating. And if invasive science represented the worst of modern society to anti-vivisectionists, it represented the best to many people, including the scientists themselves. The threat to their autonomy constituted by the anti-vivisection campaign inspired what may have been the first organization of scientists to lobby for their own interests, and they were able to persuade both the legislature and, in large measure, the public that the experimental use of animals, properly regulated but not unduly constrained, was essential to the prosecution of that great Victorian icon, progress.[13]

*

A range of analogous inconsistencies or contradictions emerged in the protracted and impassioned Victorian public debate about rabies, or hydrophobia. Throughout the nineteenth century, rabies epizootics were a recurrent source of public concern and even hysteria. Because of its association, widely recognized and often explicit, with contamination and sin, the disease evoked a degree of attention strongly incommensurate with the actual threat it posed to either human or animal populations. That is, although rabies victims inevitably suffered excruciating pain and gruesome death, the actual numbers of such victims were rather low. The annual animal death toll numbered only in the hundreds, and in 1877, by far the worst year on record, only seventy-nine Britons died.[14]

Despite the low likelihood of becoming infected with rabies, many people worried – often both compulsively and in print – about contracting the disease, and their worries reflected a range of attitudes towards the domestic dogs that were its major carriers. These attitudes even determined the positions that people took on the genesis and spread of rabies. Defenders of dogs tended to favor the spontaneous generation hypothesis, which held that rabies could arise in dogs, and even in people, who had had no contact with diseased animals, as a result of exposure to a variety of external noninfectious agents. Depending on which authority was consulted, these could include not only overfeeding and sexual frustration, but also cold weather, wet weather, hot weather, thirst, hunger, confinement, terror, pain and other violent emotions.[15] Such thinking shifted moral responsibility from the infected dog to cruel human caretakers; it could make the public health campaign to eliminate rabies seem like a conspiracy on the part of canophobes to persecute innocent dogs. In its extreme form this view might lead to the flat denial that the disease existed. Thus, according to an article in the *Worcestershire Chronicle*, 'there is no such thing as hydrophobia from dog bite, but there is a very widespread disease of insanity arising from an unnatural and causeless distrust of dogs, which appears to affect people long before they have been bitten by them'. In a similar vein, the *Kennel Review* once defined hydrophobia as 'a peculiar madness that seizes men and impels them to destroy dogs'.[16]

The contagion hypothesis, which gained favor in the course of the nineteenth century, identified infected animals as the agents responsible for the spread of rabies. Although the hypothesis itself did not carry any intrinsic moral charge, either implicit or explicit, notions of guilt and innocence almost invariably surfaced in any discussion of its public health implications or consequences. In a way, treating rabid dogs as guilty, rather than just sick, transformed an epizootic from a medical problem into a police problem; the main job of disease control became intensive moral surveillance of the dog population, in order to purge it of the errant members who had deviated from standards of moral as well as physical soundness. Decisions about whether particular types of dog were especially liable to infection revealed policy-makers' assumptions about what made a dog (and often, by metaphoric transfer, its owner) good or bad; trustworthy or dangerous. From this perspective, dogs were far from a unified category toward which a single attitude was appropriate – or even conceivable.

There were many candidates for special opprobrium, and in these judgements, as in many others involving animals, the character of the animal was inextricably confounded with that of the humans with whom it was most closely associated. The aggressive sporting and hunting dogs kept by members of the lower classes – poaching dogs in the country and fighting dogs in the towns – emerged as the most suspicious element, or at least the most frequently suspected element, of the canine community.[17] It was held that the viciousness of such dogs – their inbred eagerness to attack other animals, even rabid ones, as well as people – made them more likely to contract rabies, and more likely to spread it widely once they became ill. The pet dogs of the poor were almost equally objectionable, although less aggressive, because they intensified the squalor and insalubrity of the humble dwellings of their owners.

For different reasons, the dogs of the rich might also attract attention. The inbreeding that characterized some luxury dog breeds was considered to have 'debilitated or exhausted' their nervous systems, making them more susceptible to rabies, a tendency that might be exacerbated by exotic foreign (mainly German and French) bloodlines.[18] The overeating indulged in by some pampered dogs was often cited as a cause of rabies, as was the precocious and unusually intense sexual appetite also attributed to such animals. Thus, it was discreetly claimed that 'all veterinary surgeons have noted that male animals, and those habitually confined [and] richly fed . . . are far more liable to contract rabies', and more directly asserted that 'the first sexual excitement in the young dog [can be] followed by symptoms wonderfully like dumb rabies . . . usually amongst ladies' pets, dogs in full habit of body'.[19] Finally, the genteel rural pastimes of shooting and fox-hunting required canine auxiliaries, and both of these groups of dogs were repeatedly accused of special susceptibility to rabies. In particular, the packs of highly trained and carefully bred foxhounds that dotted the Victorian countryside seemed to be constantly at risk, and their aggressiveness and wide-ranging habits made them appear as vigorous disseminators of infection rather than stagnant pools where it merely festered.[20]

Responses to rabies outbreaks were determined by whether or not people liked dogs, and also which dogs they liked or disliked, affinities largely dependent upon attitudes toward the human groups most closely associated with the suspected animals. In turn, these predilections influenced both official decisions about rabies control and the public's acquiescence or resistance. Until the last quarter of the nineteenth century the only rabies control options open to proponents of the contagion hypothesis were forms of isolation: muzzling, confinement and quarantine. All of these measures were routinely resisted by the canophile (and therefore anti-contagion) faction, on the grounds that they merely tortured dogs, and torture of various sorts was the very thing likely to produce rabies or the appearance of rabies in the first place.

But in the 1880s word spread from Paris of Louis Pasteur's new anti-rabies vaccine, which, if administered in time, could prevent those infected by the bite of a mad dog from developing rabies. Although the fact that Great Britain is an island meant that ultimately quarantine emerged as the preferred means of rabies control, Pasteur's discovery exacerbated the disparity in attitudes towards animals that was implicit in the rabies debate. His work came under intense attack by those who had previously resisted the contagion theory, and not just because the efficacy of his inoculation conclusively proved that theory. He was also criticized as a vivisector – as with all vaccines, his were tested on animals, and also produced from animals; his laboratory was portrayed not as a center of healing, but as a focus of contamination, where humans were injected with alien animal material and where, possibly still more disturbing, genteel English people might come into contact with members of other classes and nationalities. So the love of dogs merged into the hatred of biomedical research, which was seen as the agent of contamination and decay, and into the hatred of the modern world in general. Animals were not simply objects of humanitarian concern; they also represented the traditional organic forces and social relationships cherished by conservatives who, with some justice, perceived them as under attack by the forces of public health, rational science and official bureaucracy.

*

If many citizens of nineteenth-century Britain, from cab-drivers to experimental scientists, felt that the claim of animals to humane treatment should be subordinated to a range of human claims, many of their fellow countrymen felt (or at least acted and wrote as if they felt) that animals had no claim to humane treatment at all. Economic or at least vocational motives might be held to justify the suffering inflicted in the streets or in the laboratory, but simple pleasure was the motive of suffering inflicted in the chase. Hunting and shooting were common country pastimes in Victorian Britain; Matthew Arnold famously characterized the upper classes as 'barbarians' with a 'passion for field sports' in 1860, and this predilection was by no means confined to the elite.[21] The rich might, however, have greater access to the remote hunting fields of the empire, where the quarry was larger and more exciting, and the sport bloodier and more dangerous, than at home (see Plate 6.1).

What they sought in these exotic plains and jungles was richly documented in a stream of sporting adventure narratives that flowed so copiously from the presses of London publishers in the late nineteenth century that eventually, in the view of one jaded reader, 'people have been so overdone with howdahs, and . . . hair-breadth escapes, and griffins spearing a sow by mistake, that they had rather face a royal Bengal tiger in his native jungle than in the Sporting Magazine'. One sporting author rather unselfconsciously began his book by lamenting that 'every person visiting South Africa, who has shooting pro- clivities, and is gifted with the smallest powers of description, deems it his duty to the world at large, to give information regarding the sport to be had.'[22] These complaints emphasized the point made by the sheer volume of this literature: the extent to which the goals and pleasures of big-game hunters were at least vicariously shared by their large armchair audience.

Writers about exotic hunting, among whose ranks figured many military officers and imperial civil servants, as well as recreational travelers and professional collectors, were often careful to stress the many salutary side effects of their pursuit of big game, such as its influence in developing qualities of resourcefulness, independence and courage. Further, the 'unrestrained freedom' of the field, when, as one Royal Artillery captain put it, the hunter could 'feel like a wild man . . . [and] throw off all the restraints imposed by the rules of society', was efficacious in dispelling ennui and the variety of nervous ailments that tended to afflict Britons stationed in remote colonial locations.[23] As a veteran sportsman advised his readers, 'when bile and nervousness become too intolerable; when you feel yourself too shaky and cross and yellow-faced for anything; get a leave of absence, and ride into the jungle'.[24]

But these were essentially secondary benefits. Sporting authors made it abundantly clear where the real attraction of big-game hunting lay. The remembered enjoyment that made it 'still pleasant', in later years, 'sitting over a fire, talking to congenial companions about sport . . . to fight our battles with big game over again', derived ultimately from the satisfaction of the lust for blood – the 'insatiable desire for *slaying* something' cited by one of the few female contributors to the literature of late Victorian exotic sport.[25] The greatest hunters – men whose exploits sometimes attained the status of national legend – made this point repeatedly in their narratives, and then emphasized it by the generous provision of gory details. William Cornwallis Harris, one of the first sportsmen to shoot in southern Africa, characterized killing game as a 'passion . . . one of the most powerful affections of the human mind'; later William Charles Baldwin could 'imagine no greater enjoyment than in shooting . . . till every bone in my body ached'; and Robert White delighted in 'whole hecatombs of slaughter'.[26] When Roualeyn Gordon Cumming, an addictive hunter who became the Buffalo Bill of the African plains, saw five bull elephants and felt 'that you can ride up and vanquish whichever one you fancy', he found the experience 'so overpoweringly exciting that it almost takes a man's breath away'.[27]

*

Thus, even if the development of the organized humane movement might seem to offer some basis, however tentative, for the development of concern for animals in nineteenth-century Britain, a wider sampling of Victorian interactions with their fellow creatures would tend to undermine confidence in any single characteristic attitude or even trend. Rather than helping to substantiate the claim of unity that underlies even an adjective like 'Victorian', with its implicit suggestion that it describes a homogeneous society or culture, the diversity of human–animal relations seems to broach contrary claims of disparity and even incoherence. And this incoherence spreads in both directions, implicating not only the category of 'Victorian attitudes' but also that of 'animals'. The difficulty of understanding human–animal relations according to any single principle or master narrative that would accommodate both hunting and disease control – or even both humane activism and anti-vivisection – suggests that the very notion 'animal' was not determined exclusively by the concrete zoological and economic realities embodied by the creatures, however compelling those realities might have superficially appeared. Instead, it was significantly influenced by human control or cultural contingencies.

Indeed, zoology itself, the scientific specialty devoted to the description and analysis of the animal kingdom, rather than providing any objective correlative against which less rationally derived notions could be measured, might turn out instead to provide another arena for contention and contestation. That is, zoology was also embedded in and reflective of the same complex human/animal and human/human relationships that produced the inconsistencies already described. Even systematic classification, ostensibly the abstract and authoritative distillation of the zoological enterprise, turned out to express a range of varied and often inconsistent views. There was, to begin with, no generally accepted system of classification – that is, the hegemony of scientific taxonomy was implicitly challenged by the coexistence of folk taxonomies based on such activities as animal breeding and hunting, and even among zoologists there were serious differences of opinion. Conflicts between these systems, whether acknowledged or not, often illustrated not only different ways of analysing the natural world, but also inconsistent ideas about the relationship of people to animals and to each other.

Scientific taxonomy was celebrated as one of the crowning achievements of the Enlightenment. As Benjamin Stillingfleet, one of many eighteenth-century English translators or interpreters of Linnaeus put it, the ability to give a plant or an animal 'its true name according to some system' was a *sine qua non* for serious students of nature; he observed sternly that 'he who cannot go thus far ... does not deserve the name of a naturalist'.[28] So classification (whether according to the Linnaean system, or one of several serious competitors) not only distinguished one animal from another and established their relative

114

position within the natural order, but it also marked the boundary between serious students of nature and others with ostensibly similar interests. Enlightenment naturalists disparaged both their predecessors – practitioners of the outmoded bestiary tradition – and those of their contemporaries who could be described as 'mere collectors of curiosities and superficial trifles . . . objects of ridicule rather than respect'.[29] Only the prematurely systematic Aristotle escaped opprobrium; more typical was the dismissal of the works of the Renaissance naturalist Aldrovandus as 'insupportably tedious and disgusting'.[30] Even as nineteenth-century zoologists discarded many of the specific arrangements and general principles of Linnaeus and his contemporaries, they continued to celebrate their achievement in rescuing for science a study previously the province of ignorance and delusion. The implication was that, at least within the realm of zoology, attitudes toward animals were determined by objectivity and rationally grounded consensus – or, as some might have put it – that there were no attitudes at all, only accurate information and analysis.

Such a claim would be underscored by the abstract schemata and tables that often began or concluded works of post-Enlightenment zoology, implicitly announcing that each creature would find its proper place in the system. But the detailed description of individual species that made up the bulk of most such volumes told a more complicated story. In the entry on the common cat in his popular *General History of Quadrupeds*, the final edition of which appeared in 1824, Thomas Bewick mentioned its lack of affection for humans, its price in medieval Wales, its irritability, and its relationship to Dick Whittington, along with its eyesight, its voice and its gestation.[31] In his much more elaborate and scientific compendium, Thomas Pennant, the founder of the Linnean Society, similarly included the facts that Angora cats degenerated in England but were adorned with silver collars in China, that cats purred when pleased and washed their faces at the approach of a storm, and that although many people hated them they were much loved by the 'Mahometans'.[32] Such combinations of folk wisdom (or non-wisdom) with apparently scientific data worked to connect Enlightenment and post-Enlightenment natural history with the antiquated bestiary tradition or with the many competing views of animals in the nonspecialist culture that surrounded them.

Even the categories that were the glory of scientific taxonomy often turned out, when examined, to suggest that objective information and analysis may have played a less than dominant role in their determination. Nor, when they were worked out in detail, did the systems themselves unambiguously support the assertion that they represented a new departure in the study of animals. Often, on the contrary, they reflected competing, if unacknowledged, principles of organization that seemed to undermine both their schematic novelty and their implicit claim to be based on objective scientific analysis of the natural world. These competing principles usually divided animals into groups based not on their physical characteristics but on subjective perceptions of them. An ancient category like 'vermin', long used by hunters and farmers to describe noxious animals – animals 'necessary to be hunted', as one seventeenth-century manual of venery put it – survived in the taxonomy of Ray and Pennant only superficially transfigured by the claim that it alluded to the worm-like forms of the weasels, martens and polecats most frequently so castigated.[33] Rather than analysing nature exclusively on its own terms – the claim embodied in their formal systems – naturalists often implicitly presented it in terms of its relationship to people, echoing the kind of anthropocentric and sentimental projection characteristic of the bestiary tradition they had so emphatically discarded and (then as now) of much nonscientific discourse about animals.

Richard Brookes introduced one of the most powerful and highly constructed sets of subjective categories in *The Natural History of Quadrupeds*. He proclaimed himself a follower of the seventeenth-century English naturalist John Ray rather than Linnaeus (an allegiance he shared with many of his patriotic fellow countrymen), and, like most zoologists in this camp, he used a range of physical characteristics to group mammals, with foot conformation pre-eminent.[34] This method yielded the following order: horses (undivided hoofs); ruminants (cloven hoofs); the hippopotamus, elephant and others (anomalous hoofs); camels; monkeys (the first of the animals without hoofs); humans; cats; dogs; weasels; hares; the hedgehog, armadillo and mole (divided feet and long snouts); bats, and, finally, sloths. Yet he also asserted, and in the synoptic introduction where his methodological consciousness might be presumed to be highest, that 'the most obvious and simple division ... of Quadrupedes, is into the Domestic and Savage.'[35] Obvious though it might be, however, this division implied a taxonomic structure that cut across the formal organization established in Brookes's synoptic summary (unless, perhaps, that summary was taken to represent a progression from familiar to exotic animals, rather than an analysis of mammals based on feet). It replaced a structure based, at least ostensibly, on animal anatomy with one based patently on animal bondage.

Brookes was not the only naturalist to address this dichotomy; other zoological writers shared his inclination to treat the distinction between wild and domestic animals as primary rather than contingent, the basis for taxonomic discrimination rather than the occasion for description and explanation. It was commonplace to notice, for example, that 'domestic animals in very few respects resemble wild ones; their nature, their size, and their form are less constant ... especially in the exterior part of the body'.[36] Related, if less firmly anchored in objective observation, were frequent assertions to the effect that 'all Animals, except ourselves ... are strangers to pain and sickness .... We speak of wild animals only. Those that are tame ... partake of our miseries.'[37]

Thus William Swainson defined domestication not as a human accomplishment, but as an innate, divinely inculcated propensity 'to submit ... cheerfully and willingly'. In consequence, it had systematic significance, cropping up in 'every instance among the more perfect animals [of] the rasorial type'.[38] Many naturalists used domestic animals as taxonomic models, typically claiming that 'each class of quadrupeds may be ranged under some one of the domestic kinds'; so domestic animals both exemplified and limited the range of mammalian possibilities.[39] The categories of wild and domestic might be perceived as so disparate that they required a connecting link; thus, 'as the cat may be said to be only half domestic; he forms the shade between the real wild and real domestic animals'.[40]

Another indication of the taxonomic significance of domestication was that animals perceived to differ only in this attribute – that is, animals that were anatomically similar and that were believed to interbreed – were frequently placed in separate species. Although Pennant, along with many others, identified the European wild cat as the 'stock and origin' of the domestic cat, the former was labelled *Felis sylvestris* and the latter *Felis catus*.[41] Analogously, he referred to what were known as the wild cattle of Chillingham, an unruly strain of white animals preserved in the parks of several great houses, mostly for decoration or hunting rather than for the dairy or the slaughterhouse, as *Bisontes scotici*, putting them into a separate genus or subgenus from the *Bos taurus* that grazed on ordinary British pastures.[42]

The fact of domestication appeared so important to some naturalists that they tended to accord breeds of domestic animals the same taxonomical status as species of wild animals, despite the fact that variability within species was widely recognized as one of the most frequent results of domestication. Following Linnaeus, George Shaw tagged many dog breeds with Latinate binomials that at least sounded like the names of species – for example the hound was *Canis sagax*, the shepherd's dog was *Canis domesticus*, and the Pomeranian was *Canis pomeranus*.[43] And if divisions based on the dichotomy between wild and domestic animals came into explicit conflict with divisions based on the principles of systematic taxonomy, it was sometimes the latter that gave way. So when Edward Bennett admitted that 'it would . . . appear . . . impossible to offer' a physical description of the domestic dog that would distinguish it from the wolf and other wild canines, he did not conclude that they should all be considered a single species. Instead, to reify the division based on domestication, he introduced a new and circular criterion: 'it is to the moral and intellectual qualities of the dog that we must look for those remarkable peculiarities which distinguish him'.[44]

*

If the valorization of domestic animals reflected the links of nineteenth-century naturalists to farmers and pet owners, the sense of zoological probability embodied in many of their deliberations linked them to cultural commitments perhaps even older and deeper. Although eighteenth- and nineteenth-century systematics did not depend on biblical sanctions, it turned out to have trouble dealing with some creatures that did not fit easily into the taxonomy of Genesis – 'the fish of the sea' and 'the fowl of the air' and so forth. In the late eighteenth century naturalists became aware of the echidna and the platypus, egg-laying mammals that might have seemed created to confirm the still-cherished theory of the Great Chain of Being.[45] But instead of embracing these intermediate creatures, they held them very much at arm's length. Bewick responded to the platypus, the more spectacular of the two, with confusion, characterizing it as 'an animal *sui generis*; it appears to possess a three fold nature, that of a fish, a bird, and a quadruped, and is related to nothing we have hitherto seen'. He declined not only to classify it, but even to name it, referring to it only as 'an amphibious animal'.[46] Shaw responded to it with suspicion, wondering whether 'some arts of deception' might have been practiced to produce the first specimen he saw; after he was reassured, he nevertheless described it has having 'the beak of a Duck engrafted on the head of a quadruped'.[47]

But such skepticism was not the invariable rule; folkloric traditions persisting in unlikely places might make some improbable animals seem less surprising than others. Creatures of myth sometimes fared better than startling new discoveries like the platypus – the plausible impossible, as often in nonscientific discourse, preferred to the possible implausible; the imaginary and familiar perceived as more persuasive than the actual and bizarre. For example, the zoological literature of the eighteenth and even the nineteenth century contained many references to mermaids, unicorns and sea serpents, even though the credulity of classical and Renaissance bestiarists with regard to such improbabilities was part of the standard Enlightenment brief against them.[48] Rather than simply dismissing these creatures as imaginary, naturalists often tried to account for the persistent reports of their existence. In the popular and widely respected Naturalist's Library series, William Jardine remarked of the oryx that 'this group is remarkable, as it is supposed that from some of its members the far-famed Unicorn would be made out'; Robert Hamilton identified whales, walrus and seals as 'the original types of nearly all these wondrous tales' about mermaids.[49] Others were still more open-minded, discriminating, for example, between the unicorn, which one naturalist dismissed as a creature, 'which, if it ever did exist, is now to be found no more', and the mermaid, 'partly a fish, and partly of the human species', for which, he asserted, 'there seems to be sufficient evidence to establish its reality'.[50]

Not even the most carefully elaborated taxonomy would necessarily exclude such prodigies; it could dictate the form of subsidiary categories, but not their content. Indeed, sometimes manifestly scientific systems could seem to mandate violations of the natural order; to blur rather than demarcate the boundary between myth and science. The quinary system was formulated by William MacLeay in 1819 and popularized by William Swainson a decade and a half later, at least in part as a response to the narrow restrictiveness of the chain of nature. It arranged animals within a set of complexly embedded circles, which took account of both anatomical affinities and less concrete (and often more traditional) similarities.[51] The system was designed to be predictive as well as descriptive. Each circle was supposed to contain five subcategories, and if the current state of zoological knowledge left one unfilled, it remained as a niche for some creature or group of creatures yet to be discovered. Thus Swainson took the absence of an aquatic group (one member of each group of five was supposed to be 'natatorial') in the circle of Quadrumana, which otherwise included apes, monkeys, lemurs and bats, to indicate that although 'we do not . . . believe in the existence of mermaids as depicted . . . by the old writers . . . some such animal has really been created'. Similarly, with regard to the circle of Ungulata, he reasoned that the 'obvious hiatus' . . . between the horse and the camel' would ultimately be filled 'by some animal agreeing more or less with the unicorn'.[52]

*

The competing, if unacknowledged, agendas embodied in Enlightenment and post-Enlightenment classification systems, in which explicitly scientific tax-onomical principles were often profoundly modified by unacknowledged principles reflecting more popularly based views of nature, were inevitably reflected in the nomenclature associated with them. To some extent, this was an open secret among zoologists, who inevitably encountered, in the course of their daily work, telling evidence that the Linnaean mission of unique identification and organization, however widely honored in theory, often proved difficult to implement in practice. That is, while they publicly celebrated the triumph of system over chaos, ignorance and lack of special-ization, among themselves they bemoaned the turmoil and inconsistency that surfaced whenever nomenclatural issues had to be addressed. Their claim to have given each species a single, universally accepted and systematically correct Latinate designation was belied, not only by the continued use and proliferation of popular names, but by a great deal of disagreement and contention within the scientific community.

Sometimes the profusion of competing tags reflected political rivalries, with each national scientific establishment promulgating its own terminology. Appropriating an exotic animal through nomenclature could be tantamount to claiming its habitat. Further, the zoological frontier and the political frontier were not always in the same place, and territorial boundaries were easier to challenge in scientific journals than on the battlefield. Sir Stamford Raffles, founder of both Singapore and the Zoological Society of London, once found himself in the unhappy position of having to dismiss 'two French gentlemen who [had] appeared qualified' to help him with the preservation and description of his specimens, lest, as a result of what he called their 'private and national views', 'all the result of all my endeavours . . . be carried to a foreign country'. What he feared was the integration of his specimens into a

Gallicized nomenclature, and their consequent loss, not only to himself but to his country.[53]

The existence of rival English and French nomenclatures within a system ostensibly designed to provide a unique and universally accepted designation for every species signaled a disjunction between the ostensible function of Linnaean terminology and the way it actually operated. Through much of the nineteenth century, the universality of scientific nomenclature and therefore the uniqueness of individual species names were more matters of assertion than demonstration. Anybody could present an authoritative-seeming terminology, and, as it turned out, more or less anybody did. In the late eighteenth and early nineteenth centuries this uncanonical plethora of names was often acknowledged directly – that is, natural history compendia would begin the description of a species with a synonyma, or list of all the names, both Latinate and vernacular, by which the species was known. Subsequently, zoologists tended to ignore alternative terminologies, citing only the binomials they preferred, unless they wished to criticize specific alternatives or to inveigh against the proliferation of terms.

Often, they did wish so to inveigh. And although the French drew repeated criticism for their willful and uncooperative 'rage for innovation', as one British systematizer rather mildly put it,[54] the most frequent targets of such criticism on the part of the British scientific establishment were closer to home. In 1841, in response to what was perceived as a troublesome level of confusion, the British Association for the Advancement of Science appointed a committee 'to draw up a series of rules with a view to establishing a nomenclature of zoology on a uniform and permanent basis'.[55] This committee was supposed to report back to the British Association the next year, but in fact its work was not completed for more than two decades, by which time most of the original committee members were dead.[56] Despite this long delay, the concerns expressed at the outset were those that shaped the entire discussion. It was recognized that there were unavoidable technical causes for some disparities in nomenclature – for example, legitimate disagreement about where a creature's closest affinities lay, and the occasional necessity for naming on the basis of very small samples (so that dissimilar members of a single species might be identified as two separate species) – and these unavoidable causes were generally ignored. The Nomenclature Committee instead focused its ire on a source of confusion that it took to be rooted in human nature, and therefore vulnerable to policing.

This source, castigated as an 'evil' in the committee's initial report, which was circulated for comments to a rather large circle of scientists, was 'the practice of gratifying individual vanity by attempting on the most frivolous pretexts to cancel the terms established by original discoverers, and to substitute new and unauthorized nomenclature in their place'.[57] Individual vanity was an issue because binomials were normally cited with the name of the namer appended in parentheses. Thus, even though scientific etiquette forbade discoverers of new species to commemorate themselves (an attempt at enforced gentility that was routinely compromised by the tendency of discoverers to name species after their employers or sponsors), this parenthetical convention provided a strong incitement to naturalists who might inappropriately value glory over truth.

In the view of the committee and its correspondents, these egotistical rogue naturalists were not a random sample of the zoological community, distinguished only by moral weakness. Instead, it was implied by the rules that were proposed as correctives for this situation, they were an identifiable segment of this community. The rules stressed the importance of preserving the classical flavor of zoological nomenclature, in part to supersede possible national differences, but perhaps more significantly to distinguish zoologists with the command of classical languages normally acquired only through formal education from those whose expertise had been acquired in less genteel academies.[58]

It was asserted: 'the *best* zoological names are . . . derived from . . . Latin or Greek', and namers were warned against designations that revealed a misunderstanding or half-understanding of classical texts, such as referring to an ancient name for a different animal, or a mythological figure that had no relation to the character of the animal being named.[59] (That such strictures reflected a desire to establish a binary taxonomy of Victorian zoologists, rather than a more generalized respect for traditional scholarship, was suggested by a warning to nomenclators inclined to delve too deeply into Aristotle, Pliny and other figures from the prehistory of zoology. Such propensities might result in 'our zoological studies . . . [being] frittered away amid the refinements of classical learning'.[60] Further, names were repeatedly banned on the grounds that they revealed vulgarity or lack of taste, such as nonsense names, names made up of fragments of two different words, hybrid names that combined elements of two languages (often also a telltale indication of insufficient education), and names that instead of commemorating 'persons of eminence as scientific zoologists', celebrated 'persons of no scientific reputation, [such] as curiosity dealers . . . Peruvian priestesses . . . or Hottentots'.[61] A paleontologist primarily interested in the remains of extinct sea monsters characterized the latter transgression in similar terms as 'injurious to the dignity of Science, and the Taste of the Age in which we live'.[62] And in several letters to H. E. Strickland, who headed the Nomenclature Committee, Charles Darwin enthusiastically applauded his efforts, while disparaging those naturalists in need of suppression as mere 'species-mongers' who wanted to 'have their vanity tickled' and were therefore responsible for a '*vast amount of bad work*'.[63]

Nor did non-elite naturalists pose the only challenge to the ostensibly objective viewpoint represented by a uniform, authoritative and exclusive code of zoological nomenclature. Interest in natural history was not restricted to Victorian scientific circles, however loosely or restrictively defined, and the larger audience for zoological curiosities had little interest in the hair-splitting of nomenclatural purists, or, for that matter, in any Latinate terminology at all. From this perspective, differences within the scientific community were less important than the difference between that self-defined elite, which claimed to control a certain sphere of knowledge, and others interested in the same material, who resented such claims. The same zoological nomenclature used by scientists to symbolize their intellectual hegemony could be subverted to express criticism and even ridicule. *Punch* occasionally made pseudo-scientific nomenclature the metaphor for the love of obfuscation shared by scientists and most other scholarly specialists, referring to the 'Clamour-making Cat (*Felis catterwaulans*), which is well known to all Londoners', the *Felis omnivora*, or Common Lodging-House-Keeper's Cat', the 'Learned British Pig (*Porcus Sapiens Britannicus*)', and the Rum Shrub (*Shrubbus Curiosus*)'.[64]

A more common, and perhaps also a stronger riposte to the claims implicit in the valorization of scientific expertise, was to ignore them completely – to indulge without reservation in what the British Association's Nomenclature Committee referred to as 'the vicious taste on the part of the public' for 'vernacular appelations'.[65] The public insisted on calling a buffalo a buffalo and also sometimes on calling a bison a buffalo or even a bonassus, no matter how much it was exhorted or bullied to the contrary. And when financial matters were at stake, zoologists stuck to their nomenclatural principles at their peril. For example, the failure of several mid-Victorian zoos resulted from the refusal of their directors to pitch the exhibits to the general public rather than to naturalists.[66] In the preface to a new edition of his *Observations in Natural History*, Leonard Jenyns more shrewdly assured readers that he had 'transferred to the notes all the scientific names of . . . animals'.[67]

*

Wherever we look in nineteenth-century British culture, even within the rarefied domain of scientific investigation, the role of animals appears not only multiple but contested. The appropriate conclusion is not to abandon hope of making sense of the relations between humans and animals during that period, or at any other time. But the search for a single generalization or a single unfolding narrative may be intrinsically misguided – not only doomed to failure, but likely to mislead us. By trying to fit this vast and disparate mass of evidence into a single Procrustean bed of explanation, we may be blinded to what we can genuinely learn about the condition of animals in nineteenth-century British society, a condition that was shaped as much by rhetorical and symbolic concerns as by material conditions, and as much by relationships between people as between humans and their fellow creatures. One of the things that we have been learning as historians, sometimes rather painfully, over the past generation or so, is that any society, even one whose members have much in common, is woven of many threads. The Britain of the last several centuries was certainly no exception. Class, region and gender constituted only the most striking dividing lines; the preceding discussion has touched on several others. So one thing that we can expect from the study of nineteenth-century animals (in addition, of course, to increased understanding of the conditions of the animals' own lives) is an enriched and nuanced articulation of those human differences, as projected on to their fellow creatures and as embodied in their treatment.

NOTES

1 For additional information about the economic exploitation of livestock, see Richard Perren, *The Meat Trade in Britain, 1840–1914* (London: Routledge & Kegan Paul, 1978) and the essays in F. M. L. Thompson (ed.) *Horses in European Economic History: A Preliminary Canter* (Reading: British Agricultural History Society, 1983).

2 James Turner, *Reckoning with the Beast: Animals, Pain, and Humanity in the Victorian Mind* (Baltimore: Johns Hopkins University Press, 1980), p. 15; Antony Brown, *Who Cares for Animals? 150 Years of the RSPCA* (London: Heinemann, 1974), pp. 10–11.

3 'The lion fight', *New Monthly Magazine* 14 (1825): 288; Edward Jesse, *Gleanings in Natural History, Third and Last Series* (London: John Murray, 1835), p. vi.

4 Alfred Charles Smith, 'On the persecution of birds and animals, unhappily so general in this country', *Zoologist* 11 (1853): 3901.

5 William Hamilton Drummond, *The Rights of Animals, and Man's Obligation to Treat Them with Humanity* (London: John Mardon, 1838), p. 5; 'Abattoirs contrasted with slaughter-houses and Smithfield market', *Voice of Humanity* 3 (1832): 5–6.

6 Christopher Hibbett (ed.) *Queen Victoria in Her Letters and Journals* (London: John Murray, 1984), p. 205.

7 W. J. Stillman, 'A plea for wild animals', *Contemporary Review* 75 (1899): 674, 675–6; Brian Harrison, 'Animals and the state', in *Peaceable Kingdom: Stability and Change in Modern Britain* (Oxford: Clarendon Press, 1982), pp. 102–3.

8 Accounts of cruelty to animals made up the majority of the RSPCA's annual reports, and were also prominently featured in its monthly periodical, *The Animal World*.

9 Turner, *Reckoning with the Beast*, p. 39.

10 Harrison, 'Animals and the state', p. 91.

11 David Owen, *English Philanthropy, 1660–1960* (Cambridge, Mass.: Harvard University Press, 1964), pp. 179–80.

12 For a full discussion of the debate surrounding the passage of the 1876 Act, see Richard D. French, *Antivivisection and Medical Science in Victorian Society* (Princeton: Princeton University Press, 1975), Chs 4 and 5.

13 Harriet Ritvo, *The Animal Estate: The English and Other Creatures in the Victorian Age* (Cambridge, Mass.: Harvard University Press, 1987), pp. 157–66.

14 George Fleming, *Rabies and Hydrophobia: Their History, Nature, Causes, Symptoms, and Prevention* (London: Chapman and Hall, 1872), p. 34; Report from the Select Committee of the House of Lords on Rabies in Dogs, *Parliamentary Papers*, 1877, no. 322, Vol. XI.541, 178.

15 Report . . . on Rabies in Dogs, 31, 206; *The Bazaar, the Exchange and Mart*, 8 December 1877; Anna Kingsford, *Pasteur: His Method and Its Results* (London: North London Antivivisection Society, 1886), p. 20.

16 *Worcestershire Chronicle*, 22 December 1877; *Kennel Review* 4 (1885): 191.
17 William Youatt, *On Canine Madness* (London: Longman, 1830), pp. 30–1.
18 Report ... on Rabies in Dogs, 164, 168.
19 Kingsford, *Pasteur*, p. 21; Report ... on Rabies in Dogs, 226.
20 Ritvo, *Animal Estate*, p. 181.
21 Matthew Arnold, *Culture and Anarchy: An Essay in Political and Social Criticism* (1860; repr. New York: Macmillan, 1883), pp. 77–8.
22 'Letters from a competition wallah, letter VI: – A tiger-party in Nepaul', *Macmillan's Magazine* 9 (1893): 18; Parker Gillmore, *The Hunter's Arcadia* (London: Chapman and Hall, 1886), p. 1.
23 Roualeyn Gordon Cumming, *Five Years of a Hunter's Life in the Far Interior of South Africa, with Notices of the Native Tribes, and Anecdotes of the Chase of the Lion, Elephant, Hippopotamus, Giraffe, Rhinoceros, &c* (London: John Murray, 1850), I, p. 63; Alfred Wilks Drayson, *Sporting Scenes among the Kaffirs of South Africa* (London: G. Routledge, 1858), p. 53.
24 'Bear hunting in India', *Fraser's Magazine* 46 (1852): 385.
25 Denis David Lyell, *Hunting Trips in Northern Rhodesia, with Accounts of Sport and Travel in Nyasaland and Portuguese East Africa* (London: Horace Cox, 1910), p. 42; Isabel Savory, *A Sportswoman in India: Personal Adventures and Experiences of Travel in Known and Unknown India* (London: Hutchinson, 1900), p. 202.
26 William Cornwallis Harris, *Portraits of the Game and Wild Animals of Southern Africa, ... with Sketches of the Field Sports* (London: W. Pickering, 1840), p. 41; William Charles Baldwin, *African Hunting from Natal to the Zambesi ... from 1852 to 1860* (New York: Harper & Brothers, 1863), p. 17; quoted in Christopher Hibbert, *Africa Explored: Europeans in the Dark Continent, 1789–1869* (London: Allen Lane, 1982), p. 217.
27 Gordon Cumming, *Five Years of a Hunter's Life*, II, p. 18.
28 C. Linnaeus, *Miscellaneous Tracts ...* , trans. and ed. Benjamin Stillingfleet (London: R. J. Dodsley, 1759).
29 R. Pulteney, *A General View of the Writings of Linnaeus*, preface by W. G. Maton (London: J. Mawman, 1805), p. 11.
30 Richard Brookes, *The Natural History of Quadrupeds...* (London: J. Newbery, 1763), I, p. x.
31 Thomas Bewick, *A General History of Quadrupeds* (Newcastle: T. Bewick, 1824), pp. 231–4.
32 Thomas Pennant, *History of Quadrupeds* (London: B. and J. White, 1793), I, pp. 295–7.
33 Nicholas Cox, *The Gentleman's Recreation* (London: Thomas Fabian, 1677), I, p. 121; Pennant, *History*, I, p. 269.
34 Brookes, *Natural History*, I, p. xi.
35 Ibid., p. xxvi.
36 Georges Louis Leclerc, Comte de Buffon, *Barr's Buffon* (London: H. D. Symonds, 1797), VII, p. 24.
37 [J. Gregory], *A Comparative View of the State and Faculties of Man with those of the Animal World* (London: J. Dodsley, 1772), p. 13.
38 William Swainson, *On the Natural History and Classification of Quadrupeds* (London: Longman, Rees, Orme, Brown, Green & Longman, 1835), p. 137.
39 Oliver Goldsmith, *An History of the Earth and Animated Nature* (London: J. Nouse, 1774), II, p. 302.
40 Buffon, *Barr's Buffon*, VI, p. 13.
41 Pennant, *History*, I, p. 295.
42 Ibid., 16–17.
43 George Shaw, *General Zoology* (London: G. Kearsley, 1800), I (2), pp. 277–80.

44 Edward Bennett, *The Tower Menagerie* (London: Robert Jennings, 1829), pp. 85–6.

45 Jacob W. Gruber, 'What is it? The echidna comes to England', *Archives of Natural History* 11 (1982): 1–15.

46 Bewick, *General History*, pp. 523, 526.

47 Shaw, *General Zoology*, I (1), pp. 228–9. Shaw's suspicion that the platypus had been surgically produced was understandable in an era in which stuffed mermaids, composed of the cobbled remains of three or four creatures, were familiar exhibits in London's fairs and taverns (Richard D. Altick, *The Shows of London*, Cambridge, Mass.: Harvard University Press, 1978, pp. 302–3).

48 Harriet Ritvo, 'Amateur mermaids and professional scientists: beating the bounds in 19th-century Britain', *Victorian Literature and Culture*, 19 (1991), 277–92. For the Renaissance background, see Katherine Park and Lorraine J. Daston, 'Unnatural conceptions: the study of monsters in sixteenth and seventeenth-century France and England', *Past and Present* 92 (1981): 20–54.

49 William Jardine, *The Natural History of the Ruminating Animals, Part I* (Edinburgh: W. H. Lizars, 1835), p. 201; Robert Hamilton, *Amphibious Carnivora* (Edinburgh: W. H. Lizars, 1829), p. 293.

50 W. F. Martyn, *A New Dictionary of Natural History* (London: Harrison, 1785), n. p.

51 On the quinary system, see Mario A. DiGregorio, 'In search of the natural system: problems of zoological classification in Victorian Britain', *History and Philosophy of the Life Sciences* 4 (1982): 232–6 and Adrian Desmond, 'The making of institutional zoology in London 1822–1836: Part I', *History of Science* 23 (1985): 160–4.

52 Swainson, *Natural History and Classification*, pp. 96–7, 189.

53 Thomas Stamford Raffles (communicated by Everard Home), 'Descriptive catalogue of a zoological collection, made on account of the East India Company, in the island of Sumatra and its vicinity', *Philosophical Transactions of the Royal Society* (1820): 239–40.

54 William Lawrence, 'Introduction' to J. F. Blumenbach, *A Short System of Comparative Anatomy*, trans. William Lawrence (London: Longman, Hurst, Rees & Orme, 1897), p. xvi. Lawrence's words were an early example of what proved to be a durable strain in British science.

55 Manuscript note in Scrapbook I, Nomenclature Papers, Hugh E. Strickland Collection, Cambridge University Museum of Zoology.

56 Such timetables have not been uncommon in the development of a uniform system of nomenclature. For accounts of this history, see David Heppell, 'The evolution of the code of zoological nomenclature', in Alwyne Wheeler and James H. Price (eds) *History in the Service of Systematics* (London: British Museum (Natural History), 1981), pp. 135–41; John L. Heller, 'The early history of binomial nomenclature', *Huntia* 1 (1964): 33–70; and E. G. Linsley and R. L. Usinger, 'Linnaeus and the development of the international code of zoological nomenclature', *Systematic Biology* 8 (1959): 39–47.

57 *Proposed Plan for Rendering the Nomenclature of Zoology Uniform and Permanent* (London: Richard and John E. Taylor, 1841), p. 2.

58 For extended discussions of the role of class within the early Victorian scientific community, see Martin Rudwick, *The Great Devonian Controversy* (Chicago: University of Chicago Press, 1986) and Adrian Desmond, *The Politics of Evolution: Morphology, Medicine, and Reform in Radical London* (Chicago: University of Chicago Press, 1989).

59 *Proposed Plan*, pp. 11–14.

60 Ibid., 5.

61 Ibid., pp. 11–14.
62 Thomas Hawkins, *The Book of the Great Sea Dragons, Ichthyosauri and Plesiosauri* . . . (London: William Pickering, 1840), p. 9.
63 Charles Darwin to H. E. Strickland, 29 January 1849, in Nomenclature Papers, Scrapbook I, Hugh E. Strickland Collection, Cambridge University Museum of Zoology.
64 'Our cat show', *Punch* 71 (1876): 101; 'Notes by a Cockney naturalist', *Punch* 61 (1871): 194.
65 *Proposed Plan*, p. 3.
66 Ritvo, *Animal Estate*, p. 214.
67 Leonard Jenyns, *Observations in Natural History: With an Introduction on Habitats of Observing as Connected with the Study of that Science* (London: John van Voorst, 1846), I, p. x.

Plate 6.1 The remote hunting fields of the British Empire provided upper-class colonials with exotic and dangerous opportunities to slaughter wild animals ('The dead tiger', in Williamson *Oriental Field Sports*, 1807).

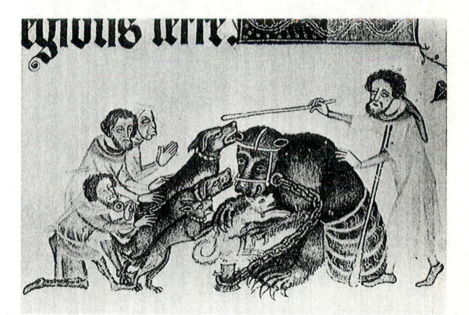

Plate 7.1 Until the nineteenth century activities such as bear-baiting were widely practised in England as popular forms of mass entertainment (The Luttrell Psalter, *c.* 1340).

Plate 7.2 In many hunting societies pet animals were often suckled at breast and treated like children.

Plate 7.3 Witch feeding familiars (A Rehearsall both straung and true, of hainous and horrible actes committed by Elizabeth Stile, Alias Rockingham, Mother Dutten, Mother Devell, Mother Margaret, Fower notorious Witches, apprehended at winsore in the Countie of Barks. and at Abbington arraigned, condemned, and executed on the 26 daye of Februarie laste Anno. 1579. London, 1579).

Plate 8.1 Dogs in an animal shelter. Working in these conditions can place people under considerable emotional strain. (Source: R.C. Hubrecht.)

Plate 9.1 German hunters by the campfire (© W. Tigner, ZEFA, Düsseldorf).

Plate 9.2 Japanese whalers in the early twentieth century (Ardea, London).

Plate 9.3 Watching for California condor at Los Padres National Forest (© Francois Gohier, Ardea).

7

PETS AND THE DEVELOPMENT OF POSITIVE ATTITUDES TO ANIMALS

James Serpell and Elizabeth Paul

INTRODUCTION

Until the early part of the nineteenth century, England was regarded by its neighbours as one of the cruellest and least sentimental nations in Europe. For centuries, violent animal abuses, such as bear-baiting (see Plate 7.1), bull-baiting, dog-fighting and cock-fighting, had been practised widely as popular forms of mass entertainment, and it was unusual for people to display strong emotional attachments to individual animals (Harwood 1928; Thomas 1983; Ryder 1989; Maehle, Ch. 5 in the present volume; Ritvo, Ch. 6 in the present volume). Even as recently as 1868, Queen Victoria observed sadly that 'the English are inclined to be more cruel to animals than some other civilized nations' (Ritvo 1987: 126).

Less than twenty years later, however, in her Jubilee Address of 1887, the same monarch noted 'with real pleasure, the growth of more human feeling towards the lower animals' among her subjects (Bensel 1984: 10), and it seems that she had good reason to feel pleased. During her reign, the cause of animal welfare became increasingly fashionable and effective, and humane organizations, such as the RSPCA and other campaigning groups, prospered as never before (Ryder 1989). Subsequently, during the early decades of the twentieth century, the combined effects of two world wars, and an intervening bout of economic recession, helped to douse the more radical flames of the animal protection movement. Despite all of this, however, the English succeeded in retaining much of their new-found enthusiasm for animals until the postwar years. In his 1947 book on *The English People*, for example, George Orwell concluded that unusual affection for animals – together with a suspicious attitude to foreigners and an obsession with sport – was a curious national characteristic that singled the English out from other peoples:

> Although its worst follies are committed by upper-class women, the animal cult runs right through the nation ... several years of stringent rationing have failed to reduce the dog and cat population, and even in

127

the poor quarter of big towns the bird fanciers' shops display canary
seed at prices ranging up to 25 shillings.

(Orwell 1947: 10)

Apart from the gradual demise of the upper-class woman, little appears to
have changed since Orwell's day. The 1960s and 1970s produced a substantial
revival of interest in animal welfare and animal rights (Ryder 1989), and this
trend shows no signs of abating. England is now justifiably regarded as a
world leader in the field of animal protection, and the RSPCA has developed
into the largest and wealthiest organization of its kind in Europe, if not the
world. So why then did the English apparently undergo such a fundamental
change in attitude? Or, to put the same question in more general terms, what
is it that inspires people, either individually or as groups, to develop a more
sympathetic and humane regard for animals?

The answers to these sorts of question are of more than purely academic
interest. The value which we place on animals, and the extent to which we
regard them in either positive or negative ways, ultimately determines their
welfare and survival in the modern world. As economic and environmental
pressures intensify, the future for nonhuman animals looks increasingly bleak,
and there is therefore an urgent need to identify the factors which initiate and
promote the development of more positive attitudes towards them.

DETERMINANTS OF ATTITUDES

The results of various recent surveys point to a number of factors that
influence people's attitudes to animals. To begin with, animals' intrinsic
physical and behavioural attributes can often affect how we view them. Large,
intelligent, anthropomorphous mammals, for example, almost invariably
inspire more favourable attitudes than, say, reptiles, fish or invertebrates (see
Burghardt and Herzog 1989; Kellert 1989; Ross et al. 1989; Driscoll 1992).
Human cultural, socioeconomic and demographic factors also exert a major
influence on attitudes; a person's age, sex, occupation, income, ethnic origins,
area of residence, educational level or religious orientation may all affect how
he or she perceives and treats animals (see Kellert 1980, and Ch. 9 in the
present volume). Unfortunately, relatively few of these animal or human
attributes are amenable to alteration once established. On the other hand,
people's perceptions of animals obviously do change quite rapidly on
occasion, and it is generally assumed in the humane and conservationist
literature that such changes can be encouraged through exposure to certain
kinds of positive animal-orientated experience (Paterson 1981; Ross et al.
1989; Ascione 1992). Most conservationists would accept, for instance, that
television has made a remarkable contribution to improving public attitudes
to wildlife. During the last thirty years, natural history broadcasts have
brought sympathetic depictions of exotic wild animals quite literally into our

living rooms. In many cases, people now *know* more and, indeed, *care* more about the behaviour and life histories of animals, such as whales, elephants or gorillas, than they do about the family living next door.

Nor is it difficult to explain why this process of familiarization with animals should give rise to increasing levels of respect or concern. Until recently, most people in the West held to the traditional Judaeo-Christian belief in the existence of an absolute moral and conceptual distinction between human and nonhuman animals (Serpell 1986). Furthermore, several recent authors have suggested that this gulf between the animal and human domains is not simply a product of human vanity, but a practical construct designed to allow people to exploit animals with a clear conscience by placing them, so to speak, beyond the pale of moral concern (Midgley 1983; Thomas 1983; Serpell 1986). As Rothschild (1986) has pointed out: 'just as we have to depersonalize human opponents in wartime in order to kill them with indifference, so we have to create a void between ourselves and the animals on which we inflict pain and misery for profit'. If this view is correct, it follows that experiences which serve to bridge this gulf – experiences which bring humans and animals closer together in any sense – should also, correspondingly, inhibit people from harming or exploiting animals, or turning a blind eye to their suffering.

By bringing the private lives of other species into our immediate consciousness, natural history television programmes represent one particular form of ethical bridge-building. Long before the invention of television, however, a very different class of animals – the ones commonly referred to as 'pets' – may have been fulfilling a similar role.

PETS AND CULTURAL ATTITUDES

The *Oxford English Dictionary* defines a pet as: 'any animal that is domesticated or tamed and kept as a favourite, or treated with indulgence and fondness'. In practice, the word is generally applied to animals that are kept primarily for social or emotional reasons rather than for economic purposes, and the recent adoption of the term 'companion animal' as an alternative to 'pet' emphasizes this distinction. Whereas most domestic animals are valued for the practical services and economic resources they provide, the rewards of pet ownership appear to derive from the relationship itself. People value their pets, not because they are necessarily useful, but because they fulfil social and emotional needs comparable, though not necessarily identical, to those fulfilled by human companions (Serpell 1986, 1989a; Council for Science and Society 1988).

It is still popularly assumed that pet-keeping – in the sense defined above – is a largely western phenomenon, fostered by modern urbanization, material affluence and bourgeois sentimentality (Serpell 1986) but this is entirely unfounded. Recent anthropological reviews (see Serpell 1986, 1987, 1989b; Erikson 1987) reveal that the practice of keeping animals for companionship is widespread in other cultures, particularly among those who obtain the bulk of their animal protein from hunting. Historically, hunting and gathering represents the most ancient form of human subsistence. It is therefore of some interest to know how pet-keeping conforms with, or contributes to, hunter-gatherer attitudes to animals.

In the majority of hunting societies, as in the west, pet animals are often named and cared for like children. As infants they may be suckled at the breast alongside human infants (see Plate 7.2). As they get older they are fed and kept out of harm's way and, when they die, they are commonly mourned and sometimes honoured with ritual burial. Among certain Amerindian groups, for example, the distinctive features which characterize the human–pet relationship are reported as being similar to

> those which define the filiative relationship, or that between human parents and their children. Children and pets alike are ideally supposed to be fed, reared and kept protected within the confines of the house. Often pets are kept secluded like human adolescents 'to make them more beautiful'.
>
> (Basso 1973: 21)

Also like children, pets are not normally expected to perform useful functions. Owners often refuse to sell their pets regardless of price, and the idea of putting them to work is typically greeted with a sort of baffled amusement (Fleming 1984). More to the point, perhaps, although such animals frequently belong to species that are normally hunted as items of food, the slaughter and consumption of pets is generally taboo (Serpell 1989b). In other words, the keeping of animals as social companions, as honorary members of the human family, appears to inhibit their use as prey. Since other animals of the same species continue to be killed and eaten, it might appear, superficially, that sympathetic attitudes towards animals in hunting societies do not generalize or extend beyond the individual pets that are adopted and befriended. But appearances, in this case, may be deceptive.

In the vast majority of non-agricultural, hunting and gathering societies, respect for the 'feelings' of animals is an important component of religious ideology and ritual (see Ingold, Ch. 1 in the present volume). Animals are believed to possess thoughts, feelings and social systems which are analogous, if not identical, to those of humans. In addition, animals are thought to possess souls, spirits or essences which are effectively immortal and endowed with supernatural powers. It is also widely understood that animals willingly submit to being killed if they approve of the hunter or his actions, but that they will seek some form of supernatural redress or retribution against the hunter if killed without prior approval or proper conduct. This retribution can take a variety of forms: members of the same species may become scarce or unapproachable, the hunter may have bad luck in future hunting, and he or a member of his family or social group may be afflicted with injury, illness, madness or even death (Frazer 1922; Hallowell 1926; Benedict 1929; Speck

1977; Campbell 1984; Nelson 1986; Serpell 1992; Ingold, Ch. 1 in the present volume). As one Eskimo informant observed:

> The greatest peril in life lies in the fact that human food consists entirely of souls. All the creatures that we have to kill and eat, all those that we have to strike down and destroy to make clothes for ourselves, have souls, like we have, souls that do not perish with the body, and which must therefore be propitiated lest they should avenge themselves on us for taking away their bodies.
>
> (quoted in Rasmussen 1929: 56)

Finally, it is often believed that animals, in a sense, *need* to be killed in order to be reborn. The hunter may actually see himself as an essential participant in an eternal and inevitable cycle of death and regeneration. The anthropologist Wenzel summarizes this idea in a description of Inuit hunting ideology:

> Contradictory as it may appear to strangers, Inuit harvesting is an ultimate sign of respect for wildlife. It conserves animals by providing them with a means of renewal, and it is a way of sharing with animals the qualities valued in human relationships through the demonstration of proper attitude and intent .... For Inuit, hunting constantly reiterates the moral balance that constitutes the basic relationship between human beings and animals.
>
> (1991: 141)

Because of belief systems like these, subsistence hunters go to considerable lengths to win the animal's prior approval and avoid inciting its posthumous revenge. Typical examples of the kinds of ritual practice that are commonly observed include dietary and sexual abstinence prior to hunting, visionary experiences induced by drugs or fasting, ritual purification of the hunter and his weapons, never speaking about the quarry in disrespectful ways, the offering of formal apologies or excuses to the slain animal, propitiatory offerings such as food or tobacco, ceremonial treatment of the animal's carcass, rules determining who may eat the animal's flesh, the avoidance of waste, avoidance of boasting, and the ritual disposal of uneatable or unusable remains (Frazer 1922; Hallowell 1926; Benedict 1929; Speck 1977; Campbell 1984; Nelson 1986; Wenzel 1991). In short, the animal that is killed for food is never perceived as merely a passive victim of human predation. Rather, it is viewed as an active and willing agent of its own slaughter. Animals are regarded as mental and spiritual equals, and the successful hunter achieves his goal of killing them, not only through his knowledge and skill, but also by virtue of his respectful attitudes and behaviour towards them. Only then will the animals consider him worthy of the gift of meat and allow themselves to be killed.

Hunting mythology thus depicts an egalitarian community of animals and people bound together by an unwritten contract of mutual respect and dependence; a sacred pact between predator and prey in which the interests of neither party are viewed as subordinate. Seen in this light, the practice of keeping some animals as pets, while killing and devouring others, poses few ethical contradictions. Indeed Erikson (1987) has even suggested that the act of caring for and indulging one individual of a species may be just another way in which the hunter and family seek to earn the respect and approval of its wild cousins. It cannot, of course, be inferred from this that pet-keeping actually helps to promote positive attitudes to other animals. But at least the affection and sympathy shown for pets in hunting and gathering cultures is entirely consistent with such cultures' attitudes to animals in general.

THE RISE OF ANTHROPOCENTRISM

The advent of farming and animal husbandry some 10,000 years ago initiated a profound change in the relationship between humans and the animals on which they depended. In particular, the idea of animals as respected coequals gave way to increasingly hierarchical notions of human separateness and superiority (Serpell 1986; Ingold, Ch. 1 of the present volume). Such ideas were clearly reinforced by religious and secular ideologies. The Book of Genesis, for example, makes explicit reference to human 'dominion over every living thing' while Aristotle's concept of a natural hierarchy placed mankind (especially Greek mankind) on a pinnacle above the rest of creation. In medieval Europe, the influential doctrine of Thomas Aquinas, which he derived from a mixture of biblical and classical sources, adopted a similar position. According to Aquinas, only humans possessed rational souls, and all animals were created in order to serve the interests of humanity (Hume 1957).

Some authors (e.g. Thomas 1983; Serpell 1986) have interpreted this change in attitudes as a necessary adaptive response to economic and ecological pressures, especially the need to intensify food animal production and eradicate competing species in order to cope with the demands of an ever-growing human population. Farmers and pastoralists, in contrast to hunters, have little choice but to set themselves up in opposition to nature. Wilderness must be cleared for cultivation, pests and predators vigorously suppressed, and domestic livestock controlled and confined, using force if necessary, to prevent them wandering or reverting to the wild. The entire system, in fact, depends on the subjugation of nature, and the domination and manipulation of plants and animals (Serpell 1986; Ingold, Ch. 1 in the present volume). According to Thomas (1983) religious doctrines, such as the one established by Aquinas, simply helped to make a virtue out of this necessity. They effectively provided the people of medieval and Renaissance Europe with a permit to use or abuse other life forms – for purposes ranging from predation and pest control to farming and vivisection – with a clear conscience, at a time when moral scruples about such practices would have constituted an impediment to both individual survival and cultural expansion.

Not surprisingly, pet-keeping – treating individual animals with indulgence and fondness – did not sit comfortably within such an anthropocentric worldview. Within the Christian church, the practice of keeping animals for companionship was officially frowned upon. Although a number of early saints and mystics enjoyed a special rapport with both wild and domestic animals, such zoophilic tendencies began to be suppressed from the thirteenth century onwards. Salimbene, for example, one of the early disciples of St Francis, considered it 'a foul blemish' that many eminent members of his order liked to 'play with a cat or a whelp or some small fowl', and this distaste became official Franciscan policy at the General Chapter of Narbonne in 1260 when it was ruled that 'no animal be kept, for any brother or any convent, whether by the Order, or any person in the Order's name, except cats and certain birds for the removal of unclean things' (Armstrong 1973: 7). Other religious orders followed suit. In 1345 Hugo de Seton, archdeacon of Ely, sent a stern letter to the abbess of a convent in Charteris: 'We forbid, therefore, dogs or birds, both great and small, being kept by an abbess or any nun within the walls of the nunnery or beneath the chair, especially during divine service' (Harwood 1928: 23). Even among the secular elite, 'overfamiliar usage of any brute creature' was frequently condemned by contemporary moralists and theologians (Thomas 1983: 40), although some of this hostility was evidently provoked by the sort of aristocratic self-indulgence exemplified by pampered lap-dogs. William Harrison's vitriolic attack on upper-class pets in the sixteenth century clearly falls within this category:

> These Sybariticall puppies, the smaller they be the better they are accepted, the more pleasure they also provoke, as meet plaiefellowes for minsing mistresses to beare in their bosoms, to keep companie withall in their chambers, to succour with sleepe in bed, and nourish with meat at bord, to lie in their laps, and licke their lips as they lie in their wagons and coches.
>
> (quoted in Jesse 1866, II: 228)

But prejudice against pet-keeping also arose from more sinister motives. Indeed, in many respects it resembled the public reaction to the crime of bestiality. At the height of the medieval Inquisition in Europe, for example, propaganda against witches and heretics often included references to orgiastic sexual rituals involving demons disguised as animals, such as dogs or cats. When witch persecution spread to England during the sixteenth century, the mere possession of an animal *familiar* (see Plate 7.3) was sufficient to arouse suspicions of witchcraft, particularly if the owner already had a reputation for promiscuous or antisocial behaviour. Judging from the surviving transcripts of English witch-trials, the ownership of pet animals – dogs, cats, lambs, hares, rats, hedgehogs, toads and a variety of birds – was one of the commonest forms of evidence used in the prosecution of suspected witches (Serpell 1986). As the historian, Rosen, points out: 'The element of affection in the alliance, which, on the Continent, took the form of surrender and worship, and bestiality with demons was in England expressed by the cosy, slighted perverted relationship of a lonely and poverty stricken woman to her pet animal' (1969: 32). Clearly, the authorities of the period felt threatened by pet-keeping, particularly when it appeared among the lower social orders. As with bestiality, it was claimed that people were debased or dehumanized by the act of cohabiting on such egalitarian and intimate terms with animals, especially since the animals in such relationships often tended to be elevated to the status of persons (Serpell 1986). In other words, by blurring the distinction between human and non-human, pet-keeping posed a serious challenge to the accepted status quo.

ENLIGHTENED PET OWNERS

Despite criticism, pet-keeping continued to be popular among the wealthy and powerful, but it did not acquire more widespread respectability until the late seventeenth century. This coincided with the gradual rejection of the narrow, anthropocentric ideas of the previous centuries, and a growing 'enlightenment' enthusiasm for science and natural history, on the one hand, and concern for the welfare of animals on the other (Thomas 1983). This change in cultural attitudes can be attributed, at least in part, to increasing affluence resulting from the growth in foreign and colonial trade, as well as to the steady migration of Europeans out of rural areas and into towns and cities. Both helped to distance growing sectors of the population from any personal involvement in the slaughter, subjugation or maltreatment of animals, and thus removed the need for belief systems designed to justify or reinforce such practices (Thomas 1983; Council for Science and Society 1988). Although socioeconomic forces probably initiated this change in attitudes to animals, circumstantial evidence suggests that pet-keeping may have helped to accelerate the process.

Since the Renaissance, many of Europe's most prominent and outspoken advocates for animals were also pet owners. In England, for example, Sir Thomas More (1478–1535), who surrounded himself with pet dogs, rabbits and monkeys, populated his *Utopia* with a tender-hearted upper class who refused to have anything to do with killing or butchering animals, and believed that the pleasure people derived from hunting denoted 'a cruel quality of mind' (Harwood 1928: 41). Similarly, the sixteenth-century French philosopher, Michel Eyquem de Montaigne (1533–92), who was among the first to challenge Aquinas's view of man's God-given right of dominion over other creatures, was also a pet owner who confessed to being of such a tender and childish nature that he was unable to resist playing with his cat or romping with his dog 'even though he invites me at the most inopportune time'. Montaigne was also the first to make specific use of his interactions with pets to strengthen his arguments: 'When I play with my cat,' he wrote who knows whether I am not more of a toy for her than she is for me? We equally amuse each other with our monkey-tricks. If I have my hour for sulking or playing, so has she. When all is said and done, there is a certain respect and human duty which binds us not only to animals, which have life and sentiment, but even to trees and plants. We owe justice to men and kindliness to other creatures: there is an intercourse and mutual obligation between them and us.

(quoted in Lowenthal 1956: 90)

As Maehle has pointed out in Chapter 5, many famous eighteenth-century humanitarians were also pet lovers. Alexander Pope (1688–1744) and Samuel Johnson (1709–84), both of whom opposed cruelty to animals and published early attacks on vivisection, were also well known for their affection for pets. Pope owned a succession of much-loved dogs, all named Bounce, while Johnson was greatly attached to his cat Hodge. Similarly, Lord Erskine (1750–1823), the champion of one of the earliest parliamentary bills on cruelty to animals in 1809, apparently lavished affection on a menagerie of pets including several dogs, a goose and two leeches (Turner 1980). Jeremy Bentham (1748–1832) – regarded as one of the founders of the concept of animal rights – admitted to loving 'everything which has four legs' including a colony of mice which he once befriended, despite having an equal affection for cats. Like Montaigne, Bentham also made use of his personal experience of animals when arguing for improvements in their treatment:

a full grown horse or dog is beyond comparison a more rational, as well as a more conversable animal, than an infant of a day, or a week or even a month old. But suppose the case were otherwise, what would it avail? The question is not, Can they reason? nor, Can they talk? but, *Can they suffer?* Why should the law refuse its protection to any sensitive being?

(quoted in Ryder 1989: 75)

Comparable nineteenth-century examples are not difficult to find. The German philosopher, Schopenhauer (1788–1860), who advocated 'boundless compassion for all living things', bequeathed a legacy of '300 gulden for the care of his dog' in his last will and testament (Lewinsohn 1954: 193). Outspoken middle-class pet owners were in the forefront of many Victorian debates on animal cruelty, a fact that did not go unnoticed by their critics. Writing sarcastically about Frances Power Cobbe, the leader of the anti-vivisection movement in the 1870s, one hostile commentator attributed her campaigning zeal to sentimental affection for her own pet dogs and cats: 'She is not defending a right inherent in sentient things as such; she is doing special pleading for some of them for which she has a special liking' (quoted in Thomas 1983: 120). Even those within the Victorian humane movement who disapproved of pets evidently found it hard to practise what they preached. Henry S. Salt, who co-founded the Humanitarian League in 1981 and was one of the intellectual beacons of the movement, regarded pet-keeping as a serious violation of animals' rights. This did not, however, prevent him from encouraging numerous animals, including a cat named 'Hodge', to share his home in a distinctly petlike capacity (Mighetto 1991: 70). Meanwhile, Queen Victoria's influential patronage of the animal protection movement was clearly founded on a lifetime of devoted dog ownership. Among her canine favourites was a Pekinese bitch named Looty – a gift of the Dowager Empress of China – of whom she commissioned a portrait by Landseer (Hutchinson 1933).

Identifying particular pet-loving humanitarians from the present century is more of a problem, perhaps because both pet-keeping and public concern for animal-related issues have become so ubiquitous. Recent estimates suggest that, of the 21.8 million households in Britain alone, over half keep pets (Pet Food Manufacturers Association 1992), and no doubt many of these pet owners contribute to animal welfare and/or conservationist causes. Although no statistics are available, it would be safe to hazard a guess that the majority of Britain's innumerable animal-based charities would be in serious financial difficulties without the membership subscriptions, donations and legacies of their pet-owning supporters (see Serpell 1992).

THE DEVELOPMENT OF INDIVIDUAL ATTITUDES

The idea that animals, and our relationships with them, might serve a formative role in the development of humane attitudes has a long historical pedigree. It must be said, however, that the chief preoccupation in early literature was not affection for animals, but the possible corrupting influence of animal abuse on those who either witnessed or inflicted such cruelties. Sections of the biblical Old Testament, as well as various Hindu and Buddhist texts, seem to advocate considerate treatment of animals for this reason, and similar notions surfaced in the classical world, probably through the assimilation of eastern theological concepts. Ovid (43 BC–AD17), for instance, attributes to Pythagoras (sixth century BC) the statement that: 'As long as man continues to be the ruthless destroyer of lower living beings, he will never know health or peace. For as long as men massacre animals, they will kill each other' (quoted in Wynne-Tyson 1990: 382). In the same tradition, the Roman writer Porphyrios (AD 233–304) emphasized the brutalizing effect of activities such as hunting or spectating at the Circus, although he also noted that Pythagoreans considered kindliness towards beasts 'to be an exercise of philanthropy and commiseration' (Porphyrios 1965, III: 130). In other words, just as it was believed that cruelty to animals could provoke a sort of generalized insensitivity, so the practice of kindness to non-humans was seen as encouraging the development of broadly compassionate feelings.

Thomas Aquinas acknowledged the importance of both concepts, first stating that: 'If in Holy Scripture there are found some injunctions forbidding the infliction of some cruelty towards brute animals ... this is either for removing a man's mind from exercising cruelty towards other men, lest anyone, from exercising cruelty upon brutes, should go on hence to human beings; or because the injury inflicted on animals turns to a temporal loss for some man,' but then adding that: 'God's purpose in recommending kind treatment of brute creation is to dispose men to pity and tenderness towards one another' (Hume 1957: 8).

The sceptic philosopher, Michel de Montaigne, appears to have been among the first to recognize the importance of childhood experience in this regard: 'Some mothers think it great sport to see a child wring off a chicken's neck, and strive to beat a dog or cat ... yet are they the true deeds or roots of cruelty, of tyranny, and of treason. In youth they bud, and afterwards grow to strength, and come to perfection by means of custom' (quoted in Wynne-Tyson 1990: 316). John Locke (1632–1704), the founder of modern educational theory, reiterated the views of Montaigne, but he also laid important emphasis on the idea of training children to eschew cruelty to animals and to develop the capacity for humaneness:

> they who delight in the suffering and destruction of inferior creatures will not be apt to be very compassionate or benign to those of their own kind .... Children should from the beginning be brought up in an abhorrence of killing or tormenting any living creature ... indeed, I think people should be accustomed from their cradles to be tender to all sensible creatures.
>
> (Locke 1699: 153)

By the nineteenth century such ideas had acquired the status of dogma within the growing humane movement. With characteristic feminist emphasis, Frances Power Cobbe declared in 1865 that, 'the hearts of men will grow more tender to their own kind by cultivating pity and tenderness to the beasts and birds' (quoted in Mighetto 1991: 51). Similarly, Henry Salt's doctrine of universal kinship included the statement: 'we may take it as certain that, in the long run, as we treat our fellow beings, the animals, so shall we treat our fellow men' (quoted in Wynne-Tyson 1990: 438).

In addition to emphasizing the developmental importance of early experience, John Locke was also the first to suggest that pet animals had a special role to play in the acquisition of sympathetic tendencies. His prescription for developing tender feelings in children followed the example of a woman he knew who indulged her daughters' liking for pets by giving them: 'dogs, squirrels, birds or any such things as young girls use to be delighted with; but then, when they had them, they must be sure to keep them well and look diligently after them, that they wanted nothing or were not ill-used. For if they were negligent in their care for them, it was counted a great fault' (Locke 1964: 154). Such liberal ideas on education flourished in the 'enlightened' climate of the eighteenth century and, judging from the content of contemporary childhood literature, anthropomorphic and affectionate animals were soon adopted as the ideal medium for cultivating children's compassion. In *Goody Two-Shoes* (1765), the first major work of children's fiction in English, the heroine, Margery Meanwell, devotes herself to fostering and caring for maltreated animals, and similar moralizing accounts of kindness versus cruelty to animals – especially companion animals – subsequently became the single most common theme of children's storybooks, at least until the end of the nineteenth century (Turner 1980; Ritvo 1987). Anna Sewell's hugely successful and consciously didactic *Black Beauty* (1877) perhaps represents the apogee of this trend, although companion animals have remained one of the most frequently used devices of childhood literature ever since (Tucker 1989).

Although the emphasis of modern humane education has undoubtedly changed since the nineteenth century, the basic principles are still the same (Finch 1989). For example, recent RSPCA guidelines on the keeping of animals in schools state that animals encourage caring and responsible attitudes in pupils: 'Teaching pet care and responsibility in school can have a major effect on the way our young people regard animals and, consequently, may make a vital contribution to the reduction of future animal suffering' (RSPCA 1986: 39). Other recent authorities preach a similar message. Richard Ryder (1989: 74), for instance, has described what he calls 'the natural bond of affection between child and pet' as one of the foundation stones of the animal welfare movement, while Konrad Lorenz (1988: 208) has claimed that childhood pet-keeping provides 'all we need in order to plant in human hearts the joy to be found in creation and in its beauty'.

EMPIRICAL EVIDENCE

Despite the prevalence of such ideas in humane education literature and practice (see Savesky and Malcarne 1981; RSPCA 1986), there is surprisingly little *empirical* evidence that pet-keeping exerts any long-term positive effect on people's overall feelings about animals, nature or their fellow human beings (Paterson 1981; Ascione 1992). Various studies have demonstrated, not surprisingly, that adults' attitudes to pets are highly correlated with previous exposure to pet animals during childhood (Kidd and Kidd 1980; Serpell 1981; Poresky *et al.* 1988), and it appears that people tend to remain loyal to the particular species of pet they kept as children. Those brought up with dogs tend to remain dog lovers, those brought up with cats prefer cats, and those raised with both species remain relatively catholic in their tastes (Serpell 1981). Only two published studies, however, have reported a statistical link between pet ownership and attitudes to other animal species. In one case, 8–12-year-old, pet-owning children were found to possess fewer fears of animals than their non-owning counterparts (Bowd 1984); while in the other study, among a random sample of Canadian adults, a positive statistical relationship was found between pet ownership and attitudes to various other categories of animal (Kafer *et al.* 1992). In the latter study, pet owners tended to be opposed to hunting and laboratory animal research, and to favour the idea of closer, more egalitarian relationships with wild animals. The authors interpret their findings as indicating a predisposition among pet owners 'to individualize relationships with animals and to have them closer to oneself' (Kafer *et al.* 1992: 104). They do not, however, speculate as to whether this predisposition is a cause or a consequence of pet ownership.

This question has been addressed by Paul and Serpell (in press) in a recent survey of university students. In this study, a detailed questionnaire was administered to some 385 students in which they were asked to express their opinions (anonymously) on a variety of animal-related topics and issues. They were also asked to provide a detailed inventory of the numbers and species of all the childhood pets they remembered, and to distinguish between pets owned by the family, pets owned by themselves, and pets they had considered especially *important* regardless of who had owned the animals. For the purposes of the study, 'childhood' represented the period from 0 to 16 years of age. The results of the survey are described more fully elsewhere (Paul 1992; Paul and Serpell in press) but some of the main findings are worth summarizing here.

It was found that childhood pet ownership was strongly positively correlated with concern for animals in general, and with the practice of some form of ethical food avoidance (i.e. veganism, vegetarianism, or avoidance of certain animal products, such as veal). It was also correlated with membership of animal welfare organizations and charities and, to a weaker extent, with membership of environmental or conservation organizations. Most of these outcome measures were most strongly correlated with the number of *important* pets reported by students and, since dogs and cats were more likely to have been regarded as *important* than most other kinds of pets, there was also a strong relationship between childhood dog or cat ownership and the development of positive adult attitudes to other species.

Such findings need to be interpreted with caution and cannot, of course, be regarded as conclusive evidence of a cause and effect relationship between childhood pet ownership and subsequent positive attitudes to animals. Rather than demonstrating any formative influence of pets, the results might suggest that some children are simply more animal-orientated that others to begin with, and that this manifests itself in more and stronger attachments for pets in childhood, and generally more sympathetic attitudes later in life. Because the data are retrospective, the possibility of inaccurate or biased recall of childhood events and feelings must also be considered. In addition, students who reported having more *important* childhood pets also described their parents' attitudes to pets as being more positive. This suggests that parental attitudes to companion animals may influence the quality and intensity of children's attachments to their pets.

If one accepts, however, that students are likely to have relatively accurate memories of childhood, and should have no obvious reason to bias their responses to an anonymous questionnaire, the results of this survey would tend to confirm the existence of a strong link between early exposure to pets and the subsequent development of positive concern for animals in general. Furthermore, the fact that childhood dog and cat ownership was associated with more positive adult attitude scores suggests that the quality and intensity of the relationship with the pet may be an important determining factor.

DISCUSSION AND CONCLUSIONS

Scientific studies of the so-called 'human–companion animal relationship' have become increasingly widespread during the last decade. Much of this research has been largely anthropocentric in focus, concentrating particularly on the putative benefits that humans derive from living or interacting with their animal companions (see, e.g., Serpell 1991; Rowan 1991). In this chapter we have examined one way in which human–pet relationships may also confer benefits on other species, albeit indirectly through their effects on people's attitudes and values.

Positive attitudes to animals are promoted through a sense of familiarity or closeness. In the case of people and their pets, expressions of closeness or kinship are an unusually prominent feature of the relationship. Pets are given personal names, they are spoken to as if they understand human speech, and they are generally treated as honorary members of the human social groups to which they belong (Midgley 1983; Serpell 1986; Council for Science and Society 1988). The question we have tried to address in this review is whether, in the process of acquiring quasi-human status, pets can also serve as ambassadors; nonhuman representatives of the interests and moral claims, not only of their own species, but of animals in general.

The answer to this question must ultimately depend on whether attitudes to companion animals ever generalize to include other species or more abstract animal-related concerns. Cultural and historical comparisons certainly provide circumstantial evidence that pet-keeping is associated with more humane and respectful attitudes to animals. Conversely, where pet-keeping is actively discouraged, its absence typically denotes a more ruthless and exploitative approach to the treatment of non-humans. In medieval and Renaissance Europe, for instance, theologians and moralists evidently regarded the keeping of pets as heretical, or even diabolical, precisely because of its tendency to subvert the notion of human superiority or uniqueness. Anecdotal and autobiographical accounts further suggest that the opinions of many early humanitarian thinkers were influenced by their relationships with pet animals. Indeed, at the level of individual development, an association between pet ownership and the development of more sympathetic attitudes to animals has long been assumed, and a small number of recent research studies have now provided some empirical support for a link between the two phenomena. Although none of these fragments of evidence is convincing on its own, taken together they represent a reasonable case for arguing that relationships with pets can at least contribute to the process of positive attitudinal change.

Clearly, it would be misleading to conclude from this that affection for pets provides some guarantee of concern for other classes of animal. After all, many lifelong pet owners appear content to disregard or contribute to the suffering or demise of other species (including humans), despite their ardent devotion to dogs and cats (see e.g. Arluke and Sax 1992). Nor can it be assumed that human–pet relationships necessarily provide the best or most reliable means of fostering respect and compassion for animals or nature. Many people with no previous history of pet ownership are nevertheless passionately concerned about animal-related issues, such as conservation or animal welfare. Conversely, like Henry Salt a century ago, some critics would argue that pet-keeping perpetuates a distorted, patronizing or dominionistic view of animals that is inappropriate in the modern context. Still others might point out (with some justification) that the depredations of free-ranging domestic pets pose a significant environmental threat to rare birds, reptiles and small mammals, particularly where they have been introduced to oceanic islands (Merton 1977). All of this serves to underline the complex and often conflicting origins of people's concerns about animals, but it does not necessarily refute the central theory.

Animals are currently exposed to greater threats to their welfare and survival than ever before. On farms and in laboratories they are subjected to increasingly intensive or invasive production systems and procedures. In the wild, they are at risk from overexploitation, environmental pollution and unprecedented habitat losses. Such trends will only be reversed through the promotion of more respectful attitudes and behaviour, and anything which appears to aid in this process of attitudinal change is therefore worthy of detailed and urgent investigation. Bowd (1989) has pointed out that: 'if we are to change the way people behave towards animals, we must learn about the origins of that behaviour in childhood'. For many children, companion animals are almost the equivalent of adopted siblings, and it is difficult to imagine how such early and significant familial bonds could fail to engender at least some sense of affinity or kinship with other nonhuman species.

REFERENCES

Arluke, A. and Sax, B. (1992) 'Understanding Nazi animal protection and the Holocaust', *Anthrozoös* 5(1): 6–31.

Armstrong, E. A. (1973) *Saint Francis: Nature Mystic*, Berkeley: University of California Press.

Ascione, F. R. (1992) 'Enhancing children's attitudes about the humane treatment of animals: generalizations to human-directed empathy', *Anthrozoös* 5(3): 176–91.

Basso, E. B. (1973) *The Kalapalo Indians of Central Brazil*, New York: Holt, Rinehart & Winston.

Benedict, R. F. (1929) 'The concept of the guardian spirit in North America', *Memoirs of the American Anthropological Association* 29: 3–93.

Bensel, R. W. (1984) 'Historical perspectives of human values for animals and vulnerable people', in R. K. Anderson, B. L. Hart and L. A. Hart (eds) *The Pet Connection*, Minneapolis: University of Minnesota, CENSHARE, pp. 2–14.

Bowd, A. D. (1984) 'Fears and understanding of animals in middle childhood', *Journal of Genetic Psychology* 145: 143–4.

—— (1989) 'The educational dilemma', in D. Paterson and M. Palmer (eds) *The Status of Animals: Ethics, Education and Welfare*, Wallingford: CAB International, pp. 52–7.

Burghardt, G. M. and Herzog, H. A. (1989) 'Animals, evolution and ethics', in R. J. Hoage (ed.) *Perceptions of Animals in American Culture*, Washington, DC: Smithsonian Institution Press, pp. 129–51.

Campbell, J. (1984) *The Way of the Animal Powers*, London: Times Books.

Council for Science and Society (1988) *Companion Animals in Society*, Oxford: Oxford University Press.

Driscoll, J. W. (1992) 'Attitudes towards animal use', *Anthrozoös* 5(1): 32–8.

Erikson, P. (1987) 'De l'apprivoisement à l'approvisionnement. Chasse, alliance et familarisation en Amazonie Amérindienne', *Techniques et Cultures* 9: 105–40.

Finch, P. (1989) 'Learning from the past', in D. Paterson and M. Palmer (eds) *The Status of Animals: Ethics, Education and Welfare*, Wallingford: CAB International, pp. 64–72.

Fleming, P. (1984) *Brazilian Adventure*, Harmondsworth: Penguin Books.

Frazer, J. G. (1922) *The Golden Bough: a Study of Magic and Religion*, London: Macmillan.

Hallowell, A. I. (1926) 'Bear ceremonialism in the northern hemisphere', *American Anthropologist*, 28 (1): 1–175.

Harwood, D. (1928) *Love for Animals and How it Developed in Great Britain*, New York: Columbia University Press.

Hume, C. W. (1957) *The Status of Animals in the Christian Religion*, Potters Bar, Middlesex: Universities Federation for Animal Welfare.

Hutchinson, W. (1933) *Hutchinson's Dog Encyclopaedia*, vol. III, London: Hutchinson.

Jesse, G. R. (1866) *Researches into the History of the British Dog*, vol. II, London: Robert Hardwicke.

Kafer, R., Lago, D., Wamboldt, P. and Harrington, F. (1992) 'The Pet Relationship Scale: replication of psychometric properties in random samples and association with attitudes toward wild animals', *Anthrozoös* 5(2): 93–105.

Kellert, S. R. (1980) *Knowledge, Affection and Basic Attitudes toward Animals in American Society*, Washington, DC: US Fish and Wildlife Service.

—— (1989) 'Perceptions of animals in America', in R. J. Hoage (ed.) *Perceptions of Animals in American Culture*, Washington DC: Smithsonian Institution Press.

Kidd, A. H. and Kidd, R. M. (1980) 'Personality characteristics and preferences in pet ownership', *Psychological Reports*, 46, 939–49.

Lewinsohn, R. (1954) *Animals, Men and Myths*, London: Gollancz.

Locke, J. (1964) *Some Thoughts Concerning Education*, ed. F. W. Garforth, London: Heinemann. First published 1699.

Lorenz, K. (1988) *The Waning of Humaneness*, London: Unwin Hyman.

Lowenthal, M. (ed.) (1956) *The Autobiography of Michel de Montaigne*, New York: Vintage Books.

Merton, D. V. (1977) 'Controlling introduced predators and competitors on islands', in S. A. Temple (ed.) *Endangered Birds: Management Techniques for Preserving Threatened Species*, Madison: University of Wisconsin Press, pp. 121–8.

Midgley, M. (1983) *Animals and Why They Matter*, Harmondsworth: Penguin Books

Mighetto, L. (1991) *Wild Animals and American Environmental Ethics*, Tucson: University of Arizona Press.

Nelson, R. K. 'A conservation ethic and environment: the Koyukon of Alaska, in N. N. Williams and E. S. Hunn (eds) *Resource Managers: North American and Australian Hunter-gatherers*, Canberra: Institute of Aboriginal Studies, pp. 211–28.

Orwell, G. (1947) *The English People*, London: Collins.

Paterson, D. (1981) 'Children's ideas on animals', in D. Paterson (ed.) *Humane Education – A Symposium*, Burgess Hill, Sussex: Humane Education Council, pp. 75–80.

Paul, E. S. (1992) 'Pets in childhood', PhD thesis, University of Cambridge.

Paul, E. W. and Serpell, J. A. (in press) 'Childhood pet keeping and humane attitudes in young adulthood', *Animal Welfare*.

Pet Food Manufacturers' Association (1992) *Profile – 1992*, London: PFMA.

Poresky, R. H., Hendrix, C., Mosier, J. E. and Samuelson, M. L. (1988) 'Young children's companion animal bonding and adult's pet attitudes: a retrospective study', *Psychological Reports* 62: 419–25.

Porphyrios of Tyre (1965) *On Abstinence from Animal Food*, trans. E. W. Tyson and T. Taylor, Fontwell, Sussex: Centaur Press.

Rasmussen, K. (1929) 'Intellectual life of the Iglulik Eskimos', *Report of the Fifth Thule Expedition* 7(1).

Ritvo, H. (1987) *The Animal Estate*, Cambridge, Mass.: Harvard University Press.

Rosen, B. (1969) *Witchcraft*, London: Edward Arnold.

Ross, A. Lien, J. and Parsons, P. (1989) 'Why people like whales', *Whalewatcher*, 23(3): 21–3.

Rothschild, M. (1986) *Animals and Man*, Oxford: Clarendon Press.

Rowan, A. N. (1991) 'Do companion animals provide a health benefit?', *Anthrozoös* 4(4): 212–13.

RSPCA (1986) *Small Mammals in Schools*, Horsham: RSPCA Education Dept.

Ryder, R. D. (1989) *Animal Revolution: Changing Attitudes towards Speciesism*, Oxford: Basil Blackwell.

Savesky, K. and Malcarne, V. (1981) *People and Animals: A Humane Education Curriculum Guide*, East Haddam, Conn.: National Association for the Advancement of Humane Education.

Serpell, J. A. (1981) 'Childhood pets and their influence on adults' attitudes', *Psychological Reports* 49: 651–4.

—— (1986) *In the Company of Animals*, Oxford: Basil Blackwell.

—— (1987) 'Pet-keeping in non-western societies: some popular misconceptions', *Anthrozoös* 1(3): 166–74.

—— (1989a) 'Humans, animals, and the limits of friendship', in R. Porter and S. Tomaselli (eds) *The Dialectics of Friendship*, London: Routledge. pp. 111–29.

—— (1989b) 'Pet-keeping and animal domestication: a reappraisal', in J. Clutton-Brock (ed.) *The Walking Larder: Patterns of Domestication, Pastoralism and Predation*, London: Unwin Hyman. pp. 10–21.

—— (1991) 'Beneficial effects of pet ownership on some aspects of human health and behaviour', *Journal of the Royal Society of Medicine*, 84: 717–20.

—— (1992) 'Animal protection and environmentalism: the background', in R. Ryder (ed.) *Animal Welfare and the Environment*, London: Duckworth, pp. 27–39.

Speck, F. G. (1977) *Naskapi*, 3rd edn, Norman: University of Oklahoma Press.

Thomas, K. (1983) *Man and the Natural World: Changing Attitudes in England 1500–1800*, London: Allen Lane.

Tucker, N. (1989) 'Animals in children's literature', in D. Paterson and M. Palmer (eds) *The Status of Animals: Ethics, Education and Welfare*, Wallingford: CAB International, pp. 167–72.

Turner, J. (1980) *Reckoning with the Beast: Animals, Pain and Humanity in the Victorian Mind*, Baltimore: Johns Hopkins University Press.

Wenzel, G. (1991) *Animal Rights, Human Rights: Ecology, Economy and Ideology in the Canadian Arctic*, London: Belhaven Press.

Wynne-Tyson, J. (1990) *The Extended Circle: An Anthology of Humane Thought*, London: Cardinal Books.

8

MANAGING EMOTIONS IN AN ANIMAL SHELTER*

Arnold Arluke

From the sociologist's perspective, what is most interesting in the study of conflicts in the contemporary treatment of animals is not to point out that such conflicts exist or to debate the assumptions that underlie them – a task more ably served by philosophers – but to better understand what it is about modern society that makes it possible to shower animals with affection as sentient creatures while simultaneously maltreating or killing them as utilitarian objects. How is it that a conflict that should require a very difficult balancing of significant values has become something that many people live with comfortably? Indeed, they may not even be aware that others may perceive their actions as inconsistent. How is it that instead of questioning the propriety of their conflicts, many don ethical blindfolds?

As with any cultural contradiction, these attitudes are built into the normative order, itself perpetuated by institutions that provide ways out of contradictions by supplying myths to bridge them and techniques to assuage troubled feelings. While researchers interested in contradictory attitudes towards different human groups have long since demonstrated the role of institutions in the perpetuation of racism, a similar focus has been strikingly absent in discussions of contradictory attitudes to animals. It may be useful, then, to begin to ask how institutions can transform everyday people, who themselves may own dogs or cats as pets, into workers who can kill these same species.

Humane and scientific institutions, for example, must teach newcomers in shelters and laboratories to suspend their prior, ordinary or commonsense thinking about the use and meaning of animals and adopt a different set of assumptions that may be inconsistent with these prior views. The assumptions are not themselves proved but rather structure and form the field upon which the activity plays out its life. Typically, these assumptions are transmitted to nascent practitioners of a discipline, along with relevant empirical facts and skills, as indisputable truths, not as debatable assumptions. They must come to accept the premiss of the institution – often that it is necessary to kill animals – and get on with the business of the institution. But exactly how do they get on with this business?

145

In addition to learning to think differently about the proper fate of animals in institutions, workers must also learn to feel differently about them in that situation. Uncomfortable feelings may be experienced by newcomers even if the premiss of the institution is accepted at an intellectual level. Although institutions will, no doubt, equip newcomers with rules and resources for managing unwanted emotions, researchers have not examined how such emotion management strategies actually work and the extent to which they eliminate uncomfortable feelings. In the absence of such research, it is generally assumed that newcomers learn ways to distance themselves from their acts and lessen their guilt. These devices are thought to prevent any attachment to and empathy for animals (Schleifer 1985) and to make killing 'a reflex, virtually devoid of emotional content' (Serpell 1986: 152).

To examine these assumptions, I conducted ethnographic research over a seven-month period in a 'kill-shelter' serving a major metropolitan area. Such a case study seemed warranted, given the sensitivity of the topic under study. I became immersed in this site, spending approximately 75 hours in direct observation of all facets of shelter work and life, including euthanasia of animals and the training of workers to do it. Also, interviews were conducted with the entire staff of sixteen people, many formally and at length on tape, about euthanasia and related aspects of shelter work. These interviews were open-ended and semi-structured, allowing workers to explore and elaborate their thinking and feeling without being unduly constrained by the limits of a formal questionnaire.

My findings suggest that learning to cope with uncomfortable feelings provoked by euthanasia in shelters may be a more complex process than assumed. Feelings such as attachment, empathy and loss were not eliminated but instead served as coping devices that enabled workers to maintain a sense of themselves as people who liked and cared for animals. Far from being completely detached from their charges, all workers became uneasy during certain killing situations. After I describe the emotional challenge faced by new shelter workers, I will identify the specific emotion management strategies they learned and assess how well these strategies worked.

THE NEWCOMER'S PROBLEM

Euthanasia posed a substantial emotional challenge to most novice shelter workers. People seeking work at the shelter typically regarded themselves as 'animal people' or 'animal lovers' and recounted lifelong histories of keeping pets, collecting animals, nursing strays, and working in zoos, pet stores, veterinarian practices, and even animal research laboratories. They came wanting to 'work with animals' and expecting to spend much of their time having hands-on contact with animals in a setting where others shared the same high priority they placed on human–animal interaction. The prospect of having to kill animals seemed incompatible with this self-conception.

146

When first applying for their jobs, some shelter workers did not even know that euthanasia was carried out at the shelter. To address this possible misconception, applicants were asked how they would feel when it was their turn to euthanize. Most reported that they did not really think through this question at this time, simply replying that they thought it was 'Okay' in order to get the job. One worker, for instance, said she 'just put this thought out of [her] mind', while another worker said that she had hoped to 'sleaze out' of (or avoid) doing it. Many said that having to do euthanasia did not fully sink in until they 'looked the animal in its eyes'. Clearly, newcomers were emotionally unprepared to actually kill animals.

Once on the job, newcomers quickly formed strong attachments to particular animals. In fact, it was customary to caution newcomers against adopting animals right away. Several factors encouraged these attachments. At first, workers found themselves relating to shelter animals as though they were their own pets because many of the animals were healthy and appealing to workers, and since most of the animals had been pets, they sometimes initiated interaction with workers. Newcomers also saw more senior people interacting with animals in a pet-like fashion. Shelter animals, for example, were all named, and everyone used these names when referring to the animals.[1] While newcomers followed suit, they did not realize that more experienced workers could interact in this way with animals and not become attached to them. Moreover, newcomers found that their work required them to know the individual personalities of shelter animals in order to make the best decisions regarding euthanasia and adoption, but this knowledge easily fostered attachments. Not surprisingly, the prospect of having to kill animals with whom they had become attached was a major concern for newcomers. This anticipated relationship with shelter animals made newcomers agonize when they imagined selecting animals for euthanasia and seeing 'trusting looks' in the faces of those killed (see Plate 8.1). They also worried about having to cope with the 'losses' they expected to feel from killing these animals.

Further aggravating the novices' trepidation was the fact that they had to kill animals for no higher purpose. Many felt grieved and frustrated by what they saw as the 'senseless' killing of healthy animals. Several newcomers flinched at the shelter's willingness to kill animals if suitable homes were not found instead of 'fostering out' the animals. In their opinion, putting animals in less than 'ideal' homes for a few years was better than death.

The clash between the feelings of newcomers for shelter animals and the institution's practice of euthanasia led newcomers to experience a caring–killing 'paradox'.[2] On the one hand, they tried to understand and embrace the institutional rationale for euthanasia, but on the other hand, they wanted to nurture and tend to shelter animals. Doing both seemed impossible to many newcomers. Acceptance of the need to euthanize did not remove the apprehension that workers felt about having to kill animals themselves or to be part of this process. Their everyday selves were still paramount and made them feel for shelter animals as they might toward their own pets – the thought of killing them was troubling. They even feared getting to the point where they would no longer be upset killing animals, commonly asking those more senior, 'Do you still care?' or 'Doesn't it still bother you?' Experienced shelter workers acknowledged the 'paradox' of newcomers, telling and reassuring them that:

> there is a terrible paradox in what you will have to do – you will want to care for the animals, but will have to kill some of them. It is a painful process of killing animals when you don't want to. It seems so bad, but we'll make it good in your head. You will find yourself in a complex emotional state. Euthanizing is not just technical skills. You have to believe it is right to make it matter of fact.

EMOTION MANAGEMENT STRATEGIES

How did shelter workers manage their uncomfortable feelings? Workers learned different emotion management strategies to distance themselves enough to kill, but not so much as to abandon a sense of themselves as animal people. These strategies enabled workers at least to hold in abeyance their prior, everyday sensibilities regarding animals and to apply a different emotional perspective while in the shelter.

Transforming shelter animals into virtual pets

New workers often had trouble distinguishing between shelter animals and their own pets.[3] Failure to make this distinction could result in emotionally jarring situations for these workers, especially when animals were euthanized. However, they soon came to see shelter animals as virtual pets – liminal animals lying somewhere between the two categories of pet and object. In such a liminal status, workers could maintain a safe distance from animals while not entirely detaching themselves from them.

One way they accomplished this transformation was to lessen the intensity of their emotional attachments to individual animals. Almost as a rite of passage, newcomers were emotionally scarred by the euthanasia of a favorite animal, leaving them distraught over the loss.[4] They also heard cautionary tales about workers who were very upset by the loss of animals with whom they had grown 'too close' as well as workers whose 'excessive' or 'crazy' attachments resulted in harm to animals – such as the person who was fired after she released all the dogs from the shelter because she could no longer stand to see them caged or put to death. Newcomers soon began consciously to restrict the depth of their attachments. As one worker observed: 'I don't let myself get that attached to any of them.'

On the other hand, certain mottoes or ideals were part of the shelter culture, and these underscored the importance of not becoming detached from their charges or becoming desensitized to euthanasia. One worker, for instance, told me that you 'learn to turn your feelings off when you do this work, but you can't completely. They say if you can, you shouldn't be on the job.' Another worker noted: 'If you get to the point where killing doesn't bother you, then you shouldn't be working here.'

While they stopped themselves from 'loving' individual shelter animals, because of their likely fate, workers learned that they could become more safely attached by maintaining a generalized caring feeling for shelter animals as a group. As workers became more seasoned, individual bonding became less frequent, interest in adopting subsided, and a sense emerged of corporate attachment to shelter animals as a population of refugees rather than as individual pets.

Workers also came to see shelter animals differently from everyday pets by assuming professional roles with their charges. One role was that of 'caretaker' rather than pet owner. As a worker noted: 'You don't set yourself up by seeing them as pets. You'd kill yourself; I'd cut my wrists. I'm a caretaker, so I make them feel better while they are here. They won't be forgotten so quickly. I feel I get to know them. I'm their last hope.' Comparing her own pet to shelter animals, another worker noted: 'No bell goes off in your head with your own pet as it would with a shelter animal, where the bell says you can't love this animal because you have to euthanize it.' If not caretakers, they could become social workers trying to place these animals in the homes of other people.

New workers came to view their charges as having a type of market value within the larger population of shelter animals. Their value was not to be personal and individual from the worker's perspective. Rather, they were to be assessed in the light of their competitive attractiveness to potential adopters. This view was nowhere more apparent than in the selection of healthy and well behaved animals to be euthanized in order to make room for incoming animals. An experienced shelter worker described these 'tough choices' and the difficulty newcomers had in viewing animals this way:

> When you go through and pull [i.e. remove an animal for euthanasia] – that's when you have to make some real tough choices. If they've all been here an equal amount of time, then if you've got eighteen cages and six are filled with black cats, and you have a variety in here waiting for cages, you're going to pull the black ones so you can have more of a variety. It's hard for a new employee to understand that I'm going to pull a black cat to make room for a white one. After they've been here through a cat season, they know exactly what I'm doing, and you don't have to say anything when you have old staff around you.

In addition, newcomers learned to think differently when spending money for the medical care of shelter animals than they would when spending on their own pets. Although an occasional animal might receive some medical attention, many animals were killed because it was not considered economically feasible to treat them even though they had reversible problems and the cost might be insubstantial. For example, while two newcomers observed the euthanizing of several kittens, an experienced worker pointed to a viral infection in their mouths as the reason behind their deaths. One newcomer asked why the kittens could not be treated medically so they could be put up for adoption. The reply was that the virus could be treated, but 'given the volume, it is not economical to treat them'.

Keeping shelter mascots further helped workers separate everyday pets from their charges, with mascots serving as surrogate pets in contrast to the rest of the shelter's animals.[5] Cats and dogs were occasionally singled out to become group mascots, the former because workers took a special interest in them, the latter because workers hoped to increase their adoptability by improving their behavior. Unlike other shelter animals, mascots were permitted to run free in areas reserved for workers, such as their private office and front desk, where they were played with and talked about by workers. Importantly, they were never euthanized, either remaining indefinitely in the shelter or going home as someone's pet. Although most shelter workers interacted with the mascots as though they were pets, one shelter worker, akin to an owner, often took a special interest in the animal and let it be known that she would eventually adopt the animal if a good home could not be found. Some of their actions toward these mascots were in clear contrast to the way they would have acted toward regular shelter animals. In one case, for example, a cat mascot was found to have a stomach ailment requiring expensive surgery. In normal circumstances this animal would have been killed, but one of the workers used her own money to pay for the operation.

Using the animal

By taking the feelings of animals into account, workers distracted themselves from their own discomfort when euthanizing. Workers tried to make this experience as 'good' as possible for the animals and, in so doing, felt better themselves. Some workers, in fact, openly admitted that 'it makes me feel better making it [euthanasia] better for the animal'. Even more seasoned workers were more at ease with euthanasia if they focused on making animals feel secure and calm as they were killed. A worker with twenty years' experience remarked that 'it still bothers you after you're here for a long time, but not as much. Compassion and tenderness are there when I euthanize, so it doesn't eat away at me.'

One way workers did this was to empathize with animals in order to figure out how to reduce each animal's stress during euthanasia. By seeing things from the animals' perspective, workers sought to make the process of dying 'peaceful and easy'. As a worker pointed out: 'You make the animal comfortable and happy and secure, so when the time to euthanize comes, it will not be under stress and scared – the dog will lick your face, the cats will purr.' In the words of another worker: 'They get more love in the last few seconds than they ever did.' Workers were encouraged to 'think of all the little things that might stress the animal – if you sense that some are afraid of men, then keep men away.' For example, one worker said that she decided not to have cats and dogs in the euthanasia room at the same time. Observation of euthanasia confirmed that workers considered animals' states of mind. In one instance, where a cat and her kittens had to be euthanized, the mother was killed first because the worker thought she would become very upset if she sensed her kittens were dying. And in another case a worker refused to be interviewed during euthanasia because she felt that our talking made the animals more anxious.

Another way that taking animals into consideration helped workers distract themselves from their own concerns was to concentrate on the methodology of killing and to become technically proficient at it. By focusing on the technique of killing – and not on why it needed to be done or how they felt about doing it – workers could reassure themselves that they were making death quick and painless for animals. Workers, called 'shooters', who injected the euthanasia drug were told to 'focus not on the euthanasia, but on the needle. Concentrate on technical skills if you are the shooter.' Even those people, known as 'holders', who merely held animals steady during injection, were taught to view their participation as a technical act as opposed to a demonstration of affection. In the words of a worker:

> The holder is the one who controls the dog. You have your arm around her. You're the one who has got a hold of that vein. When they get the blood in the syringe, you let go. But you have to hold that dog and try and keep him steady and not let him pull away. That's my job.

Bad killing technique, whether shooting or holding, was bemoaned by senior workers. As one noted: 'I get really pissed off if someone blows a vein if it is due to an improper hold.'

Since euthanasia was regarded more as a technical than as a moral or emotional issue, it was not surprising that workers could acquire reputations with the shelter for being 'good shots', and animals came to be seen as either easy or hard 'putdowns' – a division reflecting technical difficulty and increased physical discomfort for animals. If the animal was a 'hard putdown', workers became all the more absorbed in the mechanics of euthanasia, knowing that the sharpness of their technical skills would affect the extent of an animal's distress. One worker illustrated this situation:

> Old dogs, the ones that should have been euthanized two years ago, those are hard to put down because they're so old. You know, their veins are just not pumping as fast as they should. You can inject it and the vein can blow up. It's an old vein. You have to go real slow. Sometimes they

just get kind of clogged. It's really tough. It's hard to get the veins on them sometimes. You feel badly about that because sometimes you have to go use all four legs before you get a good one.

Workers could also take animals into consideration, rather than focus on their own feelings, by seeing their death as the alleviation of suffering.[6] This was easy to do with animals that were very sick and old – known as 'automatic kills' – but it was much harder to see suffering in 'healthy and happy' animals that were killed. They too had to be seen as having lives not worth living. Workers were aware that the breadth of their definition of suffering made euthanasia easier for them. One worker acknowledged that: 'Sometimes you want to find any reason, like it has a runny nose.' Newcomers often flinched at what was deemed sufficient medical or psychological reason to euthanize an animal, as did veterinary technicians working in the adjoining animal hospital who sometimes sarcastically said to shelter workers and their animals: 'If you cough, they will kill you. If you sneeze, they will kill you.'

Workers learned to see euthanasia as a way to prevent suffering. For example, it was thought that it was better to euthanize healthy strays than to let them 'suffer' on the streets. One senior worker told newcomers:

I'd rather kill than see suffering. I've seen dogs hung in alleys, cats with firecrackers in their mouths or caught in car fan belts. This helps me to cope with euthanizing – to prevent this suffering through euthanasia. Am I sick if I can do this for fifteen years? No. I still cry when I see a sick pigeon on the streets, but I believe in what I am doing.

Once in a shelter, healthy strays, along with abandoned and surrendered animals, were also thought better dead than 'fostered out'. A worker noted: 'I'd rather kill it now than let it live three years and die a horrible death. No life is better than a temporary life.' Even having a potential adopter was not enough; the animal's future home, if deemed 'inappropriate', would only cause the animal more 'suffering'. One worker elaborated:

Finding an appropriate home for the animal is the only way the animal is going to get out of here alive. The inappropriate home prolongs the suffering, prolongs the agony, prolongs the neglect, prolongs the abuse of an animal. The animal was abused or neglected in the first place or it wouldn't be here.

This thinking was a problem for newcomers who believed that almost any home, even if temporary, was better than killing animals. Particularly troubling were those people denied an animal for adoption even though their resources and attitudes seemed acceptable to workers. Some potential adopters were rejected because it was thought that they were not home often enough, even though by all other standards they seemed likely to become good owners. In one case, a veterinary hospital technician wanted to adopt a four-month-old puppy, but was rejected because she had full-time employment. Although she retorted that she had a roommate who was at home most of the time, her request was still denied.[7]

But newcomers soon learned to scrutinize potential adopters carefully by screening them for certain warning flags, such as not wanting to spay or neuter, not wanting to fence in or leash animals, not being home enough with animals, and so on, in addition to such basics as not having a landlord's approval or adopting the pet as a gift for someone else. Most workers came to see certain groups of people as risky adopters requiring even greater scrutiny before approval. For some workers, this meant welfare recipients because they might not have enough money to care for animals, Latinos because they were unwilling to spay or neuter, or policemen because they might be too rough with animals.

Although workers accepted the applications of most potential owners, they did reject some. But even in their acceptances, they reaffirmed their concern for suffering and their desire to find perfect homes; they certainly did so with their rejections, admonishing those turned down for whatever their presumed problems were toward animals. Occasionally, rejected applicants became irate and made angry comments such as 'You'd rather kill it than give it to me!' These moments were uncomfortable for newcomers to watch since, to some extent, they shared the rejected applicant's sentiment – any home was better than death. More experienced workers would try to cool down the applicant but also remind newcomers that some homes were worse than death. In one such case, the shelter manager said to the rejected applicant, but for all to hear, 'It is my intention to find a good home where the animal's needs can be met.'

Resisting and avoiding euthanasia

New workers, in particular, sometimes managed their discomfort with euthanasia by trying to prevent or delay the death of animals. Although there were generally understood euthanasia guidelines, they were rather vague, and workers could exert mild pressure to make exceptions to the rules. Certainly, not all animals scheduled or 'pink-slipped' to be killed were 'automatic kills'. As a worker noted: 'If a 12-year-old stray with hip dysplasia comes in, yes, you know as soon as it walks in the door that at the end of the stray holding period it's going to be euthanized, but not all of them are like this.' A worker described such an instance:

> Four weeks is really young. Five weeks, you're really pushing it. Six weeks, we can take it, but it depends on its overall health and condition. But sometimes we'll keep one or two younger ones, depending on the animal itself. We just had an animal last week – it was a dachshund. She is a really nice and friendly dog. In this case, we just decided to keep her.

Sometimes a worker took a special liking to a particular animal, but it was to be euthanized because the cage was needed for new animals, or it was too young, too old, somewhat sick, or had a behavior problem. The worker might let it be known among colleagues that they were very attached to the animal, or they might go directly to the person making the euthanasia selection with a plea for the animal's date of death to be delayed in the hopes of adoption.[8] One worker had a favorite cat that was to be euthanized, but succeeded in blocking its euthanasia, at least for a while, by personally taking financial responsibility for its shelter costs.

However, opposing euthanasia had to be done in a way that did not make such decisions too difficult for those making them. Workers could not object repeatedly to euthanasia or oppose it too aggressively without making the selector feel uncomfortable. One worker felt 'guilty' when this happened to her:

> There was one technician – Marie – who used to make me feel guilty. I have to make room for new animals because we have so few cages. I must decide which old ones to kill to make room for new ones. Marie would get upset when I would choose certain cats to be killed. She would come to me with her runny, snotty nose, complaining that certain cats were picked to be killed. This made me feel guilty.

More experienced workers saw these 'objections' as a problem of emotion getting in the way of 'reality'. A senior worker explained:

> Sometimes staff object because they think an animal should have longer. They'll say, 'Why does this one have to go?' But a lot of it is emotion getting in the way of the reality of what an animal shelter is. I know I regret having to euthanize particular animals, but I also know there's always a reason, whether it has been here too long – dogs go cage crazy or suffer kennel stress or we need their cage to make room for incoming animals. So there's always a reason.

If opposing euthanasia failed, workers were able to avoid the discomfort of doing it. One worker said that he would not 'be around' if his favorite cat was killed, and noted:

> There's not an animal I'm not attached to here, but there's a cat here now that I like a lot. There's a good chance that she'll be euthanized. She's got a heart murmur, I guess. It's a mild one, but . . . any type of a heart murmur with a cat is bad. She's also got a lump right here. They've already tested her for leukemia and it's negative, so they are testing her for something else. But she's just got an adorable face and everything else with her is fine. I like her personality. But I have two cats at home. I can't have a third. I won't be around when they euthanize her. I'll let somebody else do it. I would rather it be done when I'm not here.

Although workers could be exempted from killing animals with whom they had closely bonded, there was a strong feeling that such persons should be there for the animal's sake. Yet if present, they could indicate to others that they did not want to be the 'shooter' and instead be the 'holder', allowing them to feel more removed from the actual killing. A worker said:

> Especially if it's one I like a lot, I would rather be the one holding instead of injecting. If you don't want to inject, you just back up and somebody else does it. Everybody here does that. I just look at it, I don't want to be the one to do it. Even though people say that holding is the harder of the two, I would look at it as, well, I am the one who is doing this. And sometimes, I don't want to be the one to do it.

Customizing the division of labor of euthanasia to fit their own emotional limits, other workers preferred not to do the holding. One worker observed:

> One of the ways that I detach myself from euthanasia is that I do the shooting rather than the holding so that I don't feel the animal dying. I'm concentrating on the technical skill behind the actual injection. And with a dog, you literally feel the animal's life go out of it in your arms, instead of giving the injection and letting it drop.

Using the owner

Shelter workers could also displace some of their own discomfort with euthanasia into anger and frustration with pet owners. Rather than questioning the morality of their own acts and feeling guilty about euthanasia, workers came to regard owners, and not themselves, as behaving wrongly toward animals. As workers transferred the blame for killing animals to the public, they concentrated their energies on educating and changing public attitudes to pets and making successful adoptions through the shelter.

The public was seen as treating animals as 'property to be thrown away like trash' rather than as something having intrinsic value. One worker bemoaned: 'A lot of people who want to leave their pets have bullshit reasons for this – like they just bought new furniture for their living room and their cat shed all over it.' This lack of commitment resulted in many of the surrendered animals being euthanized because they were not adoptable and/or space was needed. Speaking about these owners, one worker candidly acknowledged: 'I would love to be rude once to some of these people who come in. I'd like to say to these people, "Cut this bullshit out!"' Another worker concluded: 'You do want to strangle these people.'

Even if pet owners did not surrender their animals to the shelter, they became tainted as a group in the eyes of workers, who saw many of them as negligent or irresponsible. A common charge against owners was that their pets were allowed to run free and be hurt, lost or stolen. One senior worker admitted: 'A bias does get built in. We're called if a cat gets caught in a fan belt.

We're the ones that have to scrape cats off the streets.' Owners were also seen as selfish and misguided when it came to their pets, thoughtlessly allowing them to breed, instead of spaying or neutering them. Workers often repeated the shelter's pithy wish: 'Parents will let their pets have puppies or kittens so they can show their children the miracle of birth – well, maybe they should come in here to see the miracle of death!' Workers could be heard among themselves admonishing the public's 'irresponsibility' toward breeding and the deaths that such an attitude caused. A worker explained: 'The only reason why it has been killed is that no one took the time to be a responsible pet owner. They felt the cat deserved to run free or they didn't want to pay the money to have it spayed or neutered, or that she should have one litter. Well great, what are you to do with her six offspring?' Even owners who declared great love and affection for their pets sometimes came across in the shelter environment as cruel to their animals. These were owners who let their animals suffer because they could not bear to kill them. A worker noted:

> I'll get a 22-year-old-cat. And the owner is crying out there. I tell her, 'You know, twenty-two years is great. You have nothing to be ashamed of. Nothing.' But you get some others that come in and they [the animals] look absolutely like shit. You feel like taking hold of them and saying, 'What the hell are you doing? He should have been put to sleep two years ago!'

According to shelter workers, owners should have suffered pangs of conscience about their treatment of animals, but did not. Some owners seemed not to want their pets, and this shocked workers, as one noted: 'You'd be surprised at how many people come right out and say they don't want it any more. They are usually the ones who call us to pick it up, otherwise they'll dump it on the street. And of course, we're going to come and get it. I feel like saying "It's your conscience, not mine, go ahead, do it." Of course, I don't do that.' Many surrenderers, in the eyes of shelter workers, just did not care whether their animals lived or died. At the same time that surrenderers were seen as lacking a conscience, shelter workers were afforded the opportunity to reaffirm their own dedication to and feelings for animals. A worker commented:

> Some surrenderers take them back after we tell them we can't guarantee placement. Most say, 'Well that's fine.' Like the owner of this cat, he called this morning and said, 'I've got to get rid of it, I'm allergic to it.' Of course, he didn't seem at all bothered. He goes, 'That's fine.' Or somebody is going to surrender a pet because they're moving, well, if it was me, and I'm sure quite a few other people here feel the same way, I'd look for a place where pets were allowed. People are just looking out for themselves and not anything else.

In the opinion of the workers, it was important for newcomers to learn not to bear the 'guilt' that owners should have felt. To do this, they had to see owners as the real killers of shelter animals. As one worker put it, 'People think we are murderers, but they are the ones that have put us in this position. We are morally offended by the fact that we have to carry out an execution that we didn't necessarily order.' A senior shelter worker recounted how she came to terms with guilt:

> Every night I had a recurring dream that I had died, and I was standing in line to go to heaven. And St Peter says to me, 'I know you, you're the one that killed all those little animals.' And I'd sit up in the bed in a cold sweat. Finally, when I realized it wasn't my fault, my dreams changed. After St Peter said, 'I know you, you're the one that killed all those little animals,' I turned to the 999,000 people behind me and said, 'I know you, you *made* me kill all these animals.' You grow into the fact that you are the executioner, but you weren't the judge and jury.

Shelter workers redirected their emotions and resources into changing public attitudes about pets in order to curtail the never-ending flow of animals – often called a 'flood' – that always far exceeded what was possible to adopt out. Overwhelmed by this problem, workers wanted to do something about it other than killing animals. By putting effort into adoption or public education, they felt they were making a dent in the overpopulation problem instead of feeling hopeless about it. For many, combating pet overpopulation became addictive and missionary. Rather than chew over the morality of their own participation in euthanasia, they felt part of a serious campaign – often described as a 'battle' – against the formidable foe of the pet owner and in defense of helpless animals.

Owners were used in ways other than as objects of blame. Successful adoptions helped to accentuate the positive in a setting where there were few opportunities to feel good about what workers were doing. Finding homes for animals came close to the original motivation that brought many workers to the shelter seeking employment.[9] One worker commented: 'For every one euthanized, you have to think about the one placed, or the one case where you placed it in a perfect family.' Another worker said that 'you get a good feeling when you see an empty cage'. She explained that she did not think that it was empty because an animal had just been killed, but because an animal had just been adopted. Indeed, out of self-protection, when the cage of someone's 'favorite' was empty, workers did not ask what happened to the animals so they could assume that it was adopted rather than killed. They talked about how all of their animals were 'either PWP or PWG – placed with people or placed with God'. Shelter workers felt particularly satisfied when they heard from people who had satisfactorily adopted animals. Sometimes these owners came into the shelter and talked informally with workers; at other times, they wrote letters of thanks for their animals. Besides taping this mail on the walls for all to see, workers mounted snapshots of adopters and their animals in the shelter's lobby.

Dealing with outsiders

For workers to manage their emotions successfully, they also had to learn to suspend asking hard ethical questions. While this was easy to do within the confines of the shelter, it was more difficult outside. Many reported feeling badly when outsiders learned they killed animals and challenged them about the morality of euthanasia. Workers dealt with these unwanted feelings in two ways.

Outside work, they could try to avoid the kinds of contact that gave rise to unwanted emotions and difficult questions. Workers claimed that roommates, spouses, family members and strangers sometimes made them feel 'guilty' because they were seen as 'villains' or 'murderers'. As one worker said, 'You expect your spouse, your parents, your sister, your brother, or your significant other to understand. And they don't. And your friends don't. People make stupid remarks like, "Gee, I would never do your job because I love animals too much."' Workers claimed that they had become 'paranoid' about being asked if they killed animals, waiting for questions such as, 'How can you kill them if you care about animals so much?' Sometimes people would simply tell workers: 'I love animals, I couldn't do that.' One worker claimed that these questions and comments 'make me feel like I've done something wrong'. Another said, 'So what does it mean – I don't love animals?' If workers were not explicitly criticized or misunderstood, they still encountered people who made them feel reluctant to talk about their work. One worker noted that 'I'm proud that I'm a 90 per cent shot, and that I'm not putting the animals through stress, but people don't want to hear this.'

In anticipation of these negative reactions, many workers hesitated to divulge what they did.[10] One worker said that she had learned to tell people that she 'drives an animal ambulance'. If workers revealed that they carried out euthanasia, they often presented arguments to support their caring for animals and the need for euthanasia. As one worked noted, 'I throw numbers at them, like the fact that we get 12,000 animals a year but can only place 2,000.' While concealing their work or educating others about it were by far the most common strategies used with outsiders, some workers would occasionally take a blunter approach and use sarcasm or black humor. The following worker talked about all of these approaches:

> People give me a lot of grief. You know, you tell them where you work, and you tell them it's an animal shelter. And they say, 'Well', you don't put them to sleep, do you?' And I always love to say, 'Well actually I give classes on how to do that,' just for the shock value of it. Or it's the old, 'I could never do what you do, I love animals too much.' 'Oh, I don't love them at all. That's why I work here. I kill them. I enjoy it.' But sometimes you don't even mention where you work because you don't want to deal with that. It depends on the social situation I am in as to whether I want to go into it or not, and it also depends on how I feel at

a given time. Some people are interested, and then I talk about spaying and neutering their pets.

Another way workers dealt with outsiders was to neutralize their criticism of euthanasia. The only credible opinions about euthanasia were seen as coming from those people who actually did such killing as part of the shelter community. Humor was one device that helped workers feel part of this community. It gave them a special language to talk about death and their concerns about it. As with gallows humor in other settings, it was not particularly funny out of context, and workers knew this, but learning to use it and find it humorous became a rite of passage. For instance, people telephoning the shelter might be greeted with the salutation, 'Heaven.' Referring to the euthanasia room and the euthanasia drug also took on a light, funny side with the room being called 'downtown' or the 'lavender lounge' (its walls were this color) and the drug being called 'sleepaway' or 'go-go juice' (its brand name was 'Fatal Plus').

But no ritual practice gave more of a sense of 'we-ness' then actually killing animals. No single act admitted them more into the shelter institution or more clearly demarcated the transition of shelter workers out of the novice role. As they gained increasing experience with euthanasia, workers developed a firmer sense of being in the same boat with peers who also did what they did. They shared an unarticulated belief that others could not understand what it was like to kill unless they had also done so. Even within the shelter, kennel workers often felt misunderstood by the front-desk people. As one worker reflected, 'It does feel like you can't understand what I do if you can't understand that I don't like to kill, but that I have to kill. You'd have to see what I see. Maybe then.' Since outsiders did not share this experience, workers tended to give them little credibility and to discount their opinions. By curtailing the possibility of understanding what they did and communicating with others about it, workers furthered their solidarity and created boundaries between themselves and outsiders that served to shield them from external criticism and diminish the uncomfortable feelings easily raised by the 'uninformed' or 'naive'.

THE IMPERFECTION OF EMOTION MANAGEMENT

Certainly, the killing of animals by shelter workers was facilitated by the kinds of emotion management strategies that have been discussed. Yet it would be wrong to characterize these people, including those with many years' experience, as completely detached. These strategies were far from perfect. It would be more accurate to say that their institutional socialization was incomplete. All workers, including those with many years of experience, felt uneasy about euthanasia at certain times.

For the few who continued to experience sharp and disturbing feelings,

159

quitting became a way to manage emotions. For example, one worker felt 'plagued' by a conflict between her own feelings for the animals which made killing hard to accept and the shelter's euthanasia policy with which she intellectually agreed. She said it was 'like having two people in my head, one good and the other evil, that argue about me destroying these animals'. This conflict left her feeling 'guilty' about deaths she found 'hard to justify'. After nine months on the job, she quit.

For most workers this conflict was neither intense nor constant, but instead manifested itself as episodic uneasiness. From time to time euthanasia provoked modest but clearly discernible levels of emotional distress. There was no consensus, however, on what kind of euthanasia would rattle people and make them feel uncomfortable, but everyone had at least one type that roused their feelings.

The most obvious discomfort with euthanasia occurred when workers had to kill animals to which they were attached or that they could easily see as pets.[11] While newcomers were more likely to have formed these attachments, seasoned workers could still be troubled by euthanasia when animals reminded them of other attachments. As one veteran worker reflected:

> I haven't been emotionally attached to a dog, except for one, for quite a while. I know my limit. But there are times when I'll look at a dog when I'm euthanizing it and go, 'You've got Rex's eyes.' Or it's an Irish setter – I have a natural attachment to Irish setters. Or black cats – I hate to euthanize black cats. It's real hard for me to euthanize a black cat.

Even without attachments, many workers found it 'heartbreaking' to euthanize young, healthy and well-behaved animals merely for space because they could have become pets. Without a medical or psychological reason, euthanasia seemed a 'waste'.[12]

For many, euthanasia became unsettling if it appeared that animals suffered physically or psychologically. This happened, for example, when injections of the euthanasia drug caused animals to 'scream', 'cry', or become very disoriented and move about frantically. But it also happened when animals seemed to 'know' they were about to be killed or sensed that 'death was in the air'. 'Cats aren't dumb. They know what's going on. Whenever you take them to the room, they always get this stance where their head goes up, and they know,' observed one worker. Another said that many animals could 'smell' death. These workers became uneasy because they assumed that the animals were 'scared'. 'What is hard for me,' said one worker, 'is when they are crying and they are very, very scared.' Another said that she could 'feel their tension and anxiety' in the euthanasia room. 'They seem to know what's happening – that something is going to happen,' she added to explain her discomfort.

Ironically, for some workers the opposite situation left them feeling unsettled. They found it eerie when animals were not scared and instead behaved 'as though they were co-operating'. According to one worker, certain breeds were likely to act this way as they were being killed: 'Greyhounds and dobermans will either give you their paw or willingly give you their leg, and look right past you. It's as though they are co-operating. The other dogs will look right at you.'

Killing large numbers of animals in a single day was disconcerting for nearly everyone. This happened to one worker when the number of animals killed was so great she could not conceptualize the quantity until she picked up a thick pile of 'yellow slips' (surrender forms), or when she looked at the drug log and saw how many animals had been given euthanasia injections. The flow of animals into the shelter was seasonal, and workers grew to loathe those months when many animals were brought in and euthanized. The summer was a particularly bad time, because so many cats came in and were killed. As one worker said, 'They are constantly coming in. On a bad day, you might have to do it [euthanasia] fifty times. There are straight months of killing.' Another observed, 'After three hours of killing, you come out a mess. It drains me completely. I'll turn around and see all these dead animals on the floor around me – and it's "What have I done?"' And yet another worker noted:

It's very difficult when we are inundated from spring until fall. Every single person who walks through the door has either a pillow case, a box, a laundry basket or whatever – one more litter of kittens. And you only have X number of cages in your facility and they are already full. So the animal may come in the front door and go out the back door in a barrel. It's very difficult if that animal never had a chance at life, or has had a very short life.

Even seasoned workers said that it did 'not feel right' to spend so much time killing, particularly when so many of the animals they killed were young and never had a chance to become a pet.

All workers, then, experienced at least some uneasiness when facing certain types of euthanasia, despite their socialization into the shelter's culture. The emotions generated by these situations overruled attempts by the shelter to help them manage their emotions and objectify their charges. When emotion management and objectification failed, workers felt some degree of connection and identification with the animals which in turn elicited feelings of sadness, worry and even remorse.

CONCLUSION

The initial conflict faced by newcomers to an animal shelter was extreme – because of their prior, everyday perspective toward animals, killing them generated emotions that caused workers to balk at carrying out euthanasia. However, on closer inspection, this tension was replaced by a more moderate and manageable version of the same conflict. The conflict was repackaged and softened, but it was there, nonetheless. Shelter workers could more easily live with this version, and their emotion management strategies got them to this point. These strategies embodied an underlying inconsistency or dilemma between the simultaneous pulls toward objectifying the animals and seeing the animals in pet-related terms – a conflict between rational necessity and sentimentality, between head and heart, between everyday perspective and that of the institution, and between treating creatures in Martin Buber's (1958) I–It fashion – as deindividualized things quite different from oneself – or in an I–Thou manner – in which the other is acknowledged as kin.

A final look at these strategies reveals this underlying tension. By transforming shelter animals into virtual pets, the workers could objectify the animals to some degree, while also categorizing them as something like, yet different from, everyday pets. When it came to actually killing them, workers could play the role of highly skilled technicians efficiently dispatching animal lives seen as not worth living, while simultaneously trying to take the emotional and physical feelings of animals into account. Being able to avoid or postpone killing was itself viewed as a struggle between emotion and rationality; importantly, this was allowed, thereby acknowledging some degree of emotion but within limits that reaffirmed a more rational approach. When it came to their view of owners (perhaps a collective projection of a sort), it was the public, and not themselves, that objectified animals; whatever they did, including the killing, paled by comparison and was done out of sentiment and caring. Indeed, outsiders came to be suspected, one-dimensionally, as a distant and alien group, while workers increasingly cultivated a strong sense of we-ness among themselves – humans, too, seem to have two fundamentally different kinds of relations with each other.

It is not surprising that a tension existed in the way that many shelter workers approached their animals, since the object/pet dichotomy is built into contemporary society and is behind many vagaries of human–animal interaction. Animals clearly play dual roles – utilitarian or affectionate – in the lives of many people. Sometimes a person will regard some animals as pets and others of the same species as objects. A cockfighter may retire a favorite, perhaps permanently injured rooster to the sedentary life of a barnyard fowl, despite the fact that its fighting and stud days are over (Herzog 1989). Sometimes a person will regard the same animal as both pet and object, as happens with the southern, rural American hunter who sees his dog as a significant partner for hunting and guarding, symbolically valued for its fidelity and rare abilities, but then treats it callously as a useless item (Jordon 1975). And sometimes different people will regard the same animal as either an object or a pet, as happens with children taking riding lessons – some will view a horse as little more than a cross-country vehicle, while others will relate to it as a companion (Lawrence 1988).

It is also not surprising that these strategies were sometimes imperfect, failing to prevent a penetration of the everyday perspective toward animals into the shelter. Even the most effective programs of organizational socialization are likely to be fallible when workers face situations that trigger their prior feelings and concerns. Many shelter workers may have felt uneasy because at certain times their personal, everyday thinking and feeling about animals in general may have taken precedence over the institutional 'rules' for thinking and feeling about animals. Such uneasiness is increasingly supported by growing societal attention to the ideal of humaneness and concern about the moral status of animals (Rollin 1989).

Yet, in the end, by relying on these strategies workers reproduced the institution (e.g. Smith and Kleinman 1989), thereby creating a new generation of workers who would support the humane society model and the kind of human–animal relationship in which people could believe they were killing with a conscience. Far from being a unique situation, the shelter workers' relationship with animals is but our general culture's response to animals writ small. It is not likely that we ourselves are altogether exempt from this inconsistency, as our individual ways of managing our thoughts and feelings may similarly dull the conflict just enough for it to become a familiar uneasiness. For shelter workers, the conflict is merely heightened and their struggle to make peace with their acts is more deliberate and collective.

NOTES

* This work was supported by a grant from the William and Charlotte Parks Trust. I would like to thank Andrew Rowan for his support and guidance.

1 In animal research, some newcomers want to name their animals, give them a social identity, and communicate with them on a meaningful level, but are often looked upon by more seasoned workers as 'problem children' if they continue this behavior. Scientists, in particular, usually look upon a practice such as the naming of research animals by technicians as unprofessional and amateurish (Arluke 1990a). For example, at one facility that was due for a formal site inspection, technicians were told by the principal investigator to remove all animal identification cards on cages because the cards had the names of animals written on them and to put up new cards with only animal identification numbers.

2 By contrast, many newcomers in applied biomedical research laboratories do not experience such a paradox, although they have some uneasiness sacrificing animals (Arluke 1988, 1990b, 1990c). Unlike shelter workers, few animal researchers define themselves as animal people, and those that do tend to be caretakers rather than research technicians or scientists. In medical research, many newcomers also have prior experience using animals as teaching or experimental 'tools', so their thinking is already in line with the institution's view of animals as objects. While it is true that some personnel in research laboratories treat animals in a pet-like fashion – seeing personalities in them, naming them, and playing with them – these are exceptions. Moreover, by the time medical researchers kill animals, the animals are often extremely sick or debilitated, so little alternative seems to exist except death. And medical researchers can tell themselves that this death serves a higher purpose in the form of potential clinical benefits to humanity.

3 Similarly, when everyday pets cannot be distinguished from 'X dogs', medical

students experience much greater discomfort using animals than those classmates who can separate the two in their minds (Arluke and Hafferty 1991). As one student said: 'For me, it is a big separation between having your dog at home and being a dog lover, and then doing experiments on animals. It seems that some others aren't making a division between the two, and they just don't want any part in seeing any of the animals hurt.'

4 Animal researcher technicians, too, quickly learn to distance themselves from laboratory animals after being hurt by the death of one of their favorites (Arluke 1990a).

5 There is also selective attachment in research laboratories where an occasional animal might be singled out from others for special attention, affection and privileges, although sometimes these laboratory pets remain part of the experiment rather than being put aside or 'rescued' to someone's home (Arluke 1988). In laboratories, as in shelters, the existence of animals that ape the everyday pet serves to distinguish two stances toward animals – the personal and the institutional – while at the same time blurring the way in which the entire group of animals is regarded. As a group, laboratory animals, to research staff having direct contact with them, are more sentient than objects, but they are not everyday pets.

6 Unlike shelter personnel who saw their killing as preventing or ending suffering caused by others, animal researchers cannot use suffering as an emotion management strategy. Indeed, they need to rely on strategies to blind themselves to suffering rather than to see it lurking everywhere (Arluke 1990a). In laboratories, even the word 'suffering' is avoided; instead, animals are described as in 'discomfort' or 'distress'.

7 Beck (1990) reported a more extreme instance where two veterinary school deans were denied adoptions by a shelter because all members of their households worked and their backyards did not have dog-houses.

8 In research laboratories, it is far more difficult to resist or avoid sacrificing animals. When this happens, it tends to be clandestine, with fellow technicians helping others to do so without the knowledge of investigators (Arluke 1988).

9 Interestingly, many laboratories have certain animals that are regarded as research heroes; they function much like successful shelter adoptions by confirming the essential purpose of the institution. At one point, in fact, the National Society for Medical Research created a Research Dog Hero Award given annually to a surviving and healthy-looking research dog (Lederer 1991).

10 Animal researchers also go into the closet to avoid clashes that are frustrating or uncomfortable (Arluke 1991). They, too, learn to avoid telling people exactly what they do for a living, either saying that they 'work at Bay Hospital' or 'do cancer research'. Others gradually release more details about their work as they test the interaction for acceptance and interest. And others reveal what they do and take an educational approach to these often rocky encounters. The rarest approach, as with shelter workers, is to shock outsiders by saying things such as 'I kill dogs in experiments.'

11 This is also the single greatest source of uneasiness in animal research (Arluke 1990c).

12 Although it does not wrench them as much, animal researchers are often troubled – and not only for economic reasons – when laboratory animals do not fulfil their institutional role and are 'wasted' because technical mistakes, poorly designed experiments or negligence result in 'bad' data or lost data (Arluke 1990b).

REFERENCES

Arluke, A. (1988) 'Sacrificial symbolism in animal experimentation: object or pet?', *Anthrozoös* 2: 98–117.

—— (1990a) 'Living with contradictions', *Anthrozoös* 3: 90–9.

—— (1990b) 'Moral elevation in medical research', in G. Albrecht (ed.) *Advances in Medical Sociology*, Greenwich, Conn.: JAI Press, pp. 189–204.

—— (1990c) 'Uneasiness among laboratory technicians', *Lab Animal* 19(4): 20–39.

—— (1991) 'Going into the closet with science: information control among animal experimenters', *Journal of Contemporary Ethnography* 20: 306–30.

Arluke, A. and Hafferty, F. (1991) 'Transforming dogs into tools: social death and laboratory culture in Medical School', unpublished paper.

Beck, A. (1990) 'For whom do we mourn?', Paper presented to the Delta Society, Houston, Texas.

Buber, M. (1958) *I and Thou*, 2nd edn, Edinburgh: T. & T. Clark.

Herzog, H. (1989) 'Tangled lives: human researchers and animal subjects', *Anthrozoös* 3: 80–2.

Jordon, J. (1975) 'An ambivalent relationship: dog and human in the folk culture of the rural South', *Appalachian Journal* 2: 31–48.

Lawrence, E. (1988) 'Those who dislike pets', *Anthrozoös* 1: 147–8.

Lederer, S. (1992) 'Political animals: the shaping of biomedical research literature in twentieth-century America', *Isis* 83: 61–79.

Rollin, B. (1989) 'Animals in experimentation: utilitarian objects, pets, or moral objects', *Anthrozoös* 3: 88–90.

Schlcifer, II. (1985) 'Images of death and life: food animal production and the vegetarian option', in P. Singer (ed.) *In Defense of Animals*, New York: Harper & Row, pp. 63–74.

Serpell, J. (1986) *In the Company of Animals*, Oxford: Basil Blackwell.

Smith, A., and Kleinman, S. (1989) 'Managing emotions in medical school: students' contacts with the living and the dead', *Social Psychology Quarterly* 52: 56–68.

9

ATTITUDES, KNOWLEDGE AND BEHAVIOUR TOWARD WILDLIFE AMONG THE INDUSTRIAL SUPERPOWERS
The United States, Japan and Germany

Stephen R. Kellert

INTRODUCTION

The United States, Japan and Germany collectively exert a profound impact on the global environment, not only as a consequence of massive resource exploitation, but also as models of social and economic development. Recent statistics (CIA 1990) reveal that these three countries account for nearly $8 trillion in annual gross national product (or roughly 40 per cent of the world's total) and for 34 per cent of the world's trade in resources, although they represent just 8 per cent of the world's population. This degree of economic, political and environmental influence suggests the need for increased understanding of how each country views the natural world and its conservation. This chapter examines one particularly sensitive barometer of environmental concern – attitudes, knowledge and behaviour towards animals, particularly wildlife and its associated natural habitats.

METHODS

Similar concepts and methodologies were employed to study attitudes to animals in the United States, Japan and Germany over a ten-year period from 1979 to 1989. The methods used were based on an established typology derived originally from a general population survey of people's knowledge, attitudes and behaviour towards animals and the natural world. Attitude scales were then constructed based on cluster and factor analysis of responses to survey questions (see e.g. Kellert 1979; Kellert and Berry 1981; Kellert 1983, 1991a; Schulz 1985). These scales have generated a series of basic 'attitude types' which are given shorthand names and brief definitions in Table 9.1, although more detailed descriptions can be found elsewhere (see Kellert

166

Table 9.1 Basic attitudes toward animals

Term	Definition
Naturalistic (NAT):	*Primary interest and affection for wildlife and the outdoors.*
Ecologistic (ECO):	*Primary concern for the environment as a system, for the interrelationships between wildlife species and natural habitats.*
Humanistic (HUM):	*Primary interest and strong affection for individual animals such as pets or large wild animals with strong anthropomorphic associations.*
Moralistic (MOR):	*Primary concern for the right and wrong treatment of animals, with strong opposition to the perceived overexploitation of and/or cruelty to animals.*
Scientistic (SCI):	*Primary interest in the physical attributes and biological functioning of animals.*
Aesthetic (AES):	*Primary interest in the physical attractiveness and symbolic appeal of animals.*
Utilitarian (UTIL):	*Primary interest in the practical value of animals, or in the subordination of animals for the practical benefit of people.*
Dominionistic (DOM):	*Primary interest in the mastery and control of animals.*
Negativistic (NEG):	*Primary orientation an active avoidance of animals due to dislike or fear.*
Neutralistic (NEU):	*Primary orientation a passive avoidance of animals due to indifference or lack of interest.*

1980). In the present studies, it was not possible to generate an adequate aesthetic scale, and the neutralistic and negativistic scales were combined as a single measure of negative attitudes. In addition, an effective scientistic scale was not developed for the Japanese study.

Survey questions covered knowledge of animals as well as attitudes. Various true/false-type knowledge questions were combined to construct an overall 'knowledge of animals' scale. Other survey questions also assessed attitudes towards hunting, the conservation of endangered species, animal damage control, and wildlife habitat protection. These attitude questions were asked primarily in the American and Japanese surveys and are therefore discussed only to a limited extent. Some results of questions regarding animal-related activities, such as hunting, bird-watching, zoo-visiting, pet-ownership, conservation organization membership, and wildlife-related television viewing, are also presented.

The survey of the American public involved personal interviews with 3,107 adults (aged 18 years and older) residing in the 48 contiguous US states and Alaska (Kellert 1979; Kellert and Berry 1981). A comparison of the sample with national census data indicated that the former was a relatively good representation of the American public. The survey included more than 180 questions and required approximately 45 minutes to administer.

The Japanese study involved personal interviews with 450 randomly selected individuals in Tokyo and three widely distributed rural locations, as well as 50 focused interviews with a sample of key informants (Kellert 1991b). The relatively small size of the general public sample necessitated a stratified random sample selection procedure involving age, sex and educational level quotas within each major sampling area. Census statistics suggested the sample was a relatively good representation of the Japanese adult population. The Japanese survey averaged 43 minutes and included 198 questions. Additionally, 50 focused interviews were conducted with a sample of key informants recommended (from among 300 identified) as possessing extensive knowledge of Japanese attitudes to nature and wildlife. The focused interviews included a variety of questions covering such issues as current and historic appreciation and concern for nature, attitudes toward the conservation of wildlife and biological diversity, views on economic development and conservation, and shifts in attitudes to nature.

Dr Wolfgang Schulz of the University of Munich was the principal investigator of the German study (Schulz 1985, 1986). This survey was largely a translation of the one used in the United States, although partially altered to conform with German circumstances and cultural conditions. A total of 1,484 personal interviews were conducted with individuals from all regions of Germany. The use of adult education programmes as the principal method for identifying potential respondents resulted in a nonrandom sample of the German public. When compared with national census data, the German sample included a slightly greater proportion of females, younger respondents and more highly educated persons.

Despite the use of broadly similar research procedures in all three countries, some methodological differences should be mentioned. The wording of survey questions occasionally varied to allow for cultural and language differences, and the three studies also differed somewhat in terms of sample selection procedures, methods of data collection, and year of study. Where appropriate, any problems of interpretation created by such differences are discussed in relation to the results which follow.

BIOGEOGRAPHICAL AND CULTURAL BACKGROUND

Before examining the results, some information on relevant biogeographical and cultural characteristics of the three nations will be presented. These descriptions are brief, highlighting only features of potential significance to the present findings.

The United States encompasses a wide variety of biogeographical zones, resulting in a high degree of biological diversity within a largely temperate climate. The country's human population of some 250 million, representing approximately 25 persons per square kilometre, is far less than the 248 per sq. km of Germany or the 311 per sq. km in Japan (CIA 1990) (Figure 9.1). The

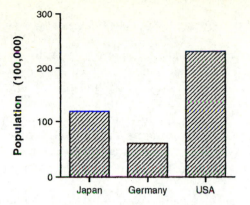

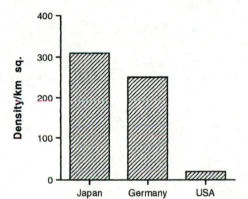

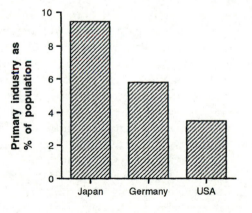

Figure 9.1 Human population, population density, and per cent of population in agriculture in Japan, Germany and the United States, 1993.

169

United States has a diverse and abundant animal fauna compared with either Japan or Germany.

America's relative wildlife abundance, as well as prevailing attitudes and needs among the largely European settlers, resulted in a tradition of open access to wildlife, particularly for commercial and sport hunting purposes (Matthiessen 1989; Dunlap 1988). A history of excessive wildlife exploitation and the existence of large amounts of public land led to the development of an elaborate system of legal protection and regulatory control of wildlife (Bean 1983; Lund 1980). A very active and influential nongovernmental sector also emerged as a prominent force in wildlife conservation and policy (Tober 1989).

The human population of Japan is approximately 125 million, or 311 persons per sq. km (CIA 1990). In relation to existing arable land, the Japanese population is 2,256 per sq. km compared to 820 in Germany and 103 in the United States (Marsh 1987). Three-quarters of the Japanese population resides in urban areas with relatively few people living in the approximate two-thirds of the country covered by mountains. As a consequence, some 70 per cent of Japan has less than 50 people per sq. km (Yano 1985). Despite the country's industrial success, in 1988 Japan still had some 4.5 million people engaged in agriculture compared to 3.3 million in the United States, which has a population roughly twice the size (CIA 1990).

Although Japan has a large human population within a small geographic area, the country possesses a comparatively rich and diverse biota: 'Compared to areas of similar size, like Great Britain and Ireland, the number of species is large in Japan' (JEA 1982). For example, 122 mammalian species are known in Japan compared to 67 in Great Britain and Ireland; over 600 bird species have been recorded in Japan, again roughly double the number in Great Britain and Ireland, while the number of insect species is roughly 4–5 times the number found in Great Britain. This high degree of biological diversity is largely due to biogeographic and oceanic factors. Three characteristics are especially important – the nation's highly mountainous terrain (occupying some three-quarters of its land mass), broad latitudinal variation (from the boreal regions of Hokkaido at 45.5°N to the neotropics of Okinawa at 24°N), and the large number of islands comprising the Japanese archipelago (over 3,900 islands with a cumulative coastline of nearly 33,000 kilometres).

It has frequently been suggested that Japanese culture has an especially strong appreciation and affection for nature (Anesaki 1932; Higuchi 1979; Ito 1972; Minami 1970; Murota 1986; Ono 1962; Oyadomori 1985; Rolston 1989; Saito 1983; Suzuki 1973; Tsutsui 1981; Watanabe 1974). Expressions of this attitude which are often cited include the religion of shintoism, the traditions of flower arranging, plant cultivation (e.g. bonsai), the tea ceremony, haiku and other poetry forms, rock gardening, various celebrations of the seasons, and a reverential attitude to particular features of the natural environment.

Saito (1983: 47) identified three important features of the Japanese appreciation of nature: '(1) Nature as friend of man, instead of servant to be used, enemy to be subdued, or an obstacle to be overcome. (2) There is no fundamental difference between man and nature. (3) The relationship between man and nature is ... harmonious and unified.' Despite this tradition of presumed affection and respect for nature, current Japanese environmental abuses reveal a pattern of widespread wildlife abuse and habitat destruction (Graphard 1985; Kamei 1983; Saiki 1988; Taylor 1990; Upham 1976, 1979). For example, Japan has been prominently criticized for its damaging whaling practices, harmful exploitation of wildlife products, destructive high seas drift net use, excessive exploitation of tropical forests, and so on (Graphard 1985; Hirasawa 1978; Kamei 1983; Linden 1989; Luoma 1988; Moreby 1982; Sneider 1989; Stewart-Smith 1987; Taylor 1990; Upham 1976, 1979; Van Wolfern 1989).

Germany has a human population of over 70 million and a density of roughly 250 persons per sq. km. It encompasses an area approximately the size of the US state of Oregon with 30 times its population. Most of Germany's land mass has been under intensive management for many centuries, and virtually no wilderness remains (Plochman 1981). Because of its geographic location and glacial history, the German landscape has been described as relatively simple in comparison to that of the United States or Japan. As a consequence, Germany has comparatively less biological diversity with, for example, only five native conifers and thirty native hardwoods, of which only three species are abundant (Plochman 1968).

Germans have further simplified their landscape through the massive conversion of natural forest to coniferous monoculture (Leopold 1933). Wildlife management has followed a similar pattern with the major emphasis on the 'production' of red deer and other preferred game species (Wolfe 1970). A strong tradition of forest appreciation, hunting and wildlife interest have, however, resulted in nearly one-quarter of the country remaining under forest since the late Middle Ages (Bundesministerium 1968). As Nelsen has noted (1987: 34), the maintenance of forest land and the German hunting tradition have been encouraged by a close cultural 'identification with wildlife, especially game animals, and the forest'. Some 70 per cent of the German population currently use the forests for outdoor recreation (Plochman 1981; see Plate 9.1). Hunting is, nonetheless, a very elitist and aristocratic sport, largely controlled by the wealthy with only 0.4 per cent of the German public holding a hunting licence compared with more than 8 per cent in the United States (Wolfe 1970; USFWS 1990). Hunters in Germany are regulated by a strict licensing and examination system requiring considerable knowledge of wildlife biology, hunting law and customs, nature protection and sportsmanship. The American system of 'the right to hunt [as] a basic right of ... citizenship' (Leopold 1933: 17), contrasts sharply with the elitist and aristocratic German hunting tradition.

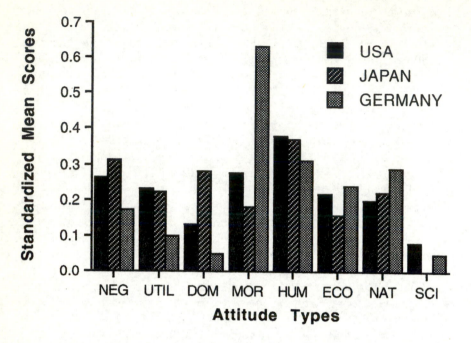

Figure 9.2 Basic attitudes toward wildlife in the United States (N = 3107), Japan (N = 450), and Germany (N = 1484) expressed as standardized mean attitude scale scores. For meaning of abbreviations see Table 9.1.

RESULTS

Before reviewing the research results, it is worth pointing out some of the limitations of the data. First, the studies reported here focus primarily on attitudes towards vertebrate animals. Other research (Kellert 1985, 1987, 1991b) has suggested that perceptions of invertebrates, as well as attitudes toward particular vertebrate species, can differ considerably. Second, the results cover contemporary attitudes toward animals, and historical views may differ from the findings reported here. Finally, the use of somewhat different methodologies renders statistical tests of significance inappropriate as the basis for comparing the three nations.

The relative rank order and scale scores of the basic attitudes toward animals in the United States, Japan and Germany are shown in Table 9.2 and Figure 9.2. The importance of strong emotional attachments to individual animals is indicated by the relatively high scores obtained in all three countries on the humanistic attitude scale. Respondents in the United States, Japan and

Table 9.2 Rank order and standardized mean scores of attitudes toward animals and knowledge scales in the United States, Germany and Japan*

Rank	United States	Germany	Japan
1	HUMANISTIC (0.38)	MORALISTIC (0.63)	HUMANISTIC (0.37)
2	MORALISTIC (0.275)	HUMANISTIC (0.31)	NEGATIVISTIC (0.31)
3	NEGATIVISTIC (0.26)	NATURALISTIC (0.29)	DOMINIONISTIC (0.28)
4	UTILITARIAN (0.23)	ECOLOGISTIC (0.24)	NATURALISTIC (0.22)
5	ECOLOGISTIC (0.215)	NEGATIVISTIC (0.17)	UTILITARIAN (0.22)
6	NATURALISTIC (0.20)	SCIENTISTIC (0.12)	MORALISTIC (0.18)
7	DOMINIONISTIC (0.13)	UTILITARIAN (0.10)	ECOLOGISTIC (0.16)
8	SCIENTISTIC (0.08)	DOMINIONISTIC (0.05)	
	Knowledge of animals mean scores		
	53	57	48

* United States data collected in 1977, N – 3107; German data collected in 1983–4, N = 1484; Japanese data collected in 1986–7, N = 450.

Germany expressed strong, positive attitudes toward large and higher vertebrates, especially mammalian and bird species generally regarded as aesthetically appealing, culturally important and historically familiar. A greater inclination in the United States and Japan, but not Germany, to indicate affection for domestic rather than wild animals, was suggested by the less frequent occurrence of the naturalistic attitude.

The Japanese, in considerable contrast to German and to a lesser degree American respondents, also revealed strong dominionistic and negativistic attitudes towards animals. In addition, key informant responses emphasized the importance of aesthetic factors in Japanese perspectives of nature. Japanese appreciation of animals generally appeared to be narrow and restricted to a relatively small number of wild and domestic species. Appreciation was typically limited to particular species possessing unusual aesthetic and cultural appeal, experienced in very controlled circumstances. Americans and Germans, in contrast, tended to evince a broader appreciation of wildlife in a wider diversity of habitats and environmental settings.

Additional insights regarding Japanese attitudes toward animals were provided by the 50 key informants. One theme repeatedly expressed by the informants was a Japanese tendency to place greatest emphasis on the experience and enjoyment of nature and animals in highly structured circumstances. The objective, as one respondent described, was to capture the presumed 'essence' of a natural object, often by adhering to strict rules of

173

'seeing and experiencing'. Rarely did this admiration go beyond single species or isolated landscapes to an appreciation of nature in general or of broad ecological processes. Environmental features falling outside the valued aesthetic and symbolic boundaries tended to be ignored, considered irrelevant or judged unappealing.

This restricted Japanese appreciation of animals and nature was described as largely emotional and aesthetic with little analytical or biological consideration. One respondent referred to it as a 'love of semi-nature', somewhat domesticated and tamed; a desire to 'use the materials of semi-nature to express human feelings'. Another respondent described this attitude as reflecting a Japanese preference for the artificial, highly abstract and symbolic rather than the realistic experience of animals and nature; a motivation to 'touch' nature but from a controlled and safe distance. In a metaphorical sense, one respondent described this perspective as a Japanese willingness 'to go to the edge of the forest, to view nature from across the river, to see natural beauty from a mountain top, but rarely to enter into or immerse oneself in wildness or the ecological understanding of natural settings'. Another described a Japanese 'love' not so much of nature and animals but of the artistic and symbolic rendering of nature. This tendency, according to another respondent, largely reflected a desire to isolate a favoured aspect of the natural world and then 'freeze and put walls around it'.

German and American results indicated a more generalized appreciation and protectionist attitude toward animals and the natural environment. German respondents expressed very strong affection, concern, and what might be called romantic feelings for animals and nature. The German sample not only had relatively high humanistic and naturalistic attitude scores, but also obtained very low scores on the utilitarian and dominionistic scales, particularly in comparison to the Japanese.

This impression of a highly romantic and protectionist attitude toward animals and nature among the German public was further suggested by exceptionally high moralistic and ecologistic scale scores. The Japanese, in considerable contrast, obtained their lowest scores on these two scales. The highly protectionist and romantic view of the German respondents was also indicated by moralistic scores twice as high as those of the next highest scoring scale, the humanistic. The German public consistently expressed considerable opposition to the exploitation of animals and strong concern for their welfare. They frequently indicated a willingness to extend rights and protected status to animals even at the loss of substantial benefits to humans.

The American public's views were generally less consistent or extreme than those of either the German or Japanese respondents. Although the American public did reveal strong affection and protectionist concern for animals, reflected in high humanistic and moralistic scale scores, they also expressed considerable indifference and highly pragmatic perspectives, as suggested by comparatively high negativistic and utilitarian scores.

Table 9.3 Selected knowledge questions (% correct)

	Japan	USA
Most insects have backbones.	45	57
Snakes have a layer of 'slime' to move more easily.	34	52
All adult birds have feathers.	49	63
Spiders have 10 legs.	37	50
A seahorse is a kind of fish.	40	71
Salmon breed in fresh water, but spend most of their life in salt water.	76	66
All the following are mammals:	20	40
Japan: impala, tanuki, iguana, killer whale;		
USA: impala, muskrat, iguana, killer whale		

This somewhat contradictory pattern may reflect the considerable heterogeneity and diversity of American society, and suggests that a better understanding of prevailing attitudes might be obtained by examining variations between key demographic groups.

On the 'knowledge of animals' scale, the Japanese public obtained the lowest scores and the Germans the highest. Table 9.3 shows that when American and Japanese responses were compared on a number of specific questions, American respondents were generally found to be more knowledgeable concerning the basic biological characteristics of animals while the Japanese seemed to have more understanding of animals that possessed economic or practical value.

The results shown in Figure 9.3 reveal that Americans were more likely than Japanese respondents to know the causes of contemporary extinction and endangerment of species. Citizens of both countries were very inclined to attribute harmful significance to chemical and industrial pollution, while ignoring the very damaging impact of introduced and exotic species.

Additional understanding of attitudes toward animals in the United States, Germany and Japan are provided by comparisons of attitude scale scores among different demographic groups. For reasons of limited space, only comparisons based on age, gender and educational effects are included here.

Young adults in each country were significantly more likely to express interest, affection and concern for animals than were other age groups, especially the elderly. A major exception was the absence of significant moralistic and ecologistic differences among Japanese age groups. Eighteen to thirty-five-year-old American and German respondents expressed considerable concern for the ethical treatment and ecological protection of wildlife, in marked contrast to the views of younger adults in Japan.

A similar pattern emerged when educational groups in the three countries

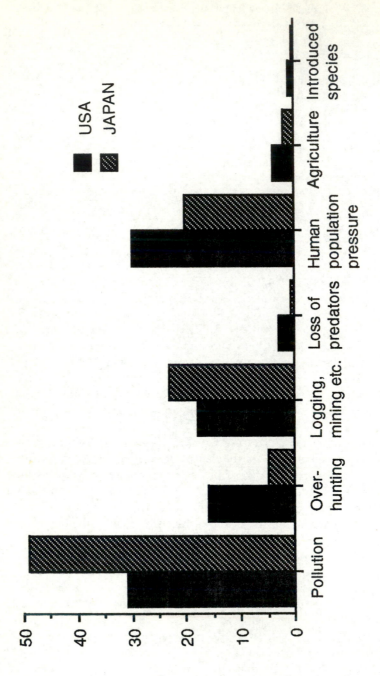

Figure 9.3 Primary reasons given for species endangerment – past 25 years, USA and Japan.

were compared. In the United States and Germany, the college-educated expressed far greater appreciation, interest and concern for animals and nature than other educational groups, particularly when compared with respondents with only grade-school education. Although college-educated Japanese also revealed more interest and appreciation for animals, they expressed no greater ethical or ecological concern than other educational groups.

In all three countries, males expressed a more general interest in and understanding of wildlife and nature, as suggested by higher naturalistic, ecologistic knowledge and lower negativisitic scale scores. Conversely, females were more likely to express greater affection for individual animals, such as pets, and for the welfare and protection of animals, as suggested by higher humanistic and moralistic scores. Gender differences across the three countries largely paralleled variations described for the nation as a whole.

Additional information was collected on views on and participation in a number of animal-related activities. Americans generally expressed more favourable views of hunting, and a greater likelihood of participating in this activity, than did Japanese respondents (Figure 9.4). Although direct comparisons with Germany are difficult owing to difference in survey methodology, it is clear that Japanese and German respondents expressed considerably less approval of hunting than Americans, the majority of whom supported hunting as long as the meat was utilized (Figure 9.5). A majority of Americans objected, however, to sport or trophy hunting.

Japanese opposition to hunting may have been related to Buddhist traditions of not killing or eating land animals. Japanese society, however, has a long history of marine animal consumption (Plate 9.2) and even today is the world's largest per capita consumer of sea products (JEA 1982). Japanese respondents reported a far greater willingness (70 per cent) than Americans (40 per cent) to kill porpoises caught in fishermen's nets, and a relatively large proportion of the Japanese public reported eating whale meat during the past five years (Figure 9.6). Japanese respondents also reported relatively frequent fishing activity, although still substantially less than occurred among the American sample.

Less frequent recreational contact with animals among the Japanese than American respondents was further suggested by participation in birdwatching and pet-ownership activities (see Figures 9.4 and 9.7 and Plate 9.3). Negligible participation differences occurred when activities involved more indirect or vicarious contact with animals, such as visiting zoological parks or viewing wildlife on television (Figures 9.7 and 9.8).

Popular environmental movements are generally regarded as being less characteristic of Japanese than American society (Kelly et al. 1976; McKean 1981; Pierce et al. 1986). This impression was confirmed by the finding that substantially fewer Japanese than American respondents reported membership of conservation or animal-related organizations (see Figure 9.8). Japanese respondents reported a far greater willingness than the American sample to

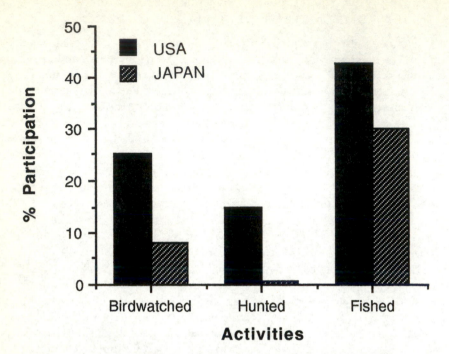

Figure 9.4 Participation in selected animal-related activities within the past two years (birdwatching, hunting and fishing), USA and Japan.

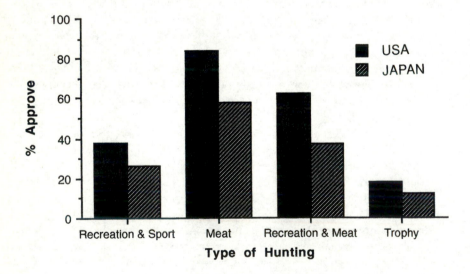

Figure 9.5 Attitudes to different types of hunting expressed as per cent approval, USA and Japan (NB: 85 per cent of German sample opposed to hunting).

drain and fill a wetland habitat critical to endangered bird-life if it resulted in increased urban employment benefits (Figure 9.9). On the other hand, Japanese and American respondents were equally inclined to approve of water projects that destroyed the habitat of endangered fish species if these produced important human benefits (Figure 9.10). A majority of respondents in both countries objected if the water benefits were only marginally significant.

DISCUSSION

Information has been presented on contemporary attitudes, knowledge and behaviour toward animals in three of the world's leading industrial democracies – the United States, Japan and Germany. While variations in research procedures limit the ability to generalize from the results, the use of similar conceptual and methodological approaches does permit some broad conclusions.

The majority of American, Japanese and German respondents expressed considerable interest and appreciation for individual animals, typically species with strong aesthetic, cultural and historic associations. Conversely, most respondents revealed limited concern or knowledge of most wildlife species or the ecosystems that support them. A more encouraging result was the finding of significantly greater wildlife appreciation, interest and concern among younger and better-educated respondents, with the exception of 18–35-year-old and college-educated Japanese respondents, who expressed no greater ecological or ethical concern for animals and the natural environment.

The American public was somewhat inconsistent, revealing great affection and concern for individual animals and their welfare, but also highly pragmatic and indifferent views of most species. Historical analyses of secondary data (Kellert 1986) similarly found that despite significant decreases in utilitarian sentiment and increases in humanistic views of animals during this century, a pragmatic view of nature and wildlife remains the dominant perspective in the United States today. The concurrent occurrence in contemporary American society of humanistic and moralistic attitudes, on the one hand, and negativistic and utilitarian attitudes on the other, may offer some insight into why so much conflict and controversy exists regarding the management and treatment of wildlife. This diversity probably reflects the considerable variation in attitudes found among diverse American demographic groups distinguished by age, gender, education, income, region and geographic area of residence (Kellert and Berry 1981). Such regional, urban–rural and socioeconomic differences are characteristic of the dynamic, highly pluralistic and heterogeneous nature of American society.

A somewhat different inconsistency was encountered in Japan. Although Japanese respondents expressed strong interest in and appreciation of a small number of preferred species, the majority indicated considerable indifference and lack of ecological or ethical concern for most wildlife and associated habitats. Despite this, various scholarly assessments have referred to an

179

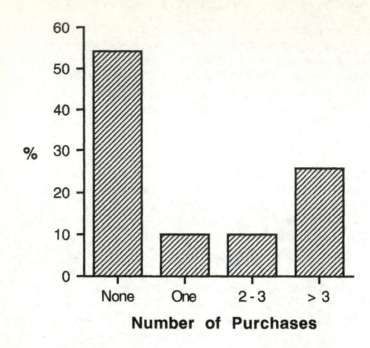

Figure 9.6 Frequency of whale meat purchases within the past five years, Japan only.

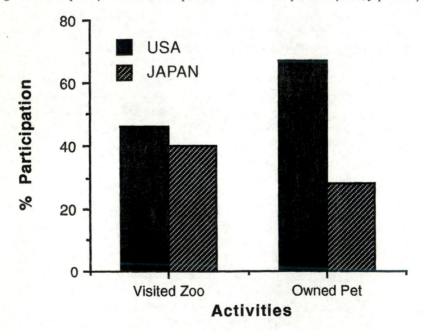

Figure 9.7 Participation in selected animal-related activities within the past two years (zoo visits and pet ownership), USA and Japan.

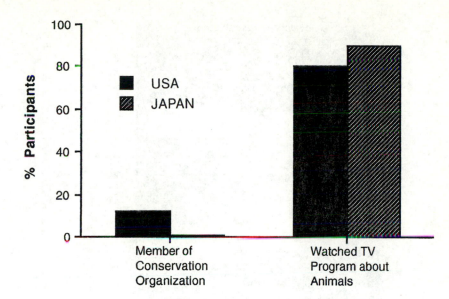

Figure 9.8 Participation in selected animal related activities within the past two years (membership of conservation organizations and TV viewing), USA and Japan.

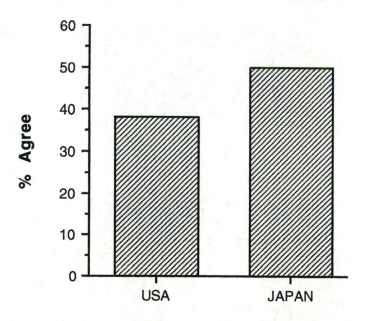

Figure 9.9 Percentage of respondents who agree that a wetland site should be filled in for industrial purposes even if this endangers a bird species, USA and Japan.

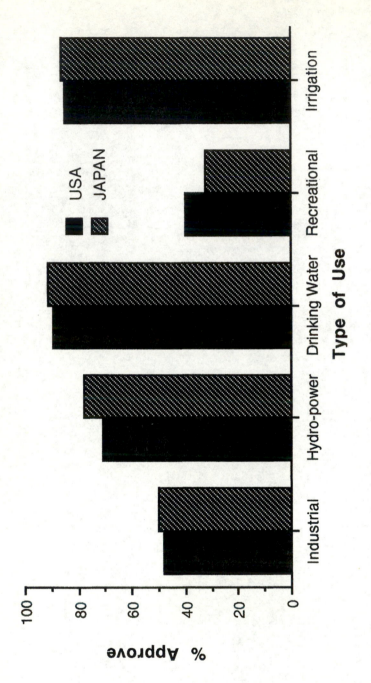

Figure 9.10 Percentage of respondents who approve various water uses even if a fish species is endangered, USA and Japan.

especially prevalent Japanese affection, respect and even 'love of nature'. Higuchi (1979: 19) suggests, for example, 'a relationship between nature and the Japanese people ... based on a feeling of awe and respect'. Watanabe (1974: 280) further remarks that a basic characteristic of Japanese culture is 'a love of nature ... [that] has resulted in a refined appreciation of the beauty of nature ... [a view] of man ... considered a part of nature, and the art of living in harmony with nature [as the] wisdom of life'. Murota (1986: 105), contrasting Japanese with European and American perspectives, argues:

> The Japanese view of nature is quite different from that of Westerners. ... The Japanese nature is an all-pervasive force. ... Nature is at once a blessing and friend to the Japanese people. ... People in Western cultures, on the other hand, view nature as an object and, often, as an entity set in opposition to humankind.

The results of this study did reveal a Japanese appreciation of nature and wildlife, although this was usually manifested in a very limited, narrow and restricted fashion. Japanese interest was largely confined to particular natural features, such as single species or individual animals, frequently admired in a context emphasizing control, manipulation and considerable contrivance. This affinity with nature was often an idealistic re-creation or artistic rendering of particularly valued aspects of the natural environment. Japanese appreciation often lacked an ecological or ethical orientation to nature, or as Saito (1983: 192) has suggested:

> nature is not lived or respected for its own sake but because it allows one to escape.... This appreciation of nature not only implies an anthropo-centric attitude ... but also suggests [an] ineffectiveness in generating an ethically desirable justification for protecting nature.

Japanese appreciation of the natural environment appeared to be largely expressed in a narrow emotional, intellectual and social context focusing on single species possessing unusual aesthetic and cultural value.

The German results are perhaps the least subject to explanatory review, given methodological limitations and restrictions on the data collected. Still, some preliminary conclusions can be drawn. The most striking impression was that of a very idealistic and romanticized German attitude toward animals and the natural environment. German respondents consistently expressed strong affection and support for animals and their welfare, reflected in an unusual pattern of high moralistic, humanistic, naturalistic and ecologistic, and very low utilitarian and dominionistic scale scores. Moreover, despite a strong hunting tradition in German culture, the public overwhelmingly disapproved of this activity. The fact that German hunting is practised as a largely elitist sport may have accounted for its limited relevance and appeal to the majority of the German public.

Strongly expressed ideals of affection, protectionist concern and naturalistic interest among most German respondents may reflect the outdoor recreational and symbolic importance of the natural environment for much of the German public. Leopold (1936), Plochman (1968) and Wolfe (1970), for example, have all noted strongly held feelings for forests and wildlife among Germans. As Nelsen (1987: 36; 53) remarked, Germans 'look to the forest . . . as a symbol of simpler times . . . and a more harmonious state of nature . . . . Game animals are a pervasive element of a traditional popular culture.'

Germany may be viewed as a country with a long and established tradition of difficult forestry and animal management decisions. The consequences of high human population density and a lengthy history of human settlement and land use have resulted in a highly managed landscape where many indigenous species have either disappeared or are currently maintained in very regulated and controlled circumstances. As Nelsen has noted (1987: 71): 'Germans have simplified their forests . . . through the conversion . . . to spruce monoculture. Game management has become correspondingly artificialized and simplified.' The average German is removed from direct contact or responsibility for wildlife and tends to appreciate animals and the natural environment from a relatively distant position. Most Germans rarely confront the need for exploiting or controlling wildlife and, for many, animals and nature constitute more an aesthetic and symbolic resource than a utilitarian one.

CONCLUSIONS

The majority of respondents in the United States, Japan and Germany expressed considerable appreciation of and affection for particular animal species. This attitude is certainly a laudable expression of wildlife interest and concern. The history of wildlife conservation has repeatedly demonstrated the importance of sympathetic feelings for particular species as the basis for mobilizing citizen support for the conservation of wildlife and the natural environment (Matthiessen 1989; Cart 1971).

The inadequacy of this perspective as a basis for wildlife appreciation is also apparent, especially in today's global conservation context. The contemporary species extinction crisis increasingly necessitates a broader concern for wildlife and the natural world. The spectre of massive extinctions is a problem that will afflict largely unknown invertebrates comprising perhaps 90 per cent of all animal species and 95 per cent of existing animal biomass (Wilson 1987). An effective and meaningful wildlife conservation movement will require an increasing recognition of the ecological and practical importance of many so-called 'lower' life forms. This expanded understanding will necessitate more than an expressed concern for individual animal species possessing unusual cultural, aesthetic and historic appeal. The urgency of contemporary wildlife conservation can no longer afford a public that remains aloof from the biological matrix of lower life forms and restricts its concern to a narrow segment of the biotic community.

The leadership of the industrial superpowers – the United States, Japan and Germany – will be critical in the evolution of this more environmentally responsible and enlightened global perspective. These three countries collectively exert an extraordinary influence on the world's biota, and their current pre-eminence necessitates a more assertive role as environmental stewards and models. It behoves the industrial superpowers to assume an ambitious agenda of creative leadership in any strategy intended to counter the ominous drift toward planetary wildlife extinction and destruction. A narrow and restricted appreciation of selected species is clearly an insufficient basis for cultivating a more environmentally responsible and literate global citizen.

REFERENCES

Anesaki, M. (1932) *Art, Life and Nature in Japan*, Rutland Vermont: Charles E. Tuttle.

Bean, M. (1983) *The Evolution of National Wildlife Law*, New York: Praeger.

Bundesministerium für Ernährung, Landwirtschaft und Forsten (1968) *Forestry in the Federal Republic of Germany*, Bad Godesburg land- und hauswirtschaftlicher Auswertungs- und Informationsdienst.

Cart, T. (1971) *The Struggle for Wildlife Protection in the United States*, Ann Arbor, Mich.: University Microfilms.

CIA [Central Intelligence Agency] (1990) *Handbook of Economic Statistics*, Washington, DC: Superintendent of Documents.

Dunlap, T. (1988) *Saving America's Wildlife*, Princeton: Princeton University Press.

Graphard, A. (1985) 'Nature and culture in Japan', in M. Tobias (ed.) *Deep Ecology*, San Diego: Avant Books.

Higuchi, K. (1979) *Nature and the Japanese*, Tokyo: Kodansha International .

Hirasawa, Y. (1978) 'The whaling industry in Japanese economy', in A. Schmidhauser and G. Totten (eds) *The Whaling Issue in US–Japan Relations*, Boulder, CO: Westview Press, pp. 82–114.

Ito, T. (1972) *The Japanese Garden: an Approach to Nature*, New Haven: Yale University Press.

JEA [Japanese Environment Agency] (1982) *The Natural Environment of Japan*, Tokyo: Environment Agency.

Kamei, N. (1983) 'Clearing the clouds of doubt', *Mainstream*: 22–5.

Kellert, S. (1979) *Public Attitudes toward Critical Wildlife and Natural Habitat Issues*, Washington, DC: US Government Printing Office.

—— (1980) 'Contemporary values of wildlife in American society', in W. Shaw and I. Zube (eds) *Wildlife Values*, Fort Collins, Colo.: US Forest Service, pp. 31–7.

—— (1983) 'Affective, cognitive and evaluative perceptions of animals', in I. Altman and J. Wohlwill (eds) *Behavior and the Natural Environment*, New York: Plenum, Ch. 7.

—— (1985) 'Social and perceptual factors in endangered species management', *Journal of Wildlife Management* 49(2): 528–36.

—— (1986) 'Historical trends in perceptions and uses of animals in 20th century America', *Environmental Review* 9(1): 19–33.

—— (1987) 'The public and the timber wolf in Minnesota', *Transactions of the 51st North American Wildlife and Natural Resources Conference*, Washington: Wildlife Management Institute.

—— (1991a) *Values and Perceptions of Invertebrates*, New Haven: Yale School of Forestry and Environmental Studies.

—— (1991b) 'Japanese perceptions of wildlife', in *Conservation Biology* 5(3).

Kellert, S. and Berry, J. (1981) *Knowledge, Affection and Basic Attitudes toward Animals in American Society*, Washington, DC: US Government Printing Office.

Kelly, D. *et al.* (1976) *The Economic Superpowers and the Environment: the United States, the Soviet Union, and Japan*, San Francisco: W. H. Freeman.

Leopold, A. S. (1933) *Game Management*, New York: Macmillan.

—— (1936) 'Deer and dauerwald in Germany', *Journal of Forestry* 34: 366–75.

Linden, E. (1989) 'Putting the heat on Japan: accused of ravaging the world's forests and seas, Tokyo starts to clean up its act', *Time*, 7 October.

Lund, T. (1980) *American Wildlife Law*, Berkeley: University of California Press.

Luoma, J. (1988) 'Japan assailed on animal imports', *New York Times*, 7 May.

McKean, M. (1981) *Environmental Protest and Citizen Politics in Japan*, Berkeley: University of California Press.

Marsh, J. (1987) *Marine Parks in Japan*, Ottawa: Environment Canada, Parks.

Matthiessen, P. (1989) *Wildlife in America*, New York: Viking.

Minami, H. (1970) *Psychology of the Japanese People*, Honolulu: East-West Center.

Moreby, C. (1982) 'What whaling means to the Japanese', *New Scientist* 31: 661–3.

Murota, Y. (1986) 'Culture and the environment in Japan', *Environmental Management* 9: 105–12.

Nelsen, A. (1987) *History of German Forestry: Implications for American Wildlife Management*, New Haven: Yale School of Forestry and Environmental Studies.

Ono, S. (1962) *Shinto: the Kanti Way*, Rutland, Vermont: Charles E. Tuttle.

Oyadomori, M. (1985) *Politics of National Parks in Japan*, Ann Arbor Mich.: University Microfilms.

Pierce, J. *et al.* (1986) 'Vanguards and rearguards in environmental politics: a comparison of activists in Japan and the United States', *Comparative Political Studies* 18: 419–47.

Plochman, R. (1968) *Forestry in the Federal Republic of Germany*, St Paul, Minnesota: L. & M. Hill Foundation.

—— (1981) 'Forestry in the Federal Republic of Germany', *Journal of Forestry* 81: 451–4.

Rolston, H. (1989) 'Respect for life: can Zen Buddhism help in forming an environmental ethic?', in *Zen Buddhism Today: Annual Report of the Kyoto Zen Symposium*, Kyoto: Kyoto Seminar for Religious Philosophy.

Saiki, M. (1988) 'Modernization of Japan with the insight of conservation', unpublished manuscript, University of Maine, Wildlife Department.

Saito, Y. (1983) *The Aesthetic Appreciation of Nature: Western and Japanese Perspectives and Their Ethical Implications*, Ann Arbor Mich.: University Microfilms.

Schulz, W. (1985) 'Einstellung zur Natur, eine empirische Untersuchung', PhD dissertation, Munich University, 1985.

—— (1986) 'Attitudes toward wildlife in West Germany', in D. Decker and G. Goff (eds) *Valuing Wildlife*, Boulder, Colo.: Westview Press, pp. 352–4.

Sneider, D. (1989) 'Japan assailed for practices that damage global environment', *Christian Science Monitor*, 7 November.

Stewart-Smith, J. (1987) *In the Shadow of Fujisan: Japan and its Wildlife*, New York: Viking.

Suzuki, D. (1973) *Zen and Japanese Culture*, Princeton: Princeton University Press.

Taylor, R. (1990) 'On the Japanese love of nature', unpublished manuscript, Department of Philosophy, University of California, Berkeley.

Tober, J. (1989) *Wildlife and the Public Interest: Nonprofit Organizations and Federal Wildlife Policy*, New York: Greenwood.

Tsutsui, M. (1981) 'Nature viewed by Japanese and a new approach to its management', *Proceedings of the XII IUFRO World Congress*, Div. 6, Ibaraki, Japan, pp. 319–22.

USFWS [United States Fish and Wildlife Service] (1990) *1990 National Survey of Hunting, Fishing and Wildlife Associated Recreation*, Washington, DC: US Government Printing Service.

Upham, F. (1976) 'Litigation and moral consciousness in Japan, an interpretive analysis of four Japanese pollution suits', *Law and Society* 8: 579–616.

—— (1979) 'After minimata: current prospects and problems in Japanese environmental litigation', *Ecological Law Quarterly* 8: 213–68.

Van Wolfern, K. (1989) *The Enigma of Japanese Power*, New York: Alfred A. Knopf.

Watanabe, H. (1974) 'The conception of nature in Japanese culture', *Science* 183: 279–82.

Wilson, E. O. (1987) 'The little things that run the world (the importance and conservation of invertebrates)', *Conservation Biology* 4: 344–6.

Wolfe, M. (1966) 'Eine vergleichende Betrachtung der jagdrechtlichen Regelungen in der BDR in der VSuA.', Harm.-Munden dissertation, University of Göttingen.

—— (1970) 'The history of German game administration', *Forestry History* 14: 6–16.

Yano, I. (1985) *Nippon: a Chartered Survey of Japan*, Tokyo: Kokuseisha Corporation.

10

BRIDGE-BUILDING AT LAST

Mary Midgley

THE BENEFITS OF CIVILIZATION

A generation ago, most academics would have been surprised to hear of a book with this title. Indeed, opinions in the learned world on this subject had not changed very much since 1787 when (as Maehle reports) 'many people could not understand at all how it occurred to an author to write about such a topic'. Interest in relations between humans and animals would have struck most scholars as hardly professional, and the topic of human *attitudes* to animals would not have sounded at all interesting.

No particular question was held to arise about finding the correct attitude to animals. Or rather (as Ritvo rightly points out) attitudes were scarcely supposed to come into the matter. It was generally held that, in an enlightened age, animals were at last being looked at objectively and scientifically. They were being perceived simply as what they were. Educated modern man had finally freed himself from the only 'attitudes' that could interfere with this objective approach. He had risen from the swamps of animism and anthropomorphism which had bogged down his ancestors, swamps where surviving primitive persons still wallowed. He had also escaped from sentimentality, though his wife – herself somewhat primitive – might well not have done so. Virility was often asserted through an exaggerated horror of sentimentality, which led people to dismiss all pet-keeping as a sinister perversion peculiar to the luxurious west – an impression which should now have been dispelled by James Serpell's recent work (Serpell 1986), showing that people have kept pets in all kinds of times and places.

In 1908 the magisterial *Encyclopaedia of Religion and Ethics* (Thomas 1908) expressed the anti-sentimental, Enlightenment point of view admirably in its article on 'Animals':

> Civilization, or perhaps rather education, has brought with it a sense of the great gulf that exists between man and the lower animals. . . . In the lower stages of culture, whether they be found in races which are, as a whole, below the European level, or in the uncultured portion of civilized communities, the distinction between men and animals is not

adequately, if at all, recognized. ... The savage ... attributes to the animal a vastly more complex set of thoughts and feelings, and a much greater range of knowledge and power, than it actually possesses.... It is therefore small wonder that his attitude towards the animal creation is one of reverence rather than superiority.

During the 1890s, Lloyd Morgan's famous Canon for assessing animal behaviour both expressed and protected this certainty (Morgan 1894). It forbade psychologists to interpret any action 'as the outcome of the exercise of a higher psychical faculty if it can be interpreted as the outcome of one which stands lower on the psychological scale'. This strange principle – which would produce most peculiar results if it were applied to humans – was seen as an austere and objective piece of parsimony. But it actually worked as rampant propaganda for human dignity and uniqueness. Psychologists became so good at explaining everything through the 'lower' faculties that notions about the species barrier slipped right back from Darwin's emphasis on continuity towards something very close to Descartes's position, regarding non-human animals as simple, unconscious machines.

This move also caused many scientifically minded people to react somewhat against the steady progress, which Maehle documents from the Renaissance onwards, from callous towards more humane treatment of animals. The move to mechanism was greatly helped by the behaviourist world-picture presented by Watson (1924), which officially showed both people and animals as machines of this kind. Common sense did eventually reject that story about people, but the idea that mechanism is the only scientific, objective and parsimonious approach to animals has lasted much longer. It has taken people some time to see that the behaviourist world-view is not itself something objective, but is – like many others with pretensions to objectivity – merely a self-flattering myth.

THE DAWN OF INTEREST

This impression about what is academically respectable still survives among many people, both learned and unlearned. In the social sciences, inter-disciplinary feuding strengthened the sense of a great gap between humans and other creatures. *Homo sapiens* counted as social territory, while the rest of the animal kingdom was alien stuff, the property of physical science. Some anthropologists, however, formed an exception to this consensus; they did at times make expeditions to see what the primitive people were doing in the animistic swamps. In 1964, one of these explorers, Edmund Leach, published an article called 'Anthropological aspects of language: animal categories and verbal abuse'. Leach's discussion now seems to us somewhat casual and slapdash. Yet it proved seminal, because it made a crack in the wall dividing social from biological science. Peering through this crack, social scientists could at last glimpse a whole new and astonishing landscape: the complex behaviour of non-human social animals.

Behaviour had become a permissible academic topic, because Konrad Lorenz and Niko Tinbergen had already begun to map it in scientific terms and annex it to zoology. Moreover, they were tentatively suggesting that their mapping methods might be of use even for territory on the human side of the wall. Ethological tools might, it seemed, have a wider application. People willing to learn this language might not only become able to understand, for the first time, animal behaviour that they had been seeing all their lives. They might also be able to use that understanding to gain new insight, by controlled analogy, into human behaviour. Perhaps, after all, an interest in other species might turn out not to be irrelevant to the social sciences . . . ?

At first, notoriously, this suggestion produced repeated explosions of mutual outrage, exasperation and incomprehension. Yet gradually this portion of the wall, like other walls, did crumble. As the dust cleared, it emerged that a co-operative exchange of tools was indeed possible. With slow, persistent, gruelling work from both sides, it turns out that both the social and the biological sciences, far from being threatened, can acquire new and important insights in this way.

THE PAINFULNESS OF THE PROBLEM

That is how we have this book. To have it at all is in a sense a kind of triumph. But it is a triumph of that special kind that attends being allowed, at last, to get down to a gruelling and overdue job of work. Here as in Europe, knocking down ancient walls brings problems.

The subject of human relations with other animals is essentially a painful one. It is not something that the learned have overlooked merely by chance. It is a topic that has been systematically evaded by our whole culture, because it makes fearful trouble.

All the chapters of this book deal with striking anomalies about it. The historical ones trace conflicts over animals in past ages, and describe defence mechanisms by which earlier peoples have tried to defuse or conceal them. They show us how we have got to where we are, which is a most necessary step to understanding our own confusions. The contemporary discussions show how deeply these conflicts are still built into our life today. They arise in different forms in all modern cultures, as Kellert shows here. Indeed, things have surely got much harder even in the last generation or two, because – at the very time when the public conscience was beginning to become more sensitive – technological efforts to put the human race in a position of total control over the natural world have immensely intensified. The resulting industrialization produces appalling problems both for practice and for theory.

How then should we now approach these problems? On the theoretical side – which is our present business – we must, of course, start by sorting them into their separate baskets for different kinds of treatment. In doing this, it is extremely helpful to listen to the historians and the anthropologists. They tell us about the various quite different ways in which these problems have been assembled in other times and other cultures, and help us to trace how we got from earlier groupings to our present ones. This makes it possible for us to see how many options are really open, and so to guess how things might now become different.

ANIMALS AND THE IMAGINATION

One central trouble about the wholesale, uncritical, pseudo-objective approach from which we are just escaping was the way in which it promoted fatalism by concealing this range of options. It treated the topic of non-human animals as an uninteresting one – something which could scarcely impinge on serious human concerns. This meant that changes in it could hardly be expected to affect our thinking on other important topics. Yet when we glance at the history, we are at once struck by the extent to which the human imagination has always occupied itself with other species, and the way in which ideas on all sorts of subjects have constantly been developed in animal terms.

If we had not yet seen any Palaeolithic paintings – if it were now announced that some had just been discovered – would we not have expected that the artists would primarily have been interested in making portraits of people? Yet the human figures that do appear in these paintings seem marginal. They are just casual sketches, standard matchstick-men. All the real interest, all the fire and vigour, goes into the animals. And for a very long time it continued to do so in later forms of art. What Schwabe tells us about bull imagery is no surprise – yet it surely deserves renewed attention.

Obviously, the point is not that people were less interested in their own lives than in those of other creatures. It is that imagery drawn from those other creatures was, for some reason, an easier and stronger language for saying what they wanted to say about their own lives than direct self-portraiture. There must surely be a parallel here with the roundabout path that we take to individual self-knowledge. Each of us learns to speak about other people before becoming able to discuss ourselves, and when we do discuss our own inner lives, we do it largely in metaphorical terms drawn from aspects of the public, physical world. We talk of seeking and finding, grasping and missing, of channels and obstacles, lights and paths, blockages and pitfalls. Just so, it seems, when we want to say something about power, even about power in a human context, our imaginations much more readily come up with a lion or a bull than with a direct description of powerful human activity. Indeed, in a sense, apparently, this language *is* more direct, more primary.

Why this symbolic link should be quite so strong is a really interesting psychological problem. But whatever its source it has, of course, had an enormous effect on our actual treatment of the animals. Whatever dealings we have with them, these creatures carry a load of symbolic meaning that goes far beyond their actual conduct and is often quite irrelevant to it. They stand in for our inner conflicts and confusions; they are often punished for our faults. In particular, they serve as stereotypes to dramatize for us the ambivalences which constantly dog our inner life and make it so confusing. As Clutton-Brock and Ingold point out, the ambivalence we feel about civilization itself is expressed in the differences of our attitudes to wild and domesticated animals. Wild ones tend to be admired more, but also feared, and credited with amazing powers to endanger us. Tame ones tend to be despised; a kind of shame attends their use, and this shame has caused an even longer delay in admitting them as a respectable object of study than that which occurred in the case of wild animals.

In both cases, it is surely transparent that it is our own motives, habitually symbolized by these two kind of animal, that are really in question. This seems a most interesting topic for further investigation. It is notable, for instance, how when human beings behave really badly, they are said to behave 'like animals', however unlike their acts may be to those that any other species could actually perform. This is a way of disowning the motives concerned and distancing them from the rest of us. It elevates the species barrier into an absolute frontier of the moral realm.

Yet in ordinary life people include their domestic animals for many purposes inside the normal realm of duty, and there has of late been increasing uneasiness about excluding other categories of animal from it. While questions about animals were regarded wholesale as negligible, this sort of anomaly attracted little attention. But today it forces itself more and more on our attention. It surely indicates an area of human life that needs a great deal more thought.

WIDENING THE GAP

As we look back now at the typical Enlightenment view that was so confidently expressed by Lloyd Morgan and the writer on animals in the *Encyclopaedia of Religion and Ethics*, what we see is surely a vigorous, deliberate widening of the gap between humans and all other animals. It was an antiseptic attempt to protect the human race from pollution by cutting its links with the rest of nature. Moreover, what was thus protected often turned out to be, not even the whole human race, but 'modern' civilization, which had to be sharply distinguished from all earlier and non-western human life. 'Animals' were often approximated to 'natives' – a point well discussed by several writers in this collection.

We confront here, surely, a peculiar consequence of modern urbanization. The towns we now live in are like an unprecedented kind of isolation hospital, cutting off their inhabitants – us – from almost all contact with other animals, and also from most of the rest of the human race, both past and present. This is not a trivial change. Most people, during most of human history, have seen their lives as roughly continuous with those of their ancestors, and have also encountered nonhuman animals in so many aspects of life that they saw them as playing a great variety of different roles – a point well made by Cohen.

This – as she says – does much to account for their powerful symbolic function in the language of our imagination, a symbolic function that has not lapsed. Unavoidably, this places animals, imaginatively, very close to us; indeed, within us. They are part of us, because our thought needs the Other – nonhuman beings of some kind to illustrate the vast range of outside possibilities. If animals do not play this role, other kinds of Other must be invented. The excesses of science fiction show how very unsatisfactory these inventions can sometimes be.

AMBIVALENCE, HYPOCRISY AND REFORM

This close imaginative involvement of humans with other species does, of course, pose enormous problems. Right from the start of human history, it must have conflicted with the straightforward, utilitarian, exploitative attitudes that were often necessary. It is very important not to oversimplify these situations. Ambivalence has always been central to most of the ways in which humans use animals; for instance to hunt (Ingold) and to herd (Schwabe). There is real reverence, there is admiration, there is some mutual trust, there is also callous and brutal exploitation.

Such conflicts are bound to give rise to hypocrisy. Yet they are also the seed of moral progress. The complex and distressing problems that Arluke documents among those working in animal shelters are typical of the conflicts that have always arisen in morally anomalous situations, conflicts that have very often finally provided the spur for reform. Relations with animals were surely among the topics that presented our earliest ancestors with the problems of guilt and evil. Bloodshed has never been seen as an entirely indifferent matter. The many myths that people invoked to justify their use of animals show that they were not indifferent to such things. Along (of course) with similar quandaries about human affairs, these worries surely provided the grit in the oyster, the stimulus to moral and cosmic thinking.

It is possible, too, that relations with animals were in a way a more direct and insistent problem than relations with human outsiders, because such outsiders are, by definition, more remote; you don't see them every day. Significantly, however, both problems tended to get the same solution. Human outsiders were ruled not to be really human at all. They could thus be placed, along with the animals, outside the species-barrier, at a distance which – it was hoped – would prevent their troubling anybody's conscience ever again.

And in this way unnumbered atrocities have been justified. But the human conscience is somewhat tougher, somewhat less easily satisfied than such simple rulings assume. It still gives trouble. It is still uneasy about vast, sweeping categorizations of this kind. It wants to know more, to make discriminations, to understand what is actually happening. It asks for serious scholarly inquiry about human–animal interactions. And, in books like these, it may at last begin to get it.

REFERENCES

Leach, E. (1964) 'Anthropological aspects of language: animal categories and verbal abuse', in E. Lenneberg, *New Directions in the Study of Language*, Cambridge, Mass.: MIT Press, pp. 23–63.

Morgan, C. L. (1894) *Introduction to Comparative Psychology*, London: Scott.

Serpell, J. A. (1986) *In the Company of Animals*, Oxford: Basil Blackwell.

Thomas, A. N. (1908) 'Animals', in J. Hastings (ed.) *Encyclopaedia of Religion and Ethics*, Vol. I, Edinburgh: T. & T. Clark, pp. 483–4.

Watson, J. B. (1924) *Psychology from the Standpoint of a Behaviourist*, Philadelphia, Penn.: Lippincott.

INDEX